PADRE

PADRE

THE SPIRITUAL JOURNEY OF FATHER VIRGIL CORDANO

Mario T. García

CAPRA PRESS
Memorable Books Since 1969
Santa Barbara

A Robert Bason Book
Published by Capra Press
155 Canon View Road
Santa Barbara, CA 93108
www.caprapress.com

Cover and book design by Frank Goad

LIBRARY OF CONGRESS CATALOGING-IN-PUBLICATION DATA

García, Mario T.
Padre : the spiritual journey of Father Virgil Cordano / Mario T. García.
p. cm.
"Selected writings by Father Virgil Cordano": p.
ISBN 1-59266-052-5 (trade pbk.) — ISBN 1-59266-053-3 (hardcover)
1. Cordano, Virgil, 1918- 2. Santa Barbara Mission—Biography. 3. Catholic Church—
California—Santa Barbara—Clergy—Biography. I. Title.

BX4705.C7765G37 2005
271'.302—dc22

2004023795

10 9 8 7 6 5 4 3 2 1

First Edition

Printed in Canada

I wish to dedicate this account of my life to my three families: the Cordano family of parents, brothers, and relatives; my family of Franciscan Friars; and my Santa Barbara family of friends.

— FATHER VIRGIL CORDANO

To my mother, Alma García Araiza, for all the love and support she has given me in my life.

— MARIO T. GARCÍA

ACKNOWLEDGMENTS
Mario T. García

I want to give my profound gratitude to Fr. Virgil Cordano for his support of this project. His willingness to share his time and his story made this book possible. But it was not only his memory that was important in constructing this narrative. It was also his contribution as co-editor, by reading the various drafts, correcting them, adding new material, and, finally, approving the final product. My inspiration to do this book could not have come to fruition without Fr. Virgil's active support.

I also want to thank anonymous friends of Fr. Virgil who through their generosity and love of Fr. Virgil made the publication of this book possible.

In addition, I want to acknowledge Marc Patton of the *Santa Barbara News-Press* who went out of his way to secure for me a copy of the *News-Press* clipping file on Fr. Virgil.

A special debt of gratitude to Susan Gulbransen who with her usual enthusiasm encouraged that I go forward with Capra Press.

Robert Bason, publisher of Capra Press, embraced this project and nurtured it through final publication, and for this I am very thankful. Richard Barre, associate publisher of Capra Press, offered insightful and sensitive suggestions for strengthening the manuscript as only a writer of his caliber is capable of doing, and for this I am equally grateful.

Darla McDavid, as she has done for several other of my oral history projects, professionally and competently transcribed my interviews with Fr. Virgil that facilitated the writing of the manuscript.

Monica Sánchez, my graduate research assistant, aided in the final preparation of the manuscript and deserves my thanks.

I want to also acknowledge the careful and professional editing of the manuscript by Grace Rachow.

Finally, I want, as always, to give my loving thanks to my family: Ellen, Giuliana, and Carlo.

MARIO T. GARCÍA
Santa Barbara, California
September 15, 2004

ACKNOWLEDGMENTS
Fr. Virgil Cordano

I wish to thank Professor Mario T. García for giving me the opportunity to reflect on my life's journey. He took the time and patience to hear, record, and write my story. I've often thought of writing my autobiography, but never got around to it. It is only through Professor García's intervention that it is now possible for my story to be told. For this, I am very grateful to him.

I am amazed at what has brought me to this day in my story: its surprises, the paradox of gains through losses, the assurance that I was never alone, the awareness of the meaning, purpose, and goal of my life; the heightened variety of things to do and people to meet.

In addition to the events in my life, Professor García has asked me to give my opinions and views on various issues. In my responses, I have relied heavily upon the insights of experts in various fields. I have added my own correlation to what scholars have written and my opinions. Much of the scholarship is very academic. In trying to "popularize" many complex theological and spiritual concepts, I hope I have not done an injustice to them. Also, on disputed issues I hope I have been fair to all.

I pray that you, the reader, as you read my story may also reflect upon the meaning of your own journey and discover, as I have, why we should be grateful for our past, how to be aware of the meaning of the present, and reasons to be hopeful for the future.

In addition to Professor García, I want to thank Capra Press for its willingness to publish my story and to all who were involved in this production. May God bless you.

I want to also give my special thanks to my dear friend and

Congresswoman, Lois Capps, for writing the Foreword. She, like her dear husband and my dear friend, Professor and Congressman Walter Capps, has been a true friend over the years and a wonderful inspiration for all of us in how to be decent and loving human beings. I pray for Walter and send a special blessing to Lois and her family.

Finally, I want to pay special acknowledgements to my mother, father, and all of my family especially June Cordano, my beloved sister-in-law, for their love and support over all of my life. My life is simply a reflection of their love.

FR. VIRGIL CORDANO
Old Mission Santa Barbara
September 15, 2004

TABLE OF CONTENTS

FOREWORD

Congresswoman Lois Capps

Lights played across the familiar stonewalls of the Old Mission as dancers twirled and flamenco music enticed the crowd gathered at the foot of the Mission steps to clap and cheer.

Yes, Santa Barbara's La Fiesta Pequena 2004, was in full swing! And there was Father Virgil, microphone in hand, dressed as usual in brown Franciscan garb, leading the festivities as he has each year since the early 1960s.

Earlier this year our beloved Padre allowed his 85th birthday to be honored by the entire community in a gala celebration and benefit. He chuckled as he contrasted his vows of poverty and humility with the grand and elegant setting. The esteem with which this cleric is held by believers and nonbelievers alike was clearly evident.

But this same priest and pastor is equally at home blessing the fishing fleet and the Los Rancheros Visitadores as he is saying Mass at the Monastery of the Poor Clares or sitting by the bedside of a dying parishioner. His goal as an academically trained theologian to simplify complex spiritual concepts is evident as he gives a short homily to elementary school students.

La Fiesta Pequena this year was no different. "It may be," Father Virgil said to the crowd, "that God is as pleased with what happens here on the steps of the Mission as with what happens inside. After all, God has created us to be happy, to have fun, to enjoy life." And how did he come, this Franciscan, to such a place and such a belief?

For me, and I trust for every reader, the value and the joy of Professor Mario García's story of Father Virgil's life is to follow the journey of the young George Cordano from his immigrant family roots in Sacramento and his traditional Catholic upbringing and education. The calling and then the pilgrimage of becoming a priest, to the spiritual leader we now know as Father Virgil is traced through the austere, even harsh light of monastic discipline and scholastic achievement.

Santa Barbara Mission and St. Anthony's Seminary were home to Father Virgil during his student days. Following his doctoral studies at Catholic University in our nation's capitol, he returned to Santa Barbara to teach and then to preside over the seminary, as well as to direct community relations at the Old Mission, a position he continues to hold. His leadership skills were tested during the tumultuous period of the 1960s. He calls it a "hectic, tense, special, and historical time. So many things we had taken for granted – in both the religious and secular worlds – were being unraveled."

It was during this post-Vatican II and Vietnam War era that my husband, Professor Walter Capps, and I moved to Santa Barbara and met Father Virgil. Profound personal respect and admiration for this dear friend inspires me to write these words, even as I keep Walter's memory alive in so doing. Walter felt especially close to Father Virgil, theoretically and spiritually, and both shared the conviction that (to paraphrase Thomas Merton) God is revealed in sacred texts and traditions, but most profoundly in the voices of the stranger. This became the title of a class that Walter taught for many years at the University of California, Santa Barbara.

One light-hearted memory comes to mind. When Walter brought visiting scholars to visit the Old Mission and to learn from Father Virgil, several wanted to return for religious services. Those not Catholic asked if they could participate in the Eucharist. Father Virgil encouraged them by saying that if asked, they should say, "It's all been taken care of." They were so impressed that at the end of their stay they ordered souvenir t-shirts with that phrase inscribed.

When Walter announced his decision to run for the U.S. Congress in 1995, he said: "The truth is that we are best as a people when we work for the common good, when we exercise regard for those who are least among us. We are strongest as a people when we are directed by that which unites us rather than giving in to the fear, suspicion, innuendo and paranoia that divide us."

It is a conviction that he and his mentor Father Virgil shared.

Indeed, in his remarks last month at La Fiesta Pequena, Father Virgil thanked me for my public service and remembered his friend Walter. He spoke of Walter looking down from above on the festive evening. And he once again invoked for all to hear the blessing that we truly are created to celebrate our diversity, even as we are united in the bond of our common humanity.

Thank you, Father Virgil, dear friend!

LOIS CAPPS
September 3, 2004

INTRODUCTION
Mario T. García

Fr. Virgil Cordano, O.F.M., is a shining example of everything that is good about the Catholic Church. In his six decades as a Franciscan priest, and at age 86, he has exemplified the key virtues of St. Francis, the founder of the Franciscans. Like St. Francis, Fr. Virgil has given up his worldly possessions and dedicated his life to helping others. It is a life filled with self-sacrifice and love of his fellow human beings. As he often says, "by giving you receive." He receives the grace of God and communion with the rest of us.

At a time in the history of the Catholic Church, especially in the United States, when suspicion, anger, and resentment are being expressed toward the Church by some, it is important to remember honest, charitable, and moral priests such as Fr. Virgil. He is not a saint, and he has faced many of the same pressures and, undoubtedly, temptations that other priests have, but Fr. Virgil has always kept in mind why he became a priest many years ago. He wanted to help others get to Heaven, and he wanted to serve God. This meant sacrificing many things that most of us would not or could not. It meant resisting temptation and living a moral life in order to be an example toward others. Because of his sacrifices and commitment, we are better off for his presence.

To those who doubt the morality of the Church and of its servants, the priests, I present the life and spiritual journey of Fr. Virgil Cordano. This does not excuse the failures of the Church and the immorality of some of its priests, nor does it excuse the need for major reforms within the Church regarding the democratization of the institution and the accountability of the bishops to the laity. But Fr. Virgil's story presented here does, I hope, bring some balance back to the sober and honest dialogue needed concerning the future of the Church.

Fr. Virgil Cordano is well known to the residents of the Santa Barbara, California community but not to many others outside of this area. If there is anyone close to being regarded as "Mr. Santa Barbara" or, in this case, as "Padre Santa Barbara" it is Fr. Virgil. He is synonymous, for example, with the historic Santa Barbara Mission. Yet, I suspect that even many within the Santa Barbara community do not know the entire history of Fr. Virgil.

This story – the life story of Fr. Virgil – is an attempt to fill in this gap and to examine the life of a long-time Franciscan priest. Fr. Virgil has been formally a member of the Franciscan Order since 1940 and a Catholic priest since 1945. Almost his entire life, with the exception of the first 15 years, has been devoted to the Franciscan way of life. Most of that life and service has been associated with Santa Barbara and the Franciscan Order at Mission Santa Barbara. Beginning with his entry into St. Anthony's Seminary adjacent to the Mission in 1934, Fr. Virgil in different capacities has served the Catholic community and the larger community from his base at the Mission. He studied his theology at the then Mission Theological Seminary in Santa Barbara and after further graduate study at Catholic University in Washington, D.C., he returned to the Mission where he filled key leadership positions such as Rector of the Theological Seminary, Guardian of the Mission, and pastor of the Mission. Today at age 86, Fr. Virgil serves as Pastor Emeritus and Director of Public Relations, linking the Mission to the Santa Barbara community. There is no retirement for him. He continues to give to others and, as he stresses, to grow spiritually.

Since coming to teach at the University of California, Santa Barbara, in 1975, I, of course, heard about Fr. Virgil and especially about his work at the Mission, with the historic Fiesta held every summer in the community, and about his other community activities. But I didn't really get to know him until just few years ago when my two children attended Marymount School, the independent Catholic school in Santa Barbara where Fr. Virgil, among his many activities, serves as spiritual advisor. He officiated, and still does, at different religious services at the school, as well as saying an offertory or opening prayer at various events sponsored by the school. Fr. Virgil loves children in the most spiritual of ways, and this was evident in how he responded to the students at Marymount. He is loved and respected by them and by their teachers. I especially remember the ecumenical Christmas service that, besides Fr. Virgil, usually includes a Protestant minister. What I appreciated was when Fr. Virgil engaged the children, especially the younger ones, about the meaning of the season. It was wonderful to see his reaction to their responses.

At these occasions, my wife and I usually spent some time chatting with Fr. Virgil and expressing to him how much we appreciated his services. This connection with Fr. Virgil at Marymount was complemented by my being invited to serve on a committee that was planning how to organize and fund an endowed Chair in Catholic Studies at UC Santa Barbara to be named in Fr. Virgil's honor. I was invited because I had been working with one of our graduate students in Religious Studies, Monica Curry, on implementing a Catholic Studies Research Focus Group on campus as part of the Interdisciplinary Humanities Center. Monica was already on the endowment committee, and, through her gracious suggestion, the committee invited me to join its efforts.

Of course, Fr. Virgil was on the committee, and this offered me an opportunity to get to know him even better and to further appreciate his contributions to the Santa Barbara community. We all worked to make the endowed Chair a reality, which it now is, raising several million dollars from many who generously donated to the fund because of their love and admiration for Fr. Virgil. The Fr. Virgil Cordano Chair in Catholic Studies will very soon be a permanent fixture at UC Santa Barbara. It will be one of the very few endowed Chairs in Catholic Studies at a public university. It is a befitting honor to Fr. Virgil and will be a living memorial to him. The mission of the endowed Chair is, in Fr. Virgil's words, "to advance the cause of ecumenism and interfaith dialogue, to discover what, at a deep level, unites all people. To achieve this desired harmony, we need an educated understanding of all religions."

The more I worked with Fr. Virgil on the committee, the more I began to think that it would be wonderful to have available his life story. I could tell that with all of Fr. Virgil's activities, even at his advanced age, and probably also due to his Franciscan modesty, he was not likely to write his own autobiography. This is often the case with active leaders, both secular and religious. So how would this story be told? I began to toy with the idea of doing it myself through oral history.

After some thought, I decided to approach Fr. Virgil about working on his life story. I think there were three main reasons why I made this decision. First, of course, was my admiration for Fr. Virgil and the sense that now, with the endowed Chair in his honor, it was important that people in Santa Barbara and elsewhere know who this man is and what he represents. Second, given my own growing interest and involvement in Catholic Studies, I saw Fr. Virgil's story as part of this expansion of my intellectual and research interests.

Finally, at a more personal level, I felt that by doing this story that it would allow me to give back (no doubt Fr. Virgil's influence) to others who have given to me. These others in this case are the larger Santa Barbara community that since my arrival 30 years ago has been good to me and my family. I am not a native of Santa Barbara and of California (having been born and raised in El Paso, Texas), but I have now spent more of my life here than anywhere else. I felt that because Fr.Virgil's story is so tied in with Santa Barbara, this would be one way to use whatever talents I have as a historian to give back something to my adopted community. I would also be giving back to my Catholic faith community by focusing on the life of such a remarkable member of that community. There is no question but that I owe much of my own life development to the Catholic Church and especially to the role of the Catholic schools I attended, taught largely in my time by the Sisters of Loretto and the Christian Brothers. I am not a perfect Catholic, and I have sinned, as all of us have, but my life has been enriched and my own spirit strengthened by my Catholic faith. I may fall as a Catholic, but I am also uplifted by my faith. By doing Fr. Virgil's story, I felt that I was giving back something tangible to my Church.

When I approached Fr. Virgil about working on his life story, he consented without hesitation. I'm not certain he understood what it would lead to, other than a series of interviews, but he was gracious in accommodating me. I think, too, that with his characteristic modesty, he didn't believe this story would be of much interest to others. I assured him, and continue to do so, that his story has much meaning and significance, not only to the history of the Santa Barbara community, but to the larger history of the Franciscan Order. We began our interviews in early 2001. For awhile we met almost every week for about an hour. I audio taped the interviews and had them transcribed by my longtime transcriber, Darla McDavid. We approached Fr. Virgil's story chronologically. With some interruptions due to our work schedules and vacation and holiday periods, we worked for over three years in the preparation of this manuscript. I taped approximately 40 hours of interviews. Not all of the material is included in the book due to repetition or lesser relevance to Fr. Virgil's story.

Working with Fr. Virgil was a pure delight. He very quickly came to appreciate what the objectives were: to write and publish his life story. He was always ready for me, and we always got right down to business. It was equally a delight to do the interviews at the beautiful Santa Barbara Mission. I always looked forward to just going there. There was something calming and, yes, spiritual, about interviewing Fr. Virgil at the Mission. Part of this was the setting, but it was also Fr. Virgil in his brown Franciscan robe. Fr. Virgil told his story at two levels. One was by responding to my questions concerning his individual and family history. This was the more life-cycle part of the story. This was impressive enough to me but there was a second level of his narrative as well. Fr. Virgil sees his life in light of his spiritual growth. Hence, as we went through his life experiences, he always reflected on the evolving stages of his spiritual development. Listening to Fr. Virgil's spiritual journey, for me was a spiritual experience. I felt that our interviews were more than a scholarly exercise but encounter sessions as well. At some points, I almost felt like confessing to him but I resisted the temptation in order to maintain a level of professional relations. But our sessions were an experience unlike any that I have ever had in my career as a historian from a religious and spiritual standpoint.

As I have noted in my previous life-narrative books based on oral history, this work is collaborative and the production is a shared one. Fr. Virgil is the subject but unlike traditional autobiography, there is an intervening element, namely me. My questions produced and structured the narrative. Although my voice is not directly in the narrative, it is there in a covert or indirect fashion. Fr. Virgil, for the most part, is addressing my questions. This is what is referred to as dual authorship and is characteristic of and, indeed, fundamental to oral history projects.

Each interview was transcribed, and it was off the transcriptions plus listening to the tapes that I wrote each initial chapter draft. Fr. Virgil read each draft and made corrections and, more importantly, additions to the manuscript. Following my making these changes, he would read again the new draft. We went through three revised drafts of the manuscript to compose the final product. I should add that it was also extremely helpful that Fr. Virgil shared with me newspaper clippings, his published and unpublished spiritual writings, other documents, and photographs, all of which helped me in doing the interviews. In addition, Marc Patton at the *Santa Barbara News-Press* graciously assisted me by securing a copy of the *News-Press* clipping file on Fr. Virgil.

Working in this collaborative fashion, we produced the life and spiritual journey of Fr. Virgil. Fr. Virgil is the subject and co-author and his name is thus prominent in the title. As producer and co-author of the project, I am listed as the author. But we both needed each other.

Fr. Virgil's story has many facets and many historical meanings. However, I would note at least four that stand out for me. The first is the ethnic context. This is a story not just of a member of the Franciscan Order in the Untied States, but of an Italian-American member of that Order. It is the story of a child of Italian immigrants who came as poor people to the United States, as so many of their countrymen did around the turn of the twentieth century. In the case of Fr. Virgil's parents they came to California and eventually met, married, and settled in Sacramento. It is here where George (later Fr. Virgil) Cordano was born in 1918. The young George along with his four other brothers grew up in a largely Italian-American neighborhood and in a household where Italian traditions, including religious ones, ruled.

But as with other U.S. ethnic experiences, acculturation and new identities are part of the normal process of change, especially generational change. Fr. Virgil grew up the child of Italian immigrants, but he is not an immigrant. He is a U.S. born citizen. English became his primary language although his Italian is somewhat retained. His cultural tastes became more eclectic and more "Americanized" especially due to the influence of the English-language Catholic schools that he attended, by his peers including kids from other ethnic cultures, and by the impact of the English-language mass media, such as the movies. Fr. Virgil fortunately did not experience overt forms of ethnic discrimination and became secure in his American identity and yet, at the same time, was and is aware and accepts that he is of Italian descent. His ethnic and religious identities are shaped by his Italian-American Catholic background. Hence, at one level this text is an ethnic text. It is the story of an Italian-American who finds his role in U.S. society through the Church. Although, because Italian-Americans by Fr. Virgil's generation were more readily accepted as part of "white" America, his ethnic identity is less pronounced as compared to Latino Catholic priests, for example. Still, Fr. Virgil's story is an ethnic one, nonetheless, and provides us insight into a facet of U.S. ethnic history.

A second issue that I would highlight in Fr. Virgil's life history concerns the complex and mysterious world of the Catholic seminary in his time. This is a part of his life that shaped his early consciousness as a Franciscan and as a member of the clergy. At the same time, it is a part of his history that he has always been struggling with in religious and spiritual terms. When Fr. Virgil entered the seminary at St. Anthony's in Santa Barbara at the age of 15 in 1934, he entered into a world that had not changed that much for hundreds of years. Through his twelve years of seminary training until his ordination as a priest, Fr. Virgil experienced a very formal, traditional, and heavily disciplined way of life. It was a time, first of all, when those who felt, or had been influenced to believe, that they had a vocation to the priesthood were taken from their families at a very early age and integrated into the seminaries. Psychologically, this took a toll on young men such as Fr. Virgil. They no longer had the nurturing of their parents and their families. This was painful. During his seminary years, there was a period when Fr. Virgil saw his mother and his family once in six years. Instead, seminarians were told that they had a new family and a new community: the Franciscans.

The seminary was also a world of conformity and of strict obedience to a hierarchical order and theology. Seminary training in the pre-Vatican Council II years was characterized by a noncritical approach to religion, spirituality, and dogma. It was the time of what Fr. Virgil calls "ghetto Catholicism" when the Church defensively closed itself in against the world and against contact with those of other faiths. This was especially true of the seminaries. Moreover, the seminary was not a place to critically think or raise questions or to explore new ideas. Instead, it was a regimented space to learn how to follow authority and a prescribed set of rules and beliefs. Despite some loosening of this strict discipline due to the reforms associated with Vatican II in the 1960s, Fr. Virgil to this day still struggles with expressing his own views and following the authority of his superiors.

It was also a time when spiritual training focused primarily on just getting to the next world or Heaven. One concentrated on the virtues of life after death and avoided this world, which was seen as the setting for sin and temptations. As a result, seminary training prepared young students such as Fr. Virgil for the next world, but not very well for this one. The social responsibility of the Church was not as well defined as it would be following the major changes in the Church as a result of Vatican II.

It is not that Fr. Virgil does not appreciate what was good about his training, especially learning discipline, hard work, and the basis of his faith and his commitment to his vocation. Fr. Virgil wanted more than anything else to become a Franciscan and a priest. The seminary years helped him to achieve his calling in life. At the same time, he looks back and laments the losses: the lack of a daily presence of a loving mother and family; the lack of a spiritual training that stressed a balance between the other world and this world; the lack of a more intellectually stimulating environment; the lack of a linkage between religion and psychology so that he and others of his age could better understand the emotional and physical changes that they were undergoing; and the lack of a more ecumenical perspective that appreciated other faiths.

Fr. Virgil's account of a seminary world that has largely faded (although some traditionalists in the Church would welcome it back) is another contribution that this narrative makes. It reminds us about and educates us to that aspect of Church history in the United States. It raises questions about this type of training. Questions that may still have relevance today given the recent sexual scandals involving priests that some believe, including Fr. Virgil, that in part may have to do with this earlier type of education and socialization that deprived young men of knowing their full selves, including their sexual identities and emotions. For those not acquainted with this closed older world of Catholic seminaries, Fr. Virgil's account of his experiences will be enlightening.

This more insular world of the Catholic Church, however, was significantly shattered due to the impact of Vatican Council II. This historic gathering of bishops called by Pope John XXIII met between 1962 and 1965 in order to bring new changes and reforms to the Church and to make it more responsible to the modern world. It challenged centuries of thought and behavior within the Church. It was not a revolution but an updating of the Church. It sent new winds of change within the Church and caused much dislocation and uncertainty to both clergy and laity.

These changes and tensions were both at the macro level and at the micro one. It affected the universal Church and the local one. Fr. Virgil's story reveals how Vatican II affected the workings of the Franciscan Order at Mission Santa Barbara. It represents a case study of the tumultuous impact that Vatican II's call for renewal had at the local level. It suggested that authority be more widely shared within the Church so that not everything came from the top, in this case the Vatican. That sounded promising but with no traditions of shared authority, it also caused ambivalence and conflict. The Franciscans including Fr. Virgil welcomed change but they did not know how to change. They had no traditions of self-rule. What changes would the Order implement and how far should they go? There was no one to tell them what to do and they had no experience in making these types of decisions themselves.

As a result, as Fr. Virgil painfully still remembers, the Order in Santa Barbara underwent some very trying times. Some (who Fr. Virgil refers to as the self-proclaimed liberals or radicals) wanted immediate and drastic changes involving self-governance and a new more relaxed rule of discipline, while others, including Fr. Virgil, wanted changes and accepted the new spirit of Vatican Council II, but believed that the changes had to be deliberate and not to the extremes desired by the others. Fr. Virgil, due to his leadership position, found himself caught right in the middle and, as such, subject to much criticism and even abuse, especially by the radicals. Changes in the liturgy and in the running of the seminaries were instituted, but never fast enough or far enough for some. At the same time, what changes Fr. Virgil supported were opposed by some of the laity who felt that they were losing "their" Church. Fr. Virgil recalls the period of the 1960s as some of the most difficult years of his life as a Franciscan. It divided friars against each other and laity against clergy and even against other laity.

Yet the spirit of renewal and an emphasis on a new worldliness by the Church were welcomed and supported by Fr. Virgil. It was a time that tested his commitment to the Church, but it was also a time that advanced his spirituality. One central aspect of this advance was Fr. Virgil's embrace of the new ecumenical spirit within the Church. Vatican II called for a dialogue with not only other Christian religions but with non-Christian faiths as well. Fr. Virgil recognized the importance and relevance of this new ecumenical movement. Having grown up sensing that his own Italian-American Catholicism was often looked down upon by Catholics of other ethnic backgrounds, Fr. Virgil understood the importance of religious understanding and tolerance. Ecumenism and interfaith dialogue became a central component of Fr Virgil's life and of his spirituality. Everyone was a child of God of whatever faith, and all were welcomed into His kingdom.

Finally, what I further find impressive in Fr. Virgil's story is how even before Vatican II, but certainly accelerated by it, Fr. Virgil understood and appreciated the importance of the Church and, in his case, the Franciscan Order reaching beyond itself to others in the community, and not just Catholics, but people of other faiths or no faiths. This is the community side of Fr. Virgil that has led, in part, to his beloved and even celebratory status in the Santa Barbara area. As head of Public Relations for Mission Santa Barbara for some four decades, Fr. Virgil has integrated the role of the Mission with the larger community. He has helped make the Mission a central aspect of what Santa Barbara means and, at the same time, integrated the community into the meaning of the Mission. As such, Fr. Virgil represents what I call a "community priest." Fr. Virgil is not an overtly political person, and yet his role as the community liaison for the Mission serves a political purpose in the best meaning of that term. It links religion to public life. Fr. Virgil sees his role as bringing people together, including people of different religious, ethnic, and economic backgrounds. His is a healing mission. He is a missionary, but a missionary to all people, and with the task not of converting to his faith, but of converting to the acceptance of the common humanity of all and of the divine nature of that humanity. We are all made in the likeness and love of God, irrespective of our particular faith or no faith, and as such we should love one another and accept each other as brothers and sisters. This is the best form of political work, and Fr. Virgil, although he would not consider it such, carries it out with great skill and yet with great modesty. Fr. Virgil holds his community together, and no one does it better than he.

These four key aspects of Fr. Virgil's life story that I have outlined above, and others as well in the narrative, represent the content of a remarkable life centered on giving to others. This is an extraordinary contribution and one that is hard for the rest of us to emulate: a life of giving. Yet, hopefully, we can be inspired to do so as much as possible in our lives by Fr. Virgil's example. It is my great pleasure to present to you Fr. Virgil's story that reminds us that there is still much good in the Catholic Church and much good in all of us. We are all sinners but there is forgiveness and redemption also for us. The future of the Catholic Church and of our world lies in our common understanding that we are all part of one humanity graced by God, and it is this shared recognition that will make for a Church and a world where everyone will have equal voices, responsibilities, and equitable shares of God's fruit on earth.

PROLOGUE

We are born of a mother to be born of God.
— FR. VIRGIL CORDANO

Our mothers are so much a part of our lives that when they die there is
left behind an immense gap in us. I can't think of any family member's
death that affects us more than that of our mothers. Our mothers gave us
life, nourished us, and lovingly cared for us until their deaths.

This is how I felt when my mother died in 1973.

My mother's death forced me to reflect on all that she had meant to
me. I said her funeral Mass and delivered the eulogy. I said a few words
but it was difficult.

I wasn't up to giving the kind of eulogy that my mother deserved. I
have no remembrance of what I said. I think I expressed my admiration
of and gratitude to her.

If I could speak that eulogy now I would praise her motherly love and
care for me. Over the years, I have come to be in reverential awe of the
vocation of a mother. Maybe the deepest expression of human love is that
of a mother for her children. It is the ultimate model and inspiration of
the giving of one's very self to others. She lives her life tenderly caring for
those born of her love and her flesh. She cherishes the life of her children
more than her own life. Children are an extension of her self. Her love is
both joyous and sacrificial. Maybe we can say that the affectionate love of
a mother is the originating source from which all other kinds of love are
developed. She is the first one to love us.

It is also the initially experienced love that points the way to our
understanding of God, who is Love. We are born of a mother to be born

of God. We are loved into existence by a mother to come to experience all other loves, especially the fullness of love in God. Often, especially at the baptism of a child, I reflect on my early days of infancy and subsequent years of growth. I (and all of us) was entirely dependent for the satisfaction of my needs on the love of my mother. Even now she lives, even now she loves and cares, one with the heavenly love of God. Life and love never die. They are eternal because they are of God. I am grateful that I am loved and that I can love in return.

We buried Mother at St. Mary's Cemetery in Sacramento. My mother left almost nothing behind. I had nothing but the greatest admiration for her. She had come to this country as a poor immigrant and had worked hard for her children as a janitor and as a cannery worker. She was a brave woman and a wonderful mother.

What I learned from my mother, and hopefully am somewhat like her, is the priority of faith in God, my serious concern for what is most important in life, a willingness to work hard, an appreciation of ties with family and friends, and, I might add, with all whom I meet a sense of duty and honesty, and a profound hope in a better future.

I only regret not having spent more time with her as I was growing up. I missed her all those years that I was in the seminary and I miss her now. May she rest in peace. I not only pray for her but ask her to pray for me. She gave me life that I might one day enjoy the fullness of eternal life with her.

1

SACRAMENTO BOY

As I look back over my early life at home, I grow in appreciation of the support, love, and sense of belonging given to me by my ties with my extended family of aunts, uncles, and cousins. We enjoyed being together.

— FR. VIRGIL CORDANO

My journey in becoming a Franciscan priest began well before I entered the seminary. It commenced with my family and my early childhood experiences. Cordano marks me as being of Italian ancestry. I'm part of the Italian-American Catholic saga in the United States.

My family comes from the province of Liguria in northern Italy. Genoa is the key city in this region. The people here are referred to as Genoese. They speak Genoese, a particular dialect somewhat different from Toscano the main Italian dialect.

The Cordanos go back generations. The Cordano name is a rather common one in this region. My mother's maiden name was Cordano like my father's. The name Cordano, I think, means rope or cord. It probably is linked to people who made rope or cord.

Both of my parents were born in a little village called Favale di Malvaro a short distance up from the Italian Riviera. The town's main claim to fame is A.P. Giannini, the founder of the Bank of America in the United States who was born there. In the piazza of the village there is a bronze statue of Giannini. On one side, he's holding his luggage and waving goodbye as he leaves for America. On the other side, he's on a ship looking at the Statue of Liberty.

Many from Favale di Malvaro emigrated during the late nineteenth century primarily for economic reasons. Curiously, more from the village went to South America than to the United States. If you go to Lima, Peru today you will find many Cordanos. Other common Genoese names are Cereghino, Boitano, and Giannini. Their dialect is somewhat French-sounding. Of course, many other Italians at this time also went to the United States.

I've often visited Favale di Malvaro. I go there almost every five years. It has a beautiful church where I've had the privilege of saying Mass. Unfortunately, the village has been dying off for some years. The young people have left because there are few economic opportunities for them. They've gone to the cities in Italy or they have emigrated. There's not even a restaurant anymore in the village but only a lone bar where you can get something to drink. Some people from the cities use the village as a summer resort. It's quite pleasant there and cooler than in Genoa. Mostly old-timers live there now including a couple of my relatives.

My mother's family home still exists, although it's been remodeled. My father's is gone. His was up on a rocky place called *la rocca* or the rock or the fortress. My father's home was on one hill and my mother's on another.

My father's name was Vittorio and my mother's was María. They probably knew each other then, but it's not clear since my mother was much younger. Parts of both families were farmers or makers of slate, who barely eked out a living. My mother's father was somewhat of a small businessman who did well enough to support his family. They were all poor but hard-working people.

Yet it was a tight-knit community and a very Catholic one. But poverty drove many of them out and many emigrated, including my father's and mother's families. Apparently my grandfather on my father's side came to the United States along with my father and his three sisters. I'm not as clear about my father's background but they came around the turn of the century, in the second half of the 1800s, around the same time as my mother's family came. Because others from the village had come all the way to California, primarily to the Sacramento and Stockton area, this is where both of my parent's families also migrated to in a form of chain migration.

Here in the Sacramento area, which was then mostly rural, many families resumed their traditions as farmers. In fact, you find more northern Italians in northern California than you do in southern California where I believe mostly southern Italians went. There's always been a bit of a rivalry between the northern Italians and the southern Italians. Both speak different dialects. Also the northerners speak of the southerners as residents of *bassa Italia*, lower Italy. When you meet another Italian for the first time, the first thing you ask is *"Da che parte di Italia viene?"* [From what part of Italy do you come?]

In northern California many Italians also settled in San Francisco, especially in North Beach, which they referred to as "Northa Beacha." Often Italians would take the English word and attach an "a" or a vowel to it, such as jump-a-la-fence-a, catch-a-la-bus-a. My father came to California when he was already in his early twenties. My mother was about fourteen. Her older brothers had come first and then they sent for her. In the Italian idiom, "they called for her."

My mother was a sickly girl. The winters can get quite cold in that part of Italy and this affected her health. Her brothers felt she might improve in the warmer California climate. So she migrated with several other Italian women. It was a big ocean trip in those days. It was also a scary one because my mother and the others knew no English.

They landed in New York and then caught a train for California. On the train, for the first time in my mother's life, she encountered a black man. Frightened by his appearance, my mother and the other women started praying right away for protection.

Some of my maternal uncles resumed farming east of Sacramento. Two of them were twins, Tony and Joe. Tony lived to be 105 years old. Another farmer was Uncle John, popularly known as "Billy." The uncles in farming apparently first worked for other farmers and then when they had saved enough, bought their own small farms.

One of my uncles was called George or GB, but his real name was Giovanni Baptista, or John the Baptist. He was a businessman. A half brother of my mother, Carmelo, lived in San Francisco. All of them, of course, had true Italian names but as children we preferred to call them by their anglicized names.

Another uncle of mine, named Luigi or Louis, was a window-washer in San Francisco who while at work tragically fell from a tall building and died.

My uncles' farms were just outside the Sacramento city limits. When I was a youngster, Sacramento ended at about 31st Street. My uncles' farms started at about 65th Street, which was considered the outskirts of the city. Today Sacramento as a metropolis extends well beyond where the farms were.

The Italians from Favale di Malvaro all re-united and re-established their earlier community bonds. They called themselves the "Favalesi." Every year the Favalesi living in California would come together at a picnic in San Jose where they celebrated their rich heritage. Gladly they would celebrate baptisms, weddings, birthdays, and anniversaries. Even at funerals their sorrow was complemented by the joyful celebration of the entry of another Italian into Heaven.

My relatives attended an Italian parish church, St. Mary's, at 7th and T Streets. The Masses were in Latin but the homilies were spoken in Italian. I was an altar boy (they're now called altar servers) at the church. The church was the setting for many social events besides religious ceremonies.

At all gatherings there was much to eat and drink. At Uncle Billy's and Uncle Joe's ranches there was always a game of bocce to be played. Italian music could be heard and Italian songs were sung. Most Sunday afternoons were spent with part of the clan at the ranches. I visited my parents' relatives often. The caring interest of the extended family gave me a very supportive sense of belonging.

I'm not sure how my parents met and began to court, but probably it was at one of these community events. The Favelesi also visited each other in their homes regularly, so it might have been on such an occasion as well.

Not all cultural traditions survived the migration to California including the one of the man asking the woman's parents permission to marry their daughter. So my father didn't have to do that, especially since my mother's parents had stayed in Italy. It's possible, however, that he at least had to talk to her brothers. In any event, they got married in the early 1900s at St. Francis Church, the Franciscan church near Sutter's Fort. I am not sure of the date nor why they got married there and not at St. Mary's, the Italian church in Sacramento. I guess this is where the Franciscan influence in my life began.

As I look back over my early life at home, I grow in appreciation of the support, love, and sense of belonging given to me by my ties with my extended family of aunts, uncles, and cousins. We enjoyed being together. I can better understand now why I felt so alone later in leaving home for institutional living with previously unknown students in new surroundings and a changed daily routine. It took a long time to be "at home" with others, a new extended family. Today I cherish my Franciscan ties and my closeness to many friends in Santa Barbara. I am never alone.

†

Both my mother and father were short in stature. In contrast with the other relatives, both were not very demonstrative or loud in speech. I never really got to know my father very well. My mother was, for all practical purposes, both mother and "father" to me and my siblings. My mother had a very pleasant face and was easily liked by all because she was very respectful of all those whom she encountered.

Unlike others in his family, my father never cared for farming. So he tried his hands at different things, at none of which he had any great success. For awhile he was a bootblack, a person who shined shoes. At another time he worked at Folsom prison as a guard. We were always moving because he kept finding new jobs. All of these jobs were within a radius of 5-100 miles from Sacramento.

It was my mother who carried the economic load for the family. I remember as a youngster my parents arguing over finances, since my father spent too much of his money in gambling. My mother worked in the canneries. She had worked there before marrying, and, given my father's very limited income, she continued to do so after as well. There were no union wages and no job benefits in the canneries. She received very little but somehow we ate well.

The canneries were only a few blocks away from home. Now and then my mother would come home very late in the night. I and my brother Ray ate the evening meal she left for us on the dining room table and then went off to bed. Sometimes we would go to the cannery and walk home with her.

The pressure on my mother kept building as the children started to come. The first child was my brother, Jim who was born in 1904. In all, my mother had five boys: Jim, Andrew, Philip, then me, George (my baptismal name), and the youngest, Raymond. I was born on December 3, 1918.

My mother always wanted a daughter but didn't have one. To compensate for this, she wrote to her family in Italy and asked them to send over a young girl. They did. This was Carmela Cereghino, my mother's niece. Carmela was like a member of the family, a beautiful young woman, very warm, affectionate and delightful company. She was already a teenager and lived with us for a few years until she married a fellow by the name of Manuel Garibaldi. They had two children, Eva and Roy, very close cousins of mine.

Andrew, the second oldest brother, died in the terrible Spanish Flu Epidemic of 1918, a worldwide health crisis. Many people died suddenly. Andrew was only eight years old at the time. My mother told me that Andrew was a very spiritual and sensitive boy. My brother Jim said that Andrew was the best one of us. Our parish priest also died during the epidemic. Jim remembers that each family had to bury its own dead. So Jim and my father buried Andrew. The coffins throughout Sacramento just stacked up at the time. My mother was pregnant with me and I was born shortly after Andrew died.

My mother wasn't feeling well. So she asked this Genoese girl, Eleanor Corsiglia, to be my godmother and to care for me because my mother was very sick and saddened by the death of Andrew. As a result, it was Eleanor who named me. She came up with the name George. Years later I asked her why she chose this name. "I don't know. I just liked the name," she said. Eleanor was a second mother for me. I always felt close to her and her family by marriage, the Coffrinis. Close ties to families added much to my happiness in my early life. Fortunately, my mother improved in health. While my baptismal name was George, my mother called me Giorgio, the Italian for George.

Because my father kept changing jobs, my parents and their growing family lived in many different homes. Jim changed elementary schools six or seven times. My parents finally settled at 6th and S Streets in the south side of Sacramento. There was a Southside park nearby, a favorite spot for our neighborhood. Many other Italians also lived in south Sacramento. That's where I was born and raised.

While many Italians lived in our neighborhood, so too did other ethnic groups. There were Portuguese, Croatians, and a few Irish and Asian persons. The Portuguese had their own church, St. Elizabeth's, while we had St. Mary's. The major social events of our neighborhood were the church ones such as the St. Mary's parish picnic. We'd go there, and, while the adults played bingo, the kids would play a variety of games. In one game, they'd have a salami hanging down from a tree. With a potato, you had to try to hit the salami to win it. For us kids, the picnic was the big social event. Everything centered around the church. Again, there was good Italian food and music that accompanied the dancing. A young girl by the name of Lena Casali, whose family lived next door to me, used to teach my brother Ray and me how to dance and sing – and we did so at parish social events and a local theater. The Casali family residence was like another home for us.

†

Among my first memories are having a wagon and playing games like marbles and jacks. I think my childhood was not very different from that of other children. I remember making my First Communion when I was around six. For my First Communion, I wore a special suit with a white tie. I recall that I was very happy on that occasion, as I was at all church events. I went to confession, I believe, once a month, and welcomed the resultant freedom from guilt over my sins or better, self-displeasure. It all made sense. I never had any doubts about the kind of God I experience in my faith.

My minor failings were similar to those of other children whose confessions I have heard. I welcomed the experience of being freed from the burden of guilt, or self-accusation. Yes, children in their own way are healthier for sharing with others what stirs deeply within themselves. I have come to know of their need to be listened to. A child who had confessed her sins to me told her parents that she came out of the confessional "feeling like an angel." Our heaviest burden in life is to fail ourselves. Often I have told children and others that when your heart accuses you, you must recall that God is greater than your accusing heart (1 John 3: 19-20).

I also enjoyed being an altar boy and serving Mass, but had no idea then that it would lead to a vocation to the priesthood. I felt very close to the Church even at an early age. My belief in God was an essential part of my Italian heritage.

I think that I felt so close to the Church because it represented community for me as did my family, my school, and my neighborhood. Not only did I feel close to others in religious services, but also in the many social events sponsored by the church. In addition, I was gladdened by the good news that God does not punish but loves and forgives. Also, I was assured of happiness in life after death. This was my deepest longing – for myself and for others.

At home, my parents mostly spoke the Genoese dialect. When they would meet non-Genoese Italians, they'd speak the Tuscan Italian dialect. Once in awhile they would speak in English. I understood Genoese, but I never spoke it. I would respond in English, strange as that may seem.

We grew up with a clear understanding that we were Italians, and we were proud of our heritage. At an early age, I realized that some people in Sacramento were anti-Italian. We were a minority population similar to minorities today such as Latinos and African Americans. Italians expected Italians to marry within their ethnic group. At times I'd hear my mother say, "He/She married an American! Italians should marry Italians."

"But Mom, we're all Americans," I responded.

"Yes, but we're Italians too," she came back with the final word.

Some of the non-Italians would call us "wops" and "dagos." We countered by calling the Slovenian kids "dog eaters." I don't know why, but we did. But aside from some light name-calling, we got along very well.

I was not ashamed of being Italian but I didn't like the exclusivity of being only Italian. I wanted to be accepted by more people than just Italians. I wanted to be accepted as the person I was, beyond the designation of being an Italo-American. I had no difficulty in accepting my being both American and Italian. I believe that I had no biases against people based on their race or religion.

I cherished extended family culture. This was a big factor in my life. Aunts, uncles, and cousins, they all were part of our lives. Looking back now, from a psychological, emotional, and cultural perspective, I was very much at home when members of the extended family got together. Often we would visit at one of the relative's home where everyone would gather for a good time. While the kids ran around and played, the adults would play bocce ball and sing and drink wine. My mother loved to visit her relatives. Besides accompanying my mother when she visited her brothers' families, I also went with her when she spent time with the families of my father's three sisters who lived in and near Stockton.

We were poor and probably even poorer during the Great Depression. But I never lamented my economic status. We had all that we needed. I knew that we had to count our pennies, as did others in our neighborhood. We were properly clothed. We always had plenty to eat. My uncles who were farmers would give us a variety of fruits and vegetables. Also we had peach, cherry, and fig trees in our backyard.

My mother cooked tasty Italian meals. Sometimes we would just have a good bowl of minestrone soup and bread. That's all we needed. My favorite dish was pasta and chicken. While we were served vegetables, Ray and I didn't care for them. I also loved dessert such as the pies and cakes made by my mother and also those bought in nearby stores. I didn't have a favorite one, but as kids we always had a sweet tooth. We'd used to go down to a store on K Street and buy three candy bars for ten cents. Sometimes we'd go to the drugstore and get a milk shake for eleven cents or an ice cream cone for five cents. Often we enjoyed buying focaccia, a kind of pizza without the varied toppings of today.

†

Because my mother was a deeply religious member of the strong Italian Catholic community in Sacramento, I and my brothers were sent to Catholic elementary schools and high school. We attended the Cathedral Parish School on 8th and S Streets close to our home on 6th and S. The school, run by the Sisters of Charity and Penance, was part of the Blessed Sacrament Cathedral parish under the direction of mostly Irish American priests. The Cathedral itself was located on 11th and K Streets in downtown Sacramento.

We were within the Cathedral parish although we attended Mass at St. Mary's, the national church for Italians within the Cathedral parish. There was a certain tension of cultural differences between the Italians and the Irish clergy. My mother and other Italians found services in Italian more to their liking. They didn't feel comfortable in a non-Italian church. But, at the same time, she wanted us to get a good Catholic education so she sent us to the Cathedral Parish School since St. Mary's didn't have one.

I started in kindergarten, and, because my mother worked all day, I and my younger brother Ray stayed there most of the day. The nuns fed us lunch that we didn't savor. It involved a complete change of diet. They would feed us cabbage that instead of eating, we stuffed into our pants pockets. We would dump it when the nuns weren't looking, but Sister Clementia finally caught us. After that, she called us the "cabbage kids." She was a delightful lady and a wonderful teacher. She used to tell me that I would be a priest. She was admired by us because her bright personality kept us interested in all that went on in the classroom.

In elementary school, the nuns had a great impact on my life. Their order was originally from Holland. Their main headquarters on the West Coast was on the peninsula south of San Francisco. They came out of a very severe Catholic Dutch church. For instance, they were not permitted to eat with laypersons. They were great women and teachers. I think that the real strength of the Catholic Church in those days is attributable to the teaching nuns. They were totally devoted and self-sacrificing, quite removed from socializing with those outside the convent.

At that time, of course, they wore their full habit that revealed only their bright and caring faces. They gave themselves fully to God and to the service of others. I admired them tremendously. Thanks to them, I acquired good study habits. After my family, they were the greatest influence in my life.

Our school had quite an ethnic mix resembling our neighborhood. Italian, Portuguese, Croatians, and Irish, and a few Mexican Americans made up the student body. Neither can I remember any ethnic tensions among the kids at school. There were the usual pranks of young people outside of school but not in the school itself. I remember Stephen Morgan, Evelyn Wear, Jim Malloy, Dave Bennett, Caroline Bianchi,

Manuel Soares, and Elizabeth Horgan.

The school charged no tuition because the diocese picked up the costs. However, my mother did have to pay for our books. Ray and I were the only ones in our family who attended this Catholic school. Jim attended St. Stephen's and various public schools during the early years when my parents were constantly moving. Andrew, of course, had died before I was born. Philip, around age five or six, caught an infection of some kind. The doctors didn't have a treatment for it and he ended up somewhat retarded. He had to be put in a home for awhile since it was difficult for my mother to adequately take care of him. He later recovered to an extent, but he still was like a child who enjoyed the little things in life.

At the Cathedral School, we wore uniforms. For the boys, this consisted of a white shirt and blue tie. For pants, we generally wore blue corduroys. The other boys liked to wear their pants somewhat dirty. It was the style. But my mother wouldn't hear of this. She always insisted on washing our pants.

"But Mom," I would say, "the other boys wear them like that."

"Give me those dirty pants," she replied. "I don't care what the other kids do."

The girls at the school also had to wear uniforms, white blouses and blue skirts.

The uniforms represented part of the discipline at the school, the discipline common to those early days. There was discipline all over the place. If you misbehaved, the nuns whacked your hands with a belt. You were disciplined at school and at home. My mother would grab anything handy and swing at us if we stepped out of line. My father only threatened us with punishment. That was part of life. I never had any trouble with that. It was part of the culture of the time. Rules had to be observed.

I was a very good student. I got mostly A's. I'd stay up late at night doing my homework. I was also well-behaved. Monthly I went to confession or what is called reconciliation today. I had friends, but I was a bit more on the introverted side. I was more reflective and serious than some of the other kids.

Throughout my elementary school years, Sister Clementia, my kindergarten teacher, remained one of my favorite teachers. I liked some of the others but can't remember their names. I liked my seventh grade teacher. She was from Germany and had a slight foreign accent. I thought she was one of the best teachers I had. She used to put on play productions and nearly always picked me to be the leading character. The plays were highly moralistic.

I also enjoyed playing sports. We had teams in basketball, baseball, and soccer. Baseball was my favorite sport. I usually played an infield position. I think I knew more about baseball than I did about religion. Mother didn't like me playing soccer because I would return home with bruised shins.

I liked girls as I grew up but never got that serious over a relationship. There was Muriel in my class throughout elementary school, whom I liked, and who was very smart. She and I were academically competitive. She was attractive and I liked her even though we were rivals. The closest I came to a girlfriend in elementary school was Caroline Bianchi. She asked me for my pin, which I won for having the best grade in religion. This, I guess, symbolized some kind of romantic attachment. I gave it to her. However, after about six months I noticed that she wasn't wearing it anymore.

"What happened," I asked her.

"Well, I lost it," she sheepishly replied.

In later years, jokingly I gave this as the reason why I became a priest.

Tongue in cheek, I said to myself, "If that's the way women are then I'm going to the seminary."

But I was silently disappointed that Caroline no longer had my pin. She actually thought of becoming a nun but didn't. Only one girl in my class, Evelyn Wear, did become a nun. I was the only boy in my class who entered a seminary, although most boys gave the priesthood much thought. It was believed to be the highest vocation in life.

I can't recall receiving any positive sex education at school. Rather, we were told to observe the sixth commandment and other moral norms. For Valentine's Day, the nuns gave us holy cards that were pictures of saints.

†

As I grew up life was centered around family, school, Church, and the leisure time spent with neighborhood kids. I had a couple of good friends like Norman Silva and Manuel Soares, two Portuguese boys. My brother, Ray, was my main friend. We'd play hockey on the street using a palm branch and an old tin can. We also played baseball on corner lots. At Christmas we'd sometimes get new roller skates and skate all around the neighborhood.

We especially liked going to the movies. My parents never gave us an allowance, but movies were cheap then. It cost ten cents for admission. The theaters were all downtown, which was close to home. There was the Senator Theater and several more. Each Saturday they'd have free admission for kids. Besides the film, they would have talent contests before the movie. You could either sing a song or lead a live band. Ray and I used to compete. After you had performed, the winner was the one who received the bigger applause by the audience. Ray always beat me. His prize was some candy.

My favorite films were the cowboy and gangster ones. Our first movies were the silent ones and then by the 1930s the "talkies" started. I especially remember a very early talkie with Al Jolson singing "Mammy, Mammy." Cowboy favorites were Tom Mix and Ken Maynard. I also enjoyed the comedies with Buster Keaton, Harold Lloyd, and Laurel and Hardy.

Our playing companions included girls sometimes as we entered adolescence. There was a neighborhood girl, Lena Caseli, who was a few years older than we were. We used to go over to her house rather frequently since my mother was working most of the time. Lena showed us how to play Post Office and Spin the Bottle at her home with some of the other neighborhood girls and boys. These were kissing games. The "postman" would come in with a letter for you. "You are to kiss Nancy." Or you would spin the bottle and when it pointed to Suzy you had to kiss her. We'd laugh and saw it as just a game. It was nice and a healthy way to begin to realize sexual differences during our pre-puberty years.

†

It was when I was ten years old that my dad died. He had been sick for some time. As a result, he used to eat a special diet of vegetables – a dislike of mine. While he was somewhat aloof, I knew that he cared for us. He finally was restricted to bed where he eventually died of cancer. His sisters, Eugenia and Teresa, from Stockton came to visit him and to help my mother take care of him. Although my father did not attend church services regularly, I remember seeing the priest come to the house to give my father "the anointing of the sick" called at that time "the last rites."

I remember going to bed and hearing my mother say the next morning, "Your father died during the night." I can recall only crying once, when I was told the news. I wasn't that close to him. If my mother had died, I would have felt it more.

There was a funeral Mass and we buried my father in the new Catholic cemetery on 65th Street that was separate from where my brother Andrew was buried. Even now when I return to Sacramento, I visit my father's and mother's graves. After the burial, my aunts, uncles, and cousins who had attended the funeral went to the house of Serafina, one of my father's sisters for a reception. That sort of eased the blow and lightened the burden. I was comforted by the assurance that my father was now in Heaven.

I felt a sense of loss in my father's dying, even though he didn't have a significant influence on my life. I didn't really know him well. As I look back, I miss not having had a more influential father figure. I would have like that. I can't recall that he ever took me aside and talked to me. I grew up with little emotional support from my dad. I don't know what affect this had on me deep inside, if any. My mother's care, the closeness of brotherly ties, and the continuing support of my extended family lessened the sense of loss. Besides, at funerals, I became accustomed to facing up to and accepting the reality of death.

My father's death didn't necessarily increase the financial pressure on my mother since she was carrying the load already. Jim also began to earn money for the family. My father provided very little. My mother had gone from working in the canneries to doing janitor work downtown at the Mitau Building on 8th and J Streets. Ray and I used to help her. Every day at 5 P.M., we'd go to the building and empty wastepaper baskets and do other work such as dusting. We worked for about two hours. If we got there late, my mother would threaten to hit us with a mop. She especially expressed her anger at Ray, who was much more rebellious than I. An Italian friend, Emilio, was in charge of the building. He'd come along and claim that Ray and I hadn't cleaned properly. Ray would be defiant and say, "We're through here, goodbye. Let's go, George." So we'd leave.

However, I had to return some of the evenings to run the elevator. I would go on my bike to begin operating the elevator at 10 P.M. when young women would finish secretarial school and needed to exit the building. Ray and I didn't get paid for our work. They only paid my mother and she didn't get much. For awhile, I also delivered certain handouts for some businesses. Because of our financial difficulties, Jim, as the oldest brother, had dropped out of high school to start working full time.

†

When I was at the Cathedral Parish School, I was very serious about religious matters and in time came to believe that I had a vocation to the priesthood. This was in part due to the influence of the nuns, and also to the general Catholic culture of my home and of the Italian community.

My mother was deeply religious. She attended daily Mass at St. Mary's while I was the altar boy. Without her faith, she wouldn't have held up. Her faith was her strength. I remember one night looking into her room and seeing her on her knees praying next to her bed. That made a tremendous impression on me. God really matters.

At home, my mother also had many religious icons. There were all the traditional Italian Catholic saints such as St. Francis and St. Anthony. Of course, she had a special devotion to Mary – María "La Madonna" – the Blessed Mother. She also was devoted to St. Giuseppe or St. Joseph. She would attend many novenas and devotions at the church. A novena is nine consecutive days of prayer in preparation for the celebration of a feast. I would sometimes accompany her to these services. I don't recall saying particular family prayers at home or regular grace before meals. I guess my mother figured that the nuns took care of our religious instruction. Instead, she taught us by her example of caring love and hard work.

Outside of home, besides Sunday Mass, we'd also participate in the Italian Catholic festivals at St. Mary's. These included the *festa* of Mary and the Saints. On Corpus Christi day, there would be a procession around our school. Religion and Italian culture were closely linked. These people were Catholic because of their Italian culture. I later noticed that among the succeeding generations of Italian Americans, the less Italian they became, the less Catholic they were. Culture carries religion. For me, it was a nice blend to be Catholic and Italian.

Next to Christmas and in some ways even more important to Italian Catholics were the services of Holy Week. This would be preceded by the Lenten season. Every Catholic was expected to do penance during this six-week period. Of course at that time, eating meat was forbidden on all Fridays of the year, but especially during Lent. This was particularly painful for me at times. Sometimes we would go see the local Sacramento minor league baseball team, the Sacramento Senators, play. Each Friday during the season was kid's day and besides the free admission, you could also get a hotdog. But since it was Friday I would not dare to eat a hotdog. It wasn't easy since a ball game seemed to call for a hotdog. I was tempted, but I didn't give in. In my youth, I was very observant of rules and regulations.

During Lent, my mother insisted that we give up something. We gave up candy but the hardest penance was my mother insisting that we give up going to the movies. I thought that the best movies came out during Lent!

On Holy Thursday, my mother would take us to visit several of the Catholic churches in Sacramento such as St. Mary's, the Cathedral, and St. Elizabeth's where we admired the lavish floral decorations. I particularly remember having to attend with my mother very long services on Holy Saturday at St. Mary's. The priests read twelve long readings in Latin. At parish missions I had to also listen to lengthy sermons. At times I fell asleep because they went on and on. All this would last three to four hours. The missionaries would talk and talk. I don't recall much of what they said other than the emphasis on the importance of living a good life to avoid hell and to go to Heaven.

Growing up in this religious environment meant that Catholicism became as natural to me as the air I breathed. I was just as sure that God existed as my mother existed. It was that simple. In that setting, I began to realize that I had a calling to the priesthood. Nothing was more important than religious faith, and maybe I was being called to give myself full time to my Church.

I must have been eleven or twelve when I was sure that I had a vocation. But this was not a sudden revelation. I was very religious early in life. I remember very well my First Communion. I didn't have a deep theological understanding of it, but I knew that it brought me closer to God. I had the same feeling about my Confirmation. I was well prepared to answer the bishop's question about my being prepared to become a soldier of Christ. In my graduation class from elementary school, I achieved the highest marks in religion. I took religion very seriously.

At home, I would always say my evening prayers before going to bed. God was important to me at all times. During the day, if I did anything wrong, I'd right away feel guilty. It was a healthy guilt. I had no trouble in going to confession and telling the priest that I lied or that I stole something at home. Confession was a welcome release from my sense of guilt.

I went about once a month. We'd line up and go into the confessional like an assembly line. One hurriedly after another. Also I believed that according to a devotion to the Sacred Heart of Jesus, if you went to confession on nine consecutive First Fridays, you would go straight to Heaven when you died.

I took all of this seriously. I would say that my religion at that time was what I would call today eschatological or very other worldly. It's a big theological word that means that the other world – Heaven – mattered so much more than this life on earth. Later, I became incarnational – another big theological word meaning that this world mattered also, and that God was also in the present world. But these distinctions would come later in my theological education.

At school, the focus in religion was on morality, acceptance of the Church's teachings, and obedience to authority. I memorized the answers to all the question asked in the Catechism. I recited the customary vocal prayers such as "O God I love you, trust in you, help me." We sang many hymns to the Blessed Mother, such as "On this day, O beautiful Mother, daily, daily sing to Mary, Mother dearest, Mother fairest."

Part of my religious socialization was being an altar boy. I began when I was five or six years of age. I liked it. I was proud to be one. It seemed very natural to me. Since the Mass was said in Latin then, I had to learn the Latin responses that altar boys made. But I didn't have a problem learning and memorizing them. I didn't know what they meant but I recited them. Responses such as "*Et cum spiritu tuo*" followed the priest's "*Dominus vobiscum*" or "*Confiteor Deo omnipotenti.*"

Being an altar boy was serious, but it did have its light moments, even for me. At that time, the priest said Mass with his back to the people. We, as altar boys, knelt behind the priest so sometimes we'd goof off by giggling. Once the priest caught me and another boy doing this and he turned around and instead of saying "*Dominus Vobiscum*" [God be with you], he instead looked right at us and in the same prayerful tone said "One-a by one-a, walk off the altar." We left as directed. My mother heard about this and severely reprimanded me.

I never sipped the altar wine like some of the other kids did, but once in awhile I'd eat the non-consecrated hosts or wafers. I never liked wine very much, even though we had it at home. I liked bottled soda water or "pop" as we called it.

There was also an occasion when I and several other boys threw rocks against the church to frighten the girls who were inside for choir practice. One of the priests came out, very agitated, and scolded us. He asked me why I had done this. I don't remember what I said, but I must have responded in the wrong way because he went and reported me to my mother.

"That's no way to speak to a priest," she scolded me.

I served Mass as often as I could, often daily. Once on a Christmas day, I served six Masses. I felt that that was an achievement!

Whenever incense was called for, Father Taverna would give the order "go get the tobacco," instead of "bring in the incense." He was being lighthearted.

All of this church-related activity gradually convinced me by the time that I was in the eighth grade that I had a calling to be a priest. In addition, the priests and nuns at school encouraged it. The ideal for a young Catholic boy in those days was to become a priest and for a young Catholic girl to become a nun. "Have you ever considered the priesthood," the nuns asked. They'd talk about vocations. The priest would come to our classes and do the same. This began in the very early grades. They began to pay me particular attention. I guess that because I was a good student and basically a good kid that they figured I had a calling. My brother Ray also expressed an interest in becoming a priest. He was influenced by a Sister Damian, whom he liked very much. However, when she was transferred, he "lost his vocation." Ray didn't have the deep conviction that I had.

I eventually concluded that there was nothing more important than directing people in the way to get into Heaven, and the leader in all this was the priest. I don't think that any of the priests I knew were particular role models for me. I just felt that this was something that I was called to do. I was still just a kid, but I knew that this would involve sacrifices such as being unable to marry. I was attracted to girls and wanted to marry and have children later. I also knew that I would have to leave home. For a long time, I didn't tell anyone yet about my feelings, including my mother. Generally, I kept my feelings to myself.

I felt that it was my problem and no one else could help me. I could only talk it over with God, and I alone could make the decision of "yes" or "no." I did not understand why I had this calling. It was inexplicable to me, and I had no way of explaining it to others. I felt utterly alone. It was a kind of melancholy deeply seated within me. I had to accept it and live with it. Now I can see that I would have been helped by talking it over with others. Why I did not I do not know. I have always spent time both reflecting on what goes on deep within me and also in seeking guidance in the written word of scholars.

But all of this was still ahead of me. All I knew was that I was called to be a priest.

Yet although I knew that I had a vocation to the priesthood, I was at first tentative about talking to my mother about it. I had a feeling that she would not like the idea of my going away from home at such a young age. I hesitated to tell anyone in the family.

However, some of the priests came to know of my vocation to the priesthood. Before my family knew of my calling, a priest showed up at our house while I was still in school and talked to my mother.

"I understand that your son is thinking of the priesthood," he said.

"Yes, Ray," my mother responded. Since Ray talked openly of his desire to become a priest.

"No, no. George. He's talked to me about it."

When I got home that day I immediately sensed that something was wrong.

"George, a Salesian priest came by to see me today, and he said you've talked to him about becoming a priest. Is that true?"

"Yes, Mom. I've being meaning to talk to you about this."

Inside I was disturbed and even a bit disappointed that the priest had talked to my mother.

"Why do you want to become a priest?" Mother added.

"I don't know," I uncomfortably muttered. "I've got this call from God I think."

What I didn't tell her was that in my own mind, I felt that by becoming a priest that I would have greater assurance of saving my soul. I probably picked this up from the emphasis placed on the high priority of the next world over life on earth. In those days, the focus was on Heaven and what we as Catholics could do or should do to get there. You had to save your soul.

There was less stress on this world and the meaning of this world in relationship to the next wasn't linked. This has all changed now especially due to the influence of Vatican Council II in the 1960s. Today, we in the Church are more concerned with what is human than we were in pre-Vatican II times. God is present in our world and expects us, in imitation of God, to have compassion for all that is human. By contrast, when I was a kid, we were told that we were on the way to God. The focus for me was on morality: live a good ethical life and go to Heaven. This inhibited, I think, a deeper personal relationship with God in the present moment. I have more of that awareness now in my present spirituality.

My mother certainly wanted me to go to Heaven. What good Catholic mother didn't want that for her children! But she felt that I could go to Heaven without having to become a priest. This feeling on her part was more maternal than anything else. She was a very strong Catholic, but also a mother. She didn't want to lose her son. She wanted me to stay home, go to high school, find a good job, marry a good Italian Catholic girl, and give her many grandchildren. Her motherly instinct prevailed over her Catholic faith.

I don't know if her feelings were typical of other Italian-American mothers. I know that they seemed to be different from that of many Irish mothers. The Irish seemed more supportive of priestly and religious vocations than the Italians. Proportionally speaking, I believe there have not been over the years that many Italian-American priests. This is different from the Irish. I'm no expert on Ireland, but my sense is that it was strongly dominated by the Catholic clergy. They were the leaders in Irish society. Many priests left Ireland and came to the United States. The diocese of Sacramento had a large number of Irish-born priests. This was not the case with Italian priests. Few arrived with the Italian immigrants. Our Catholic parish had many Irish priests.

I think too that my mother had reservations about my age. Leave home right after elementary school! But in those days, that's when kids went to the seminary. That's no longer true today.

I felt like telling my mother "don't blame me, blame God. He's the one who's given me this calling."

I didn't say this, but the fact was that I myself was torn as to what to do. Perhaps this was in part because of my mother's feelings. Part of me didn't want to go. I loved my mother and my brothers. I was happy at home. I didn't want to leave all of this and go to a strange place called a seminary. It would be too unlike home. I was scared of this.

These divided feelings actually put me in a state of depression and sadness.

"Okay," I told my mother. "I'll stay and go to high school here and see how I feel later." I was temporarily relieved at this decision, but I knew it was only a postponement.

†

So after my graduation from the Cathedral School in 1932, I went to Christian Brothers High School in Sacramento which at that time was on 21st and Broadway. It was farther away from my home so I bicycled there each day. It was a good experience. I enjoyed the classes, especially Religion and Latin. It was an all-boys school and the Brothers were very demanding. But I appreciated that. Intellectuals were to my liking. Like my elementary school, it was quite ethnically mixed: Irish, Italian, Portuguese, and Mexican. The Irish kids predominated.

I worked hard and stayed up late at night doing my homework. I also continued to help my mother at her cleaning job downtown.

I was relatively happy going to the Brother's school, but still I felt this weight or pressure about becoming a priest. Would I say no to God? At the end of my sophomore year, I finally decided that I had to follow through on my vocation and go the seminary.

I felt that I had to be true to my self. I must trust God. In some way God would bless me for my acceptance of this calling. Eventually I would be happy. I was being given the opportunity to be of service to others in their ways to God. Nothing was more important.

The only question for me was whether I should become a diocesan priest – not affiliated with a particular religious order – or join one of the orders. I finally decided on the Franciscans. This wasn't because of any particular appeal or mystique about this Order, which originated in Italy with St. Francis. I had this Chicano friend, Ignacio Reyes, who was a year ahead of me. At the end of elementary school, he decided to become a Franciscan priest and went to St. Anthony's Seminary in Santa Barbara. We stayed in touch and when he returned during vacations, he talked me into joining him. Wouldn't you know it? He later left the seminary and I remained. After I became a priest, I much later officiated at his funeral.

My biggest obstacle again was telling my mother about my decision. This wasn't easy. I had one conversation with her and while I could see that she didn't approve, to my surprise, reluctantly she went along with it. But I got no emotional support from her or from my brothers. Jim thought I was neglecting my obligations to support the family. "Stay at home, get an education, and support your family," he said. Ray didn't want me to go because we were the best of friends. I got no "hurrahs" for my decision, no expressed approval by relatives and friends. That would be given later when I was ordained. I was the only one in the clan, in Italy and the United States, who became a priest. My father had two sisters in Italy who were cloistered nuns.

I didn't expect the approval of others since the decision was clearly my own. Yet I knew that their love and support of my person (not my decision) would accompany me. I could look forward to the day when we would celebrate my ordination.

As for me, I was utterly alone. But I was committed.

That summer I went and talked to the Franciscan pastor at St. Francis Church. He gave me an application form and other information. He interviewed me but in no great detail. Today we have much better screening of candidates. My mother, I believe, also had to sign a form that she reluctantly did. The next thing I knew is that I received a letter welcoming me to St. Anthony's Seminary in Santa Barbara and informing me what items, such as clothing and other things, I should bring.

There was no turning back now. I had taken my first major step in my surprisingly ever-new spiritual journey.

†

As I look back at my early years at home before I left for the seminary, I grow in gratitude for a highly blessed beginning in my journey in life. I was the heir to a long-standing Italian Catholic tradition that celebrated the goodness of life. *Tutto e buono*, everything is good; *Dio e buono*, God is good; *Buon Natale*, a good Christmas; *Buona Pasqua*, a good Easter; *Buon giorno*, a good day; *Buona sera*, good evening; *Buona Notte*, good night; *Pasta e vino, son buono*, pasta and wine are good.

St. Francis of Assisi went about greeting people with *Pace e bene*, peace and every good thing.

Life in the family, *la famiglia*, was enjoyable. The love, attention, security of home life, my education in Catholic schools, my wholesome neighborhood, my interest in sports, especially baseball, the strong ties with relatives, a desire to learn as much as I could, a basic optimism and hope for the future, the enjoyment of little things like an ice cream cone, a candy bar, a movie, all of this was part of my youth.

Overall, the goodness of human living and the security of a faith in God and its promise of future happiness filled my life.

I had a sense of belonging. I was very much at home.

I had no problem in believing what I was told at church, school, and home. Life made sense. There was no need to prove anything. I was secure. I had only to accept life as it was and respond with good behavior. Even then, when I failed, God's forgiveness and that of others offered me the joy of a new beginning.

2

BECOMING FRANCISCAN

I did not doubt that I had a vocation. The challenge facing me was: will
you say 'yes' or 'no'? I knew that I was free to respond or not respond, and
God would accept my decision.

— FR. VIRGIL CORDANO

I left home for St. Anthony's Seminary in Santa Barbara in late August of
1934. St. Anthony's was the minor seminary of the Franciscan Order on
the West Coast. I felt awful and even depressed. The thought of leaving
home, my mother, my brothers, was agonizing. So much of me didn't
want to go through with this.

I was scheduled to leave in the very early morning hours. The day
before I made my final preparations. I packed my clothing and toiletries.
There was a pall over the house that day. I didn't sleep very much that
night. I cried.

I felt numb, frozen. I was doing what was expected of me. I was
resigned that I had to leave home. No satisfactory explanation could be
given them. We would not love one another any less. The distant future
would be much better. I thought this but I could not say it to them.

Since my train to San Francisco where I would connect to Santa
Barbara left Sacramento at 4 A.M., we got up very early. It was pitch black.
I don't remember how we got to the station. My mother and Ray accompanied me, but not Jim.

Ray cried. I cried. My mother didn't say much. She, unlike other

Italian relatives, was not particularly expressive of her emotions. She was a serious person, nondemonstrative but blessed with profound affections.

We hugged and said goodbye. It was a sad departure.

I felt depressed, stunned all the way to Santa Barbara. There were other young boys on the train out of Sacramento and the Bay Area also going to the seminary. They seemed to be happy and excited. I felt just the opposite.

Later that day, we arrived at our destination. We were picked up and driven up to the seminary that was adjacent to the Santa Barbara Mission. Little did I know then that I would spent most of my life here at the Mission, next door to St. Anthony's.

The next morning after breakfast, I and the other newcomers separately were interviewed. This was primarily to determine at which level we would be placed. I had already had my first two years of high school, but because I was missing some classes that the seminary felt I should have already taken, I was placed in the sophomore class. I didn't particularly like this, but I had no choice.

I was still feeling sad and depressed and homesick, but I had to also quickly adjust to my new living arrangements. We lived in large dormitories with one bed next to the other very much in military style. There were thirty or forty kids in my class and about two hundred in the seminary.

We didn't have to wear uniforms just our regular clothes. Every time we moved from one activity to another, there was the sounding of bells – bells, bells, and more bells. The bell sounded and we marched off to chapel, to class, to dinner. At each dinner, advanced students read from a book of some sort with a religious connotation.

One of the most radical changes for me was the food. We always at home ate Italian style, and I rarely ate vegetables, which I didn't like. All of this changed at St. Anthony's. Not only were we served many vegetables, but the meals offered dishes that were different for me. These included many German ones. This was because several of the Franciscan brothers (the non-ordained Franciscans who did most of the cooking and cleaning) were German. We had sauerkraut and things like that, which didn't appeal to me. On the other hand, we had corn bread and syrup three times a week that I did like. Occasionally, we had pasta, but it wasn't my mother's pasta and certainly not her sauce. Each Friday we were served fresh baked pies for dessert. This was a big treat and we looked forward to it. But all of this still smacked of institutional living. Naturally it was not home.

These changes only made me feel even more depressed and home-sick. But what made me feel a bit better and began to distract me from how I felt was the beginning of classes. I always enjoyed the intellectual life, and I did very well. The curriculum was heavily classical. It covered not only high school years but the first two years of college as well. Our teachers were Franciscan priests, some of German descent. The German connection at St. Anthony's and, for that matter, at the Santa Barbara Mission went back to the period shortly after the U.S. takeover of California in 1848 at the conclusion of the war against Mexico. Since nearly all of the earlier Spanish and Mexican Franciscans had left the missions, Rome decided to sent new Franciscans of the Midwest to the West Coast. They were mostly friars of German descent whose families had emigrated from Germany. This German influence was manifest in the curriculum and in the discipline at St. Anthony's and in subsequent years.

In addition to learning Latin, Greek, and Spanish, we had to also learn German. I had to take five years of German. We read German texts and sang German songs. We memorized some of Schiller in German.

Like any other high school, we had the usual curriculum. There were science and math that never appealed that much to me. We read Demosthenes in Greek and Don Quixote in Spanish. History, English liter-ature, music, and, of course, religion rounded out the curriculum. My favorites consisted of languages, literature, history, and religion. By the time I graduated, I could read Cicero and Virgil in Latin and classical Greek literature. I must say that the Franciscans gave us an excellent education and a very formal one.

Fr. Owen Da Silva also offered classes in music and drama. I took a liking to drama. I had the main role in a play called "The Nervous Wreck." In another play, a musical, "Ten Nights in a Bar Room," I played the daughter of the drunkard. In one scene, I entered the bar to bring my father back home. I sang, "Father, dear Father, come home with me now. Come home, come home, come home O Father, come home."

All of this extra curricular activity helped to dispel my feelings of homesickness, as did my growing appreciation of the companionship of fellow students.

All of our studying and, in fact, every aspect of our lives in the seminary was affected by the strict discipline imposed by the faculty. Discipline was part of our education and our socialization to Franciscan life. We awoke at six in the morning. We then went to chapel. This was followed by study hall before breakfast. In study hall everyone sat at his own desk while a priest paraded up and down to make sure we studied. After breakfast, we went off to classes. At mid-morning we had another study hall. Then more classes, lunch, and another study period in the afternoon followed by recreation and study period before and after dinner. At nine o'clock we were in bed. I don't regret this early discipline. I acquired good study habits.

Some of the students couldn't take all of this and soon dropped out or were dismissed. It was always sad when a student left. Maybe I should leave too, I thought. It added to my depression. If you goofed off in study hall, you were punished by having to stand while studying. Or you were called to the office and reprimanded by the Rector, the head of the school. Every month we received a conduct grade. If you got a 70 or under, you were in trouble. I remember one fellow who sneaked in some wine to the dormitory. He was discovered and had to leave immediately.

Overhanging all of our academic activities and living arrangements was, of course, our religious practices and training. After all, this was the purpose for us coming to the seminary: to become priests. We attended daily Mass and confessed our sins once a week. All of this became part of our routine and part of our lives.

But the seminary was not all classes and religious devotions. We also had some time for sports and recreation. I particularly enjoyed that because it took my mind off my sadness.

We had a good sports program. I played baseball, football, basketball, track, and tennis. We had enough players among all the seminary students to form two or three teams in all sports. We played against each other. We had all the equipment that is used in sports. Our coaches were the better players. I played running back in football. Fortunately, I didn't get hurt playing football or any other sport for that matter.

But my favorite sport, of course, was baseball. Earlier at home I had developed a great interest in baseball and baseball players. I dreamed of becoming a player in the major leagues. At the seminary, I played first base, second base, and even did some pitching. My favorite position was first base and I was a pretty good hitter. I even coached the junior team in baseball.

I always maintained my love of baseball and in later years when I became a priest, I came up with a particular blessing that uses baseball terms. It goes in part like this:

"The same God of us all, we are grateful that you assign each one of us an important *position* on your *team* and on many other teams – teams of family, church, country, city, school, sports, neighborhood, business and social life. We are always in the *starting line-up*. We just don't *sit on the bench*. You ask for *team effort*. We are to cooperate with others in the *game* of life. May we come to believe that on a team each *player* and each *player's position* matters to you and to all on the team. It is only team effort that makes all the players winners. May we gratefully acknowledge that we need the help of others if we are to succeed. In baseball the *pitcher* needs the *catcher* to *catch* his best *pitch*. The *infielders* need the *first baseman* to catch their *throws* especially when they are *in the dirt*. Every player needs the *good play* of the others."

Besides sports, physical activities, likewise, involved doing chores around the seminary. We took turns washing the dishes. We cleaned up and did minor fix-up jobs around the grounds. The most arduous task consisted of hauling stones down from Mission Canyon in order to help put together the wall at the seminary. Father Louis, the Rector, supervised us. Occasionally, we were allowed to go into Santa Barbara. But this was rare. You had to get permission and you couldn't go alone. Some of the kids would go downtown to get an ice cream. I didn't have any money, so I almost never went.

Although seminary life at St. Anthony's in time became very routine and part of my life, we did return home for Christmas and summers. This was a two-edged sword. It was good to see my mother and brothers again, especially that first Christmas, but going home also reminded me again of what I was losing by attending the seminary. It only made me more depressed when I had to return to Santa Barbara in early January.

These returns to home awakened within me the pain of separation I had experienced when I first left home. The healing "wound" of home-sickness was re-opened when I returned to family life.

During the summers, I helped mother out by working again at the building where she cleaned. I turned over all of my earnings to her. But summer also meant playing baseball and cards with Ray and old friends in our backyard. Of course, I didn't date girls. You gave up girls when you went to the seminary. This was difficult. I remember one summer seeing one of my fellow seminarians from Sacramento out on a date. I didn't say anything, but he soon dropped out of the seminary. I never got started in dating and so I didn't miss it. This person eventually married. After I became a priest, on one occasion I visited him and his wife. They were not getting along. In anger his wife told him: "You should have remained in the seminary." Later, they divorced. In fact, he went through two or three marriages.

Not only in my first year, but throughout most of my high school seminary years in Santa Barbara, I wavered in coming to a final decision regarding my calling. I didn't doubt that I had a vocation. The challenge facing me was will you say "yes" or "no." I knew that I was free to respond or not respond, and God would accept my decision. I could be a good and generous Catholic layman and yet I would not be pleased with myself if I were to refuse to accept God's invitation. I had to be true to what was sensed in the depths of myself.

I was certain of my calling but did not welcome what my vocation asked of me. I had to get used to being away from home at such a young age. I was lonely in a totally different setting. During that first year, I often cried while in bed. I felt like I was in exile. Daily I would stop by the chapel after meals and pray "God help me!" or in my better moments "I give myself to You and Your plan for me."

Getting mail from my mother helped a bit. She would write in Italian and occasionally sent packages of candy or some other treats. I wrote back in English but couldn't make myself express my loneliness to her. I didn't want to add to her suffering.

All this was a big burden for a youngster. I'm sure this affected me emotionally and impeded some aspects of my emotional development. My affective life was probably stymied and injured. After awhile, I became stoical about it and failed to express my feelings to others.

My life was one of "cold dutifulness," tempered very much by my growing interest in matters spiritual and intellectual. I regretted that I was not enthused about my vocation. It seemed to me that other seminarians laughed and smiled more than I did. I became more and more introverted and felt stifled giving expression to love and friendship.

Seemingly, not all of the other boys reacted the way I did. Some possessed sparkling personalities and were as happy as could be. I wasn't like that. I was serious and pensive. I wasn't happy and kept it all to myself.

I thought sometimes that it might help if I transferred to another seminary. Perhaps it was St. Anthony's that was depressing me. But then the next day, I would catch myself and realize that going to another place wasn't the answer. I would probably feel just the same there. Then I thought that maybe I should try to become part of another order such as the Salesians or perhaps a diocesan priest. But the same realization would set in. None of these options were the answer.

What compounded these doubts and anxieties was that I couldn't or wouldn't talk it out with anyone. One time, one of my professors recognized that I was troubled. He asked:

"George, what's the matter? You seem pretty down. Did you fall in love with somebody over the summer?"

"No," I shyly responded. "I'm just working things out."

But I didn't talk further with him or anyone else. Each seminarian had to have a weekly talk with one of the priests assigned to him, but I never in these conversations talked about the dilemma in which I found myself. I figured that I could take care of all this by myself. I didn't get in the habit of sharing with others. I believed I could make it alone.

What in the end encouraged me was the thought that someday I would be a priest. This sadness will end and I'll be happy as a priest. The hope of a better future sustained me during a dismal present. This was aided by my prayers. I prayed that I could adjust to seminary life. The idea that I was doing what God wanted me to do steeled me. I had confidence that I could endure into the future, although it wasn't a happy endurance.

Looking back over these very early years in the seminary, I believe that my emotional and affected life was somewhat impaired. I had to make a decision without being supported by accompanying emotional or heart-stirring feelings. I did not know how to deal with this depressing homesickness. There was no meaning in it except that I had to put up with it and do what was expected of me. Only in my years from the novitiate on did I put all this in perspective as I began to understand somewhat that in fulfilling my vocation in life, I would have to pay the price of giving of myself to others. Only in this way could I become the kind of religious and priest that God expected me to be.

After three years, I completed my high school or minor seminary years at St. Anthony's in 1937. I thought it would never end. But it wasn't over yet. In fact, there was no real break. I went straight from high school into my first two years of college at the same St. Anthony's. There was no high school graduation, no parents coming down, no parties, certainly no prom, and, in fact, nothing. But that was no problem for me. I was pleased to know that I was that much closer to the priesthood.

These first two years of college at St. Anthony's were very similar to high school with respect to routine, living arrangements, and discipline. The only difference was that the courses were more demanding. There was more advanced Latin and Greek. By this time, we were reading the classics in Latin and Greek. There was also more science and math. These last two years at St. Anthony's were more like an extension of high school than a traditional college. We continued to be the same student body; the scheduling was the same; we didn't as yet wear the Franciscan habit; and there were no classes in formal philosophy.

†

After these two years of college, I graduated from St. Anthony's Seminary in 1939. This time it was a big deal. We were now eligible to go on to the novitiate for one year and then complete our college education at San Luis Rey Mission after novitiate.

Our graduation ceremony was held in the study hall on the grounds of St. Anthony's Seminary. This was a special day for me. I graduated as student body president and gave one of the valedictorian addresses. It was a very formal occasion. Valedictorian presentations were given in English, Latin, Greek, German, and Spanish. I gave the one in Latin. I can't remember what I said. Probably that we should be grateful for our faith and for what we had learned.

Many parents came for the ceremony. My mother couldn't. She had to work, and, what's more, she couldn't afford it. I was alone in my spiritual journey up to this time, and my mother's presence at graduation would not have helped that much. Seeing all of the mothers and fathers and other relatives and not having my family around didn't bother me. I had become accustomed to living away from home. I knew that I was loved by them.

That summer we were allowed to go back home for what, at least for me, would be my last visit in six years. Facing me was one year of my novitiate, two more years of college, and then three additional years of theological studies in preparation for the priesthood and a year after my ordination. We would not be permitted to go home for six years once we entered the novitiate. Part of me was sad to think about this, but by then I was totally committed to the priesthood. My mother didn't say much about this, but I knew that it affected her. All she could say was that she would try to visit me when she could. She was very accepting of the demands of my calling.

On my last summer at home, I worked for the last time helping my mother with the janitorial work. It was also a time to be with my brothers. Ray and I were still very close. We did things together but not everything. By now, Ray had girlfriends and went out on dates. I stayed home. I saw Jim but not often since he was working most of the time to help provide for the family. Phil by then was in a care home in Sonoma. A few years later, when Jim was doing better economically, he arranged for Phil to come and live at home again where he was good company for my mother.

As for myself, I was more accepting of my life by now. I looked forward to the novitiate, another big step toward the priesthood and full membership in the Franciscan Order. I wanted to become a priest, but it seemed to be still far off in the future. I wanted to get there in a hurry.

†

Despite my impatience, there was still much in store for me before I could be ordained a Franciscan priest. The next step was the novitiate. This would take place at San Luis Rey Mission near Oceanside, California and north of San Diego. That's where the Franciscan novitiate on the West Coast was located. The novitiate was a one-year period of immersion into the Franciscan way of life and thought. It was not formally academic but a time to learn about and live the Franciscan life. Upon completion, I stayed at San Luis Rey for the last two years of college.

Part of the move to San Luis Rey involved three important personal changes. First, I had to adopt a Franciscan name. Once you entered into the novitiate, you had to leave behind your given name and select a religious one. This was a sign that you were entering an entirely new way of life. My baptismal name was George, but now I had to look around for a new one. What made this particularly difficult was that you couldn't take on the more popular names of the apostles such as Peter, Paul, and John. All of these names were already taken by others. Some of the names suggested to us by our old German Provincial, Fr. Ildephonse Moser, the head of the Franciscan Order on the West Coast, were unappealing to me. Some you couldn't even pronounce. There were names such as Oscar, Beno, and Cuthbert. I said to myself, "Oh no!"

We had to select our new names while still in Santa Barbara and before going on to San Luis Rey. So on one of the few occasions that I went into downtown Santa Barbara, I and a classmate, Chester Drake, now Fr. Sebastian, went to the public library to look for a listing of names. We found a book entitled *What Shall We Name Baby*. In it, I saw the name "Virgil." At least it was pronounceable. So I selected it not knowing if there was even a St. Virgil. Fortunately there was. I found out later that he was an Irish monk who left Ireland to convert parts of non-Christian Europe. He ended up as the Bishop of Salzburg, Austria. Many years later on a trip to Europe, I visited and prayed at his grave.

I felt lucky to get a name like Virgil approved by the Provincial. Some of my classmates weren't as fortunate. One got stuck with the name Benignus. We used to call him "Benign." His mother couldn't even spell it much less approve of it.

So as I entered San Luis Rey Mission that July in 1939, I was no longer George but Virgil. It is a strange feeling to undergo a name change. It affects your sense of identity. But perhaps that was the whole point. You are no longer just the son of your mother. You now belong to the family of Franciscans and that calls for a new identity and a new role in life. I'm not saying this is right, but that's the way it was then.

Changing my name was not the only radical transformation that I underwent upon entering the novitiate. If the name change was symbolic, the other was physical, although also symbolical. All of us novices had to have our hair cut in a particular way called a "tonsure." The top was cut very close leaving a circle of more hair around the lower part of the head. It was like putting a bowl on your head and then cutting. This was called a corona, a crown.

The corona symbolized consecration to religious life. In a way, by cutting your hair you were leaving lay life to become a person dedicated to a life of poverty, chastity, and obedience. This sounded okay except that we didn't have a professional barber to give us uniform cuts. Someone from our class without previous experience was assigned as the barber. The result was a variety of strange-looking coronas. We'd laugh at seeing all of the different bumps on each other's head. Because the top was left bald, some of us used to get a bad sunburn there while working outdoors.

Each month the assigned "barber" trimmed our hair. Fortunately, I was never given that assignment.

The third change involved donning the habit of the Franciscan Order. This was a welcomed change. We shed our school clothes and now each day wore the brown robe associated with St. Francis, the founder of the Franciscans. This was a wonderful feeling. It made me feel as if I was now really a priest although my ordination was still a few years away. The robe, like any other uniform, says "you're now one of us, a follower of St. Francis. Welcome!" I was twenty years old.

This feeling of acceptance was formalized in a Mass and a welcoming ceremony following a week's retreat after we arrived at San Luis Rey. After the retreat where we meditated on the meaning of entering the novitiate, a ritual was held in the mission church. Here our superiors put the habit on us. You also removed your shoes and socks and accepted the brown sandals that went with the robe. In addition, we novices had a little piece of extra cloth pinned to our robes that identified us as a novice. At the end of the year when you took your first vows, you removed that piece of cloth.

We also were now called "fraters" which is Latin for "brother." I was Frater Virgil until at ordination when I became Father Virgil.

This was an impressive ceremony attended by many of the parents. Again, the trip from Sacramento was too long for my mother. I felt lonely not having her and my brother, Ray, there, but I consoled myself with the aura of now looking like a Franciscan.

I stared at myself in the mirror. It was a different person. But more important to me than the new look was that it meant I was onto a new stage that would eventually culminate in my ordination. That was my goal and that's what I tried to keep my mind on.

There were ten novices including myself in my entering class. While we were all regarded as Franciscan brothers there were two tracks that one could follow: one involved ordination and the priesthood, and the other was not to be ordained and to serve as a Franciscan brother. Those studying for the priesthood, such as myself, were called "fraters" while the others were " brothers." The non-ordained would engage in meaningful ministries other than that of the priesthood. All of us, however, took vows to be Franciscan "brothers."

The novitiate itself reflected a kind of class or hierarchical structure. At the top, you had the ordained priests. Then you had the brothers who took vows but were not ordained. Then there were us, the novices, study-ing for the priesthood or brotherhood. The highest priority went to the priests. In those days, the brothers or the non-ordained were not given equal recognition. You could sense a tension between the ordained and the non-ordained. The brothers did all of the manual work. They cooked, sewed habits, made sandals, did maintenance, and lived a more secluded life. The priests, by contrast, moved more freely in public.

I heard a funny story about this relationship either while I was at San Luis Rey or later. A stranger notices the division of labor at the novitiate and asks one of the brothers:

"How many classes of people do you have here?"

"We have three classes," the brother replies. "We have the fraters, the brothers, and the priests. The fraters study, the brothers work, and then there are the priests!"

This story, although humorous, was actually quite true. The fact was that the priests enjoyed a much higher standard of living. They served not only the novitiate, but the parish at San Luis Rey. As part of the parish, they weren't secluded. They could mingle with the parishioners, be invited to people's homes, and receive gifts. They went out to movies, baseball games, and had cars. So naturally, there were tensions between them and the hard-working brothers who were much more isolated. Much of this inequality, fortunately, has now changed.

†

Almost immediately in the novitiate, we were socialized to the Franciscan way of life. This life was very "otherworldly" and far removed from contact with others in the world. The routine was very demanding. You must do this and you must avoid that. In living in a community you were not to do your own individual thing. You had to obey your Superiors and follow the rigid schedule, rules, and regulations. I took all of this in stride. In my earlier years, I had already accustomed myself to obey authority and do what was expected of me.

I had so much to learn about St. Francis, about his life and his spirit, especially in a modern culture so different from his times, the 13th century. There was also the Rule of Life that he gave to his followers. What most impressed me about St. Francis was his love, joyous and grateful, of God and all of creation. But I also learned that aspiring to St. Francis' love was costly. St. Francis was a restless, young, wealthy man and he used to go out with his friends and enjoy life. But he was, at the same time, also hungry for something more than just a good time. But he didn't know what he really wanted. From deep within himself he heard the call from Jesus "leave all things and come follow me." That he did, but it would ask much of him. He left his wealth and other interests to be one with the poor and neglected. Now he could joyfully sing of the goodness of God and God's creation. All this impressed me about St. Francis, although I had to admit to myself that I had a long way to go before I could be anywhere like him, if that was even possible.

We came to admire Francis's idealism and to wonder how we would observe the sacrificial directives of a Franciscan life. I would try to be sacrificial. Of course, I had by this time developed some degree of self-discipline, but in the novitiate the demands came down in heavy dosages. But I and the other novices accepted this. We hoped to be like St. Francis, even though we knew that we could never match his sacrifice and his generosity. These were all necessary steps in becoming a true Franciscan, and they still are.

What also struck me during my novitiate was that the route I was taking to become a priest was a bit more involved than I expected. I desperately wanted to become a priest, but I also had to understand that this wasn't enough. I learned that in specifically becoming a Franciscan priest you were at the same time becoming a member of a community, the Order of St. Francis. I would not be just an individual Franciscan and priest, but I would have to be truly a brother in community. I had to put my Franciscan way of life before my priesthood and even my family. I was becoming a member of a new family. This initially was not easy for me to grasp. I didn't at first fully realize the importance of communal life in my spiritual journey.

In a way, we were being asked to give up our own personal identities and self-interests for the sake of a new life. While this would take sacrifice, at the same time, we learned that we'd be supported by the community. We need not fear. To be a Franciscan was to become a member of a fraternity from the Latin *fraternitas*. St. Francis said to his followers "we're all brothers." He stressed an equalitarian bonding of brothers. He de-emphasized hierarchy. Franciscan brothers should not view themselves as superior to others but give themselves to the service of all.

I began to understand much more about the idealism and practice of the life and spirit of St. Francis. St. Francis, himself, was not a priest but a deacon. He didn't want to be a member of the ruling power of the Church: the pope, the bishops, and the clergy. "We're simple brothers," he said. His whole emphasis was on serving God by serving the poor and others. Give of yourself and don't seek the power of authority associated with the institutional church. He reminded us, and still does, that Jesus came into the world not to be served, but to serve.

St. Francis understood and lived a radical self-emptying that did not seek ecclesiastical or clerical honor and authority. Franciscans were to be humble servants, "lesser brothers."

What impressed me about St. Francis' life was his heroic generosity and his simplicity. He was able to leave everything of material value behind and do this with joy. His vision of inclusive universality and his openness to all of creation attracted me. Everyone for Francis was brother or sister. Even death was a sister. He was open to all people. He was very catholic in its true sense. He lived the paradox of life as witnessed to us through the gospel of Christianity. He gave evidence that total self-sacrifice and giving of self make it possible for a person to receive much more in return. There is profound self-fulfillment in self-emptying, as I would better understand later in life. In this, St. Francis emulated Jesus who gave totally of Himself and the Resurrection or fullness of life followed. St. Francis was such a living example of what basic Christianity is all about.

✝

In addition to studying and living the life and spirit of St. Francis we also reflected on the Rule of the Order and other directives and practices. Since at the end of the novitiate year we would take the religious vows of poverty, chastity, and obedience, we gave much of our time to serious thought of what would be expected of us in living these three vows. I must say that at this time my understanding of the vows was too negative. I would possess nothing. I would give up marriage and children and I would obey my superiors. Later on I would come to view these vows in a more positive light. They would be aids in growing in heroic love of God and others. They would free me to give more of myself and receive much more in return – this paradox I came to understand better in the years beyond the novitiate.

Seemingly, I had little difficulty in accepting these vows. For many years I had learned to accept the directives of the Church, the discipline at school, and the orders given by my parents. I could go on to obeying my Franciscan superiors. Regarding the vow of chastity and celibacy by this time I had become resigned to giving up marriage. Compensation for the absence of a wife and children was the assurance of the continuing love of my family in Sacramento, my family life with fellow Franciscans, and the many friends I would have in my priestly ministry. I would never be alone. The lost hope of becoming a husband and father with children was perhaps less disappointing than life away from the close ties of family. I especially missed being with my brother Ray and doing what we enjoyed doing together. This loss was immediately present while the issue of marriage was off in the distant future.

Taking the vow of poverty was no problem. I had become accustomed to living without an abundance of possessions. All my needs would be met. I would be taken care of the rest of my life. I would have the use of whatever I would need personally and in my service to others. We would be happy "communists" holding all things in common.

†

The daily routine of the novitiate didn't vary much. The day began around 4:40 A.M., when one of the friars would come down the corridor to your room, knock on the door, and say "Ave Maria." You had to respond *gratia plena* to assure him that you were awake. He wouldn't leave until he heard the response. We then had twenty minutes to wash up and dress. Because we had no running water in our rooms, we filled a washbasin the night before in order to wash our faces in the morning. At San Luis Rey, we had small individual rooms rather than dormitories. These consisted of a bed, desk, lamp, chair, and a nightstand. That was it. We had communal showers.

Dressed in our brown robes we went down to chapel for 5 A.M. short morning prayers followed by meditation until 5:30 A.M. This consisted of someone reading a passage from scripture for us to reflect on. There were three readings with ten minutes to meditate on each passage. There was no allowance for individuation. Everyone had to listen to the same readings. The emphasis was not on uniqueness but on commonality and uniformity. Your ego was supposed to be subsumed into common living.

Following meditation, we then recited the hours of Prime and Terce, attended Mass, and then the recitation of Sext and None. Breakfast followed around 7. We ate in silence while someone read from *The Imitation of Christ*. Then you went to your room in silence. Our first class started around 8:30 A.M. Generally all through the day you were expected to observe silence. You could only talk at certain times of the day. Just before lunch, we returned to the chapel for an examination of conscience. This was about a five-minute period. You faced up to a particular fault of yours. The Angelus prayer followed at noon. Then we went to lunch. Again, we ate in silence while someone read from the scriptures or from a spiritual text. On special feasts, we had permission to talk during the latter part of the meal.

After lunch, we again returned to the chapel for a particular service called the Cross Prayer. We'd extend our arms out in the form of a cross to say six Our Father's and six Hail Mary's. We then were free to socialize or take a siesta if we wanted. At 2 P.M. we returned once more to the chapel to visit the Blessed Sacrament and recite the Hour prayers of vespers and compline. This was followed by our afternoon class for about an hour. We were then allowed an hour or so for recreation and sports. We generally played volleyball or baseball. Around 4:45 P.M. it was back to chapel again for the recitation of Office called Matins and Lauds, morning prayers anticipated the night before. That brought us to 5:30 P.M. We'd remain in the chapel for our second meditation of the day.

There was a slight modification to this schedule on Mondays, Wednesdays, and Fridays. Following the late afternoon meditation on these days, we returned to our rooms and participated in what was called "discipline." You lifted your habit, lowered your drawers, and then with a heavily shellacked cord with knots in it, you whipped your posterior while outside of the rooms one of the friars chanted *Miserere me, Deus* or "Have Mercy on me O God." The whipping was as hard as you wanted to give yourself. It was symbolic of self-discipline and of freeing the self from all that impeded growth in love for God.

Dinner followed at 6 P.M. We called it supper and ate in silence. Afterwards, we walked to the chapel reciting "Mary's Magnificat" followed by evening prayers. We could then have some time to ourselves for about thirty to forty-five minutes for conversation, card playing, or whatever we wished to do. At 7 P.M. we returned to our rooms in silence and studied or prayed until evening prayer and then lights out at 9 P.M. Silence was observed throughout the night.

There were certain exceptions to this routine. For example, if a visitor stayed for lunch or dinner, in order not to make him feel uncomfortable, we were allowed to talk during certain parts of the meal. On particular feast days of the Church the same applied. These included Christmas, Easter, the feast day of St. Francis, and a few others called First Class Feasts.

Meals were generally simple, but tasty, consisting of much soup and bread. We had enough to eat. One of the traditions – if you can call it that – that carried over from St. Anthony's Seminary was cornbread and syrup that was served three times a week at breakfast. We loved it and the fellows did justice to it. On feast days, the meals were a bit more elaborate. Our main meal was always at noon with a light supper at six.

Each Friday we had to fast and, of course, at that time all Catholics couldn't eat any meat at all. During Lent we fasted each day except Sunday. Fasting involved having a very light breakfast, a regular lunch, and then an even lighter supper than usual.

At meals we always sat according to seniority. Our superiors and professors sat up front at the head table. Then, in descending order, were those fraters who had advanced from the novitiate and were completing their last two years of college. Finally, the novices were seated toward the back of the dining room, followed by the non-ordained brothers. We were assigned seats and always sat by the same fellows.

†

Our classes were not academic as they would be later in college and theology. They had to do primarily with spirituality. The entire year was all about the religious life and what it means to be a Franciscan. We had lectures on St. Francis; we studied the Psalms; the understanding of the breviary with its traditional hours as noted: Prime, Terce, Sext, None, Vespers, Compline, Matins, and Lauds. These classes were conducted by Fr. Leo Simon, our novice master, who was also our spiritual director. He gave the lectures and you went only to him for spiritual counseling. He was our only professor. He was a highly disciplined person although, I thought, a deficient teacher. I felt that I had to complement his instruction by reading as much on my own as I could.

So much of the novitiate consisted of an imposed discipline that was to promote our interior self-discipline. We, of course, were no strangers to some of this from our experience at St. Anthony's. But the discipline was upped a notch at San Luis Rey. Everything here was strong on structure, rules, and regulations. All of this intended to teach us discipline and order so that later on, once we were ordained a friar and a priest, hopefully, these years of formation would sustain us and direct us when we needed self-discipline. It's like socializing a child. Unless children learn discipline when they're young, they probably won't practice it readily when they're older.

I think that I adjusted well to this, including the extended periods of silence. I had never had difficulty in being alone. During silence, I developed the practice of reciting a *mantra* or aspiration throughout the day. A *mantra* is a word or a phrase that facilitates awareness of God's presence. I'd have a different *mantra* for each day. On Mondays, my *mantra* which I would repeat to myself throughout the day might be "Oh, God, I trust you." And the next day, it might be "Thy will be done." This might be followed by "My God and my all." And so on. These prayers would move me to be generous in responding to the reality of the day. *Mantras* can lead to an experience of being one with God beyond words and thoughts in truly contemplative or mystical prayer. But I was very slow in advancing to higher forms of prayer.

Everyone in my class pretty much adjusted to the discipline including the silence. Occasionally, we had lapses. We'd confess them during what was called the "chapter of faults." This was a community confession every Friday at lunch. Each one of us would, one by one, get on our knees and admit our faults.

"It's my fault that I didn't observe silence."

We'd mention one small infraction. All of this would be done in Latin. The "chapter of faults" did not replace the regular weekly confession. There we'd confess more major sins if we had them. Those confessions would be in English and in private.

†

Because I felt that I was not getting much from my classes since they focused too much on rules and regulations and books that in my limited thought were not easily relevant, I began to do a lot of reading on my own. There was a small library, and it was limited in choices, but I think I read most of what it contained. My teachers became more the authors that I read rather than those I had in the classroom. In this way, I began to come to some idea of what spirituality is all about.

What I was looking for had to do with the spiritual and psychological changes that I felt I was undergoing, but which my classes didn't seem to be addressing. I was trying to understand my changing relationship with God. How I was growing in that relationship. Part of the problem, as I look back on this period, was that spiritual training had little connection to psychology and the insight into what was going on deep within me. Now it has everything to do with it. But not then. There was no effort at self-understanding or of analyzing one's stages of human and spiritual growth.

Instead, seminary training heavily focused on doctrine, scripture, morality, tradition, and discipline. You learned the rules and said your prayers. But understanding one's humanity and complex psychological makeup was not part of the curriculum. I instinctively knew that I was experiencing powerful emotional changes, but there was no formal education about what was going on. You had to figure it out for yourself if you could. I didn't talk to my spiritual director about this or to anyone else. Perhaps I should have rather than just keeping it to myself.

So I struggled on my own throughout my seminary years. I immersed myself in reading and personal reflection. I read certain books that I perhaps shouldn't have, because, although at the time I thought that they held out a high ideal for me, I wasn't that far advanced. This frightened and discouraged me. I especially felt this after reading the great mystic St. John of the Cross. He wrote about self-emptying. You must go through the dark nights of spiritual growth. "Gee," I said to myself, "I'll never be able to live up to that."

But I continued to read and re-read many spiritual writers. In a way, I was very much self-taught. Gradually, I began to realize that everyone that I was reading was a different expression of what was essential. I began to understand this, although I could see that it would take me many years to understand fully the message and live it. Spirituality is marked by negative and positive poles. It involves dying to self and being alive to God. It is the paradox of death and resurrection, loss and gain.

The problem with the novitiate was, in my estimation, that these two poles were not put into a balanced perspective. The emphasis was too much on the negative rather than on the positive side of spirituality. There was too little sense of what you received for your giving. Here, everything was giving, sacrifice, dying to oneself. It would take more time for me to realize, based on continuing my reading and thought, that I should focus more attention on what is positive: a deep personal relationship with and love of God and others, sacrificial though this would be. The Resurrection validates the cross.

In the novitiate and in most of my seminary training the emphasis was on the divine, the other worldly, or what is referred to as the eschatological with not enough attention given to the human, the this worldly. Instead of seeing the divine in the human, I thought that we were told to pay little attention to our humanity and concentrate on the divine. You deny yourself and live virtuously then you will be rewarded in the next world. God was more the judge of whether one went to Heaven or hell based on one's behavior. There was not even direction on how to enter into a deep personal, loving relationship with God. Do what God asked of you, make sacrifices in life, and you will merit Heaven.

What I came to understand later was that instead of denying yourself to begin with, you must first fall in love with God. Love would call for a healthy self-sacrifice. That sacrificial love will lead to the rewards of joy and peace already in this life. Here, I found St. Teresa of Avila more appealing than St. John of the Cross. Although a mystic herself, St. Teresa seemed to have more of a human touch. What I learned from her life and her writings was that the incentive for giving is positive – to experience God's love for me – and not negative – I hate myself or what I am. I began to get a sense that God demands more than just obedience. God invites a close and loving relationship. Self-sacrifice would free me to love all the more. The true self is freed when the false self is disciplined.

It was in this context that I discovered and read an inspiring book that really addressed some of my concerns. This was a text by Jean-Pierre De Caussade, a French priest, entitled *Abandonment to Divine Providence*. In a later edition, the title was changed to *The Sacrament of the Present Moment*. It's a classic. De Caussade's point is that in every moment God is present, awaiting, inviting our response. Hence, we need to accept the gift of every present moment. God is at the core of reality. Prayer is a faith response to real life. God is in all that is human. It has taken a long time to grow in this awareness.

Early in life, I looked mostly to the future, the otherworldly. Though I still do, I now – and this began at San Luis Rey – have integrated the present and the future. DeCaussade helped me to begin – and I stress "begin" because this has been a life-long journey – to do this. It was the most formative book I have ever read. It was powerful. It was just what I needed. It was the positive thing I was looking for in the midst of so much negativity and emphasis on self-denial. It has helped me to come up with a definition of holiness. Holiness is a heroic response in faith to present reality. God is in human reality.

The negative or sacrificial approach to spirituality that I encountered at San Luis Rey mirrored what I believed to be the state of Catholic spirituality at that time and for many years. The emphasis was too much on the negative. The Church was known more for what it was against than what it was for. It stressed many rules and regulations. "Thou shalt not." Seminarians, religious, and priests were to avoid the temptations of the world. There was not enough stress on the richness of Catholic spirituality. Doctrinal purity and uniformity was promoted. There was little discussion of pluralism within the Church, much less ecumenism with other religions.

I remember a statement read at our breakfasts from *The Imitation of Christ* warning that every time you left the monastery, you might come back less a man. So be very careful. We wanted to keep the walls of the cloister up, not bring them down. We had to be on our guard especially with respect to protecting our celibacy. Priests were cautioned, for example, not to attend wedding receptions. It was all very penitential and puritanical.

This protective and defensive attitude reflected the legacy of the Counter Reformation. One of the tendencies that crept into the Church in the 17th and 18th centuries was what was called Jansenism, which was a rather negative attitude toward what was other than the divine and the sacred. Some of the expression of this dualistic view of life were: you were to deny yourself every human indulgence; this was a sinful world. Human nature was in great part corrupt. To grow in holiness one was to entertain a rigorous moral attitude toward the flesh that was in conflict with the spirit. There was no clear balanced correlation or integration of divine grace and human nature.

All of this tied in with the Inquisition of the Counter Reformation era. It propagated the purity of the Catholic faith and failed to give enough recognition of the good in the human. It was anti-psychological in the sense that the human didn't matter that much. It posited a huge and irreconcilable gap between the sacred and the profane, both theologically and in practice.

This tradition excluded anything that smacked of ecumenism. Protestant and other religions were still considered to be heretical. Lay Catholics were warned against going to Protestant churches or institutions such as the YMCA or YWCA much less to Jewish synagogues. I don't recall in my seminary training that I was explicitly told to look down on people of other faiths. However, the implication was clear that Catholics represented the one true religion. For example, the New Testament was sufficient for us. The Old Testament, the Jewish faith, gave way to the new covenant in Christ. All this has changed now, thank God. Today there are many opinions regarding the relationships between the Jewish and Christian covenants. The Jewish covenant still has validity. But all this was not the case in my past. We were to learn just about our Catholic theology and spirituality and that's all. This would save us and so why bother with anything else.

As I wrestled with these thoughts at the novitiate and later in my theological studies, I was inspired by the universality and inclusiveness of St. Francis. He had this tremendous appreciation of being loved by God. He put the emphasis on the positive. He believed that everything on earth, from the animals to humans, was good. In my early years a little phrase of St. Francis expressed the spirituality that I longed to live: "My God and my all." At that time, I came to appreciate Francis' way of integrating love and sacrifice.

Yes, he lived a sacrificial life motivated by God's initial love and the example of Jesus. More of God's love would be received in return for self-emptying. Self-sacrifice was not to punish yourself, but to free yourself for immersion in God's love. St. Francis fell in love with God. He made the point that religion is primarily falling in love with God. It's similar to what should happen to human relationships. You fall in love with someone and that motivates you to merge your own individualism with your beloved. You become one with your love. Falling in love is not a negative experience; it's a positive one. In our relationship with God we gratefully and humbly welcome His love for us and joyfully detach ourselves from all that impedes that love.

I didn't necessarily understand all of this too clearly as a student, but looking back I certainly, in my own way, was grappling with trying to balance the negative and the positive sides of my evolving spirituality.

If I could go back and re-do my novitiate, and for that matter my entire seminary training, especially in light of the changes of Vatican II, I would stress a better comprehension of the God who loves us. The God who wants you to rejoice in Him. I would emphasize more reflective, contemplative prayer of resting in God's love at all times and places and in every daily activity and experience. The divine is right here with us now and not only to be experienced in Heaven. God became human because He loved us and willed to be at the core of all that is human.

My novitiate training might have stressed what's good about being human rather than just the denial of what is human. It would acknowledge what's good about marriage and sex. It would downplay rigid uniformity and encourage more pluralism, allowing each one to develop his own spirituality and way of prayer. It would be less penitential and more resurrectional.

†

Although the emphasis at San Luis Rey was on discipline and silence, we did have many enjoyable moments among ourselves. But as novices, we weren't supposed to mix freely with those already professed. As we were learning about the initial vows that we would take at the end of the year, our superiors didn't want us to be influenced about what this meant to the older students. We remained separate from them except for a couple of times a year when we could enjoy an evening in recreation. Otherwise, we were to give full time to what was proper to our novitiate year.

Amongst ourselves, we were allowed to form friendships but, at the same time, cautioned of developing particular or too close relationships. We were to be friends with all the novices and not just with one or a few. Such close one-to-one relationships were strongly discouraged. Community life called for openness to all friars. I developed strong ties with the members of my class. We were true friends. I enjoyed their companionship. They were becoming my new family.

Of course, there weren't many of us to begin with. My class had only ten novices and one dropped out after he became sick. Like me, they were mostly of different ethnic backgrounds: Irish, Italian, German, Portuguese, Polish. I don't recall any Latinos in my class.

I made friends with everyone, although still favored some over others. You gravitated to personalities that complemented your own.

Once a month, members of one's family could visit. But in many cases, this didn't happen. For my mother and brothers, for example, San Luis Rey was too far away. Unlike at St. Anthony's, at San Luis Rey you also weren't allowed to go home for Christmas or summer. You really left the world behind and became a member of a new home.

We could receive and send mail, although it was subject to censorship. Our letters had to be unsealed and inspected by our superiors. I would do this later myself when I became the director of students at Mission Santa Barbara. If there were some seminarians that you wanted to know more about, you'd read their letters to give you more insights.

Other than these contacts, we were pretty much insulated from what was happening outside of San Luis Rey. We received no newspapers, but we did have a radio in the recreation room. While we didn't hear too much news, we were aware of certain things such as the outbreak of World War II. I remember hearing Hitler's voice over the radio. We would pick up bits and pieces of news, but the whole focus was to be taken up with life in a new world and home.

You only ventured outside if you needed to see a doctor or a dentist. Even just to literally step outside the Mission, you needed permission.

†

After this intense novitiate year, I felt that I had grown in my spirituality. It brought a lot of things into focus. I took more seriously the whole question of growing in holiness. It heightened my intent to become saintly. For me, this meant to be generous, to give of myself glowing in love of God. This was clear to me. What was lacking, however, was still the need to reconcile, to integrate the negative and positive aspects of spirituality and also formal religion and the rest of life. Prior to Vatican II, there was God and prayer and religious life, on the one hand, and then, on the other, there was worldly life: politics, sex, sports, and the rest of secular matters. Life was highly dualistic. This is the way I viewed the situation at that time.

This dualism has been corrected now, but then it was still quite pronounced. Then you were spiritual if you engaged in what was considered to be religious activity. Everything else was profane, not necessarily in a bad sense, but still secular and worldly and certainly not religious and spiritual. The world was seen as filled with temptations and the prudent response, at least for us, was not to spend too much time in it and then return home to the monastery. God was, as it were, more actual in the monastery than outside. We never quite said it in these terms, but there wasn't much of a link between life in the Franciscan community and life outside of it.

Thank God, all of this has now changed. I wish it had changed while I was in the novitiate and the rest of my seminary training. I would have been spared anxiety about my role within the Church and outside of it. Today, everything is seen as graced by God's presence. In theory, there's no separation between the divine and the human. The human is graced by the presence of God. Any aspect of human life is created by God. Spirituality has to go beyond just Mass and prayer. You need a multi-dimensional spirituality: a spirituality for recreation, for sex, for politics, for social life. There's a spirituality for everything that is human. Through all that is human we can encounter God. Nothing human is foreign to God. There is no revelation or grace outside of human experience. God meets us where we are, in the reality of human life.

In addition, we have gone beyond the earlier popular belief that the priestly and religious vocations were superior to the vocation of the laity. Although this view was not the official teaching of the Church, it was at least implied in the training that I received. But today we acknowledge the teaching that holiness is for all. One does not have to be a priest or religious to become a saint or to live a heroically holy life.

†

At the conclusion of the novitiate, one year after we entered, we came to another rite of passage. We took our first vows for three years. These were not the final ones for life that we would take after the temporary vows of three years when we would be at the theological seminary in Santa

Barbara. Those would come later. The ritual of temporary vows took place at a "High Mass" officiated by our Franciscan Provincial on the West Coast who played a role for us similar to a bishop's for diocesan priests.

I welcomed taking these vows since I enjoyed being a Franciscan on the way to becoming a priest. This was one more move in that direction. Taking the simple vows was an important step, although in my heart I had already made my final commitment to the Franciscan Order and the priesthood.

It was a joyous occasion, especially since many parents and relatives attended. My family couldn't come, but that was okay. I understood why they couldn't attend. I loved and missed them, and I was much more accepting of my homesickness. But I also knew that if they came, I would only get more homesick after they left. I felt that it would be even more painful if they came and left. It would re-open the wound in my heart.

We took our vows on July 17, 1940. We were now professed and eligible to move up to our final two years of college. This would get us back into the academic track especially in philosophy. There was a lot more still ahead of me, but I welcomed it.

Following my novitiate year, I remained, along with my other eight classmates, at Mission San Luis Rey. We separated ourselves from the new novices and joined with the professed senior students one year ahead of us.

Our daily routine of prayer, meals, and recreation remained the same. One difference was that we now had different quarters. The other major difference was that we resumed our academic training after that year of intense spiritual exercises. As college students we primarily focused for these two years on classical philosophy. It was mostly scholastic and Catholic. We read St. Thomas Aquinas, Duns Scotus, St. Bonaventure, and others. I liked the readings since I enjoyed abstract thought, although, in retrospect, the classes themselves were quite traditional. More modern philosophy including that of non-Catholic writers was not prominent. We also took classes in Hebrew, literature, ethics, and psychology.

Our classes included exams and were quite textbookish. They were very organized and highly structured. Learning involved mostly memorization. We rarely were requested to write papers where we could express our own interpretations. Our professors – Franciscan priests – gave us the interpretations.

Our faculty consisted of only about four or five professors and our classes, of course, were quite small since they only involved the nine of us who had gone through the novitiate and a class ahead of about the same number.

I found these classes, especially the philosophy ones, to be too restrictive and not very stimulating. They didn't have much appeal. I didn't think they were expansive or diverse enough. For one thing, the presentations were too one-sided. It was mostly all lectures. There was little dialogue with our professors or even amongst ourselves.

There was one exception to this rigid curriculum. There was Father Finbar Kenneally who had been a diocesan priest in Ireland before he became a Franciscan. He attempted to initiate a new trend, although on a very small scale, at San Luis Rey. In his classes in philosophy and psychology, he made some effort to go beyond a text-centered approach. He allowed for a bit more creative thought. Father Kenneally also initiated the building of a new library that included more and diverse books. He was a breath of fresh air. But, he was more the exception than the rule. The rest of our teachers were very traditional and lacked innovation.

To tell the truth, during these two years of college course work, I didn't advance intellectually as much as I anticipated. We mainly memorized, and it wasn't even from the original texts in philosophy. The professors made us read from textbooks and our library was limited. The changes that Father Kenneally introduced only began to mature many years later.

In my spiritual life during these two years, I experienced a continuation of my growth as a Franciscan. Although I still wrestled with the more negative approach to spirituality stressed at the seminary; nevertheless, I deepened my prayer life. I was becoming more habituated to the Franciscan way of life. It was less a mystery for me.

Still, these college years were uneventful and not a high point in my life.

If little of momentous change was occurring inside of the seminary, much of historic importance was taking place outside. World War II had broken out in 1939 and following the Japanese attack on Pearl Harbor on December 7, 1941, the United States entered this horrible conflict. But for all that this meant in disrupting American lives, the war barely affected us. This is how sheltered and out of touch we were with the rest of the world. We knew that our country was at war. While we didn't have access to newspapers, we did have a radio and heard news about the conflict. Our professors occasionally said something about the war, but not often. I still can't believe how ignorant I was about the war and what was happening in the world at this crucial time.

The war wasn't purely an abstraction for me because it affected my family. Both Jim and Ray served in the military. Jim was in business then, and after he was drafted into the army, he was assigned to do some real estate transactions for the military. Jim served for only a short period of time. Ray, on the other hand, after being drafted went into the Army Air Corp as a ground crew technician. He went in around 1943 or 1944. He didn't see combat but was sent to Panama and the Galápagos Islands. I really missed Ray then. Although we didn't see each other very much, we both still considered each other as best of friends. Neither Jim nor Ray ever wrote much to me in the seminary. I kept up with their lives through my mother's letters.

I think that part of our distance from the war in the seminary was that we didn't have to worry about being drafted. As members of a religious order, we automatically were considered 4-F or not eligible for duty. Some civilians were 4-F for physical or emotional problems. We were 4-F because of our religious status. Some Franciscans did go to the war as chaplains, and some even gave their lives for their country.

What we did do during the war was to pray that it would end. Since my two brothers were in the service, I had a personal interest in praying for peace. However, the war remained remote for us. We concentrated on becoming Franciscans. You left the world behind. You picked it up later. That was the dualism in our religious socialization.

Before Ray went into the service, he and my mother and my friend Lena Casali visited me at San Luis Rey. This was the only time in six years that I saw my mother. They drove down from Sacramento. Part of me felt good to see them, but another part felt pain because I knew that my mother still found it difficult to let me go. In faith, she accepted my vocation, but still as a mother she didn't easily let me go. I felt that she wanted me back home. This made me uncomfortable to see her sorrow. But she never kept me from the choice I made.

We didn't talk about my vocation anymore. What could we say? There were no more explanations that I could give. So there was no soul-searching on this visit. We just talked about the family and what was happening back home.

After they arrived, I received permission to leave the Mission grounds, and we went into Oceanside and walked along the beach. Before they left, my superior invited them to stay for supper. Unfortunately, the meal was terrible that evening. My mother was a good cook, and I was embarrassed that she had to eat our food, so unlike hers.

When they left, I was relieved, not because I didn't love my mother and Ray, but because their visit had brought back all of my own pain and homesickness. I wanted, even hungered, to be a priest, but a part of me was still a young boy that wanted to be with his mother and family. I missed them so much. My visit with my mother, brother, and close friend, Lena, awakened feelings of loneliness. The visit was a mixed blessing. I did not want to go back with them. By this time I was totally committed to continuing my journey toward the priesthood. "I'll spent time with them at the end of this solitary journey," I told myself.

Those two years of college at San Luis Rey passed relatively fast, and, before I knew it, I had graduated from there in 1942. This time there was no elaborate ceremony. In fact, there was no ceremony at all. You just graduated and prepared to leave the Mission. I was just as glad. This meant one additional step forward toward my ordination. The next and final step would involve four more years of theological training back in Santa Barbara in the Mission Theological Seminary adjacent to St. Anthony's Seminary.

†

I arrived in Santa Barbara later that summer but after my other classmates from San Luis Rey. Since I had enlarged tonsils, the superior arranged for me to go to Queen of Angels Hospital in Los Angeles for the operation. After a day or so of recovery, I got on the train and went up to Santa Barbara.

I arrived late at night, and there was no one to greet me since it was very late. I paid for a taxi that deposited me at the front door of the theological seminary. The door was locked and I had no idea how to enter. I saw no doorbell. But I found a rope that I pulled and eventually someone came and opened the door.

"Yes, what can I do for you?" the figure of the Franciscan in his robes asked me.

"I'm Frater Virgil. I'm one of the new theology students."

"Oh, welcome. I'm Father Maynard Geiger."

That was my reintroduction to Santa Barbara and to my next four years. Father Geiger, whom I would come to know very well for many years, led me down the dark corridors to my room. Like my last three years at San Luis Rey, I occupied an individual room. I thanked God that night that I had arrived safely and that I was now entering the last phase of my seminary education.

This involved two stages. The first included the first three years of intense theological study. At the end of this period, I would be ordained and become what was called a simplex priest. "Simplex" or "simple" meant that I could only do a few things as a priest, such as say Mass. But I still couldn't hear confessions or preach or administer the other sacraments of the Church. But I would now be "Father Virgil!" At the end of my fourth year, and, if I successfully passed my exams, I would function fully as a priest. The final examination was named the *cura* examination, prior to being commissioned to engage in the care of souls (*cura animarum*).

But before the completion of my studies in theology, and after my first year at the Mission, I would take my final vows as a Franciscan. I would then be a full-fledged member of the Order for life. You first became a Franciscan, and then you were ordained a priest, in that order.

The Franciscan life at the theological seminary was almost identical to what we experienced at San Luis Rey. This included rising early and going to chapel; silence during meals; daily prayers; and practicing discipline, including a mild form of self-flagellation three times a week. All of us also had to participate in the choir where we learned Gregorian chants and traditional church music. Again, we couldn't go out in front of the Mission without permission.

One afternoon a week we could go walking, but we couldn't go alone. On picnic days, we'd walk to Tucker's Grove or to the top of La Cumbre Peak or to the beach. Some of the friars who really wanted to exert themselves would walk up to La Cumbre, down to Gibraltar Dam, back up to La Cumbre, and then return to the Mission. They were great walkers.

On these walks, we'd be the focus of attention, since we had to walk in our robes. We always had to wear them, even in sports. Some times we'd walk all the way to Hendry's Beach that is now called Arroyo Burro. We'd wear our swimsuits under our robes. We'd throw our robes on the beach and plunge into the ocean. At that time very few persons frequented that beach.

On all of these excursions, the brothers who worked at the seminary brought us our lunch. Sometimes we'd even have dinner at the beach.

Besides the encumbrance of having to wear our robes on our walks, we even had to wear them when we cared for the Mission garden and played baseball at the Mission. At first it was clumsy, for example, having to bend down to snag a grounder with a heavy robe on, but we got used to it. The field was an open patch where the dining room of the Mission is now located.

Besides the nine in my class, the total student body varied between 30 and 40. We weren't as split up between classes as we were at San Luis Rey, although we still had to sit by seniority during meals.

Overall, the daily routine was quite the same as I had been used to at Mission San Luis Rey. We were still very sheltered from the outside world. We didn't receive newspapers even though the war continued to rage. We'd pick up bits and pieces. You could receive visitors, but that didn't affect me since I didn't have any.

†

At Mission Theological Seminary, as its title indicated, the course of study was heavily theological. Over the first three years, I studied Systematic Theology, Moral Theology, Christology, Mariology (about the Blessed Virgin Mary), Eschatology (about life after death), Canon Law, Church history, Spiritual Theology, Liturgy, Homiletics (how to deliver homilies or sermons). It was all very traditional, staid, inflexible, and dogmatic. It was quite poor in light of later post-Vatican II theology.

Most of the texts were in Latin. They were very simplistic. Our textbook for Systematic Theology was by a German theologian, Lercher. It was elementary. For example, a thesis read: "Jesus is divine and human." Then you proved it with a statement from scripture and from tradition. It was mostly memorization. There were no discussions, just lectures. The lectures were usually in English, but occasionally the professor would break into Latin that we struggled to understand. It was the old approach to theology. There was no pluralism, no ecumenism, no humanism, and no cultural or literary approaches to the study of scripture that would come to characterize later Catholic theology after Vatican II.

Now I look back and see the deficiencies in this approach, but at the time I did enjoy most of these classes, and I learned from them. They were an advance over what I had at San Luis Rey. I think too that I enjoyed them because they were dealing with what I would need to become a priest, not only theologically, but practically, such as learning to say Mass, preaching, administering the sacraments, etc.

My teachers also were all quite competent, if very traditional. There was Father Patrick Roddy and Father Noel Moholy in Systematic Theology. Father Damian Lyons and Father Silvano Matulich who taught Scripture. Father Alfred Boeddeker instructed us in Moral Theology and Canon Law. Father Robert Schmidt was in charge of Church history. These were some of the key professors I had. Most of them had doctorates in theology.

While the classes, for the most part, reflected a dogmatic approach, some changes were beginning to take place. For example, in the study of scripture, for both the Old and New Testaments, certain literary genres were becoming acknowledged as well as the limiting cultural aspects of the Word of God. Not everything was being taken literally. Instead, the human and fictional aspects of the Bible were being recognized. But this was in very small doses. Still, it was the start of new breakthroughs that would reach fruition during Vatican II and thereafter.

But such teaching was the exception. For the most part, this phase of our seminary training was very uniform and took all of its directions from Rome. There was a dearth of new and innovative thought. Indeed, such thought was discouraged.

In addition to the more strict theological classes we attended, we also took classes on Liturgy and Homiletics, how to preside at Mass, administer the sacraments, and how to give a homily. The latter, at least for me, was quite intimidating and nerve-wracking. You were given some theory and then you were asked to give a practice sermon in the Mission church but not at any public ceremony. This wasn't easy. Some students just froze and forgot what they had planned on saying. It was awkward. The exercise involved each one of us giving a homily while the rest listened and then critiqued. The criticism could be very harsh. They'd "let you have it."

"Virgil, you have to speak louder. We can barely hear you."

"Virgil, you need to look at us and not just at your notes."

"Virgil, you don't seem to have any organization in your homily. You're just rambling."

"Virgil, you don't seem to understand at all the scripture that you're addressing."

Part of the problem with Homiletics was that it was very poorly taught. The same was true of Liturgy, since the focus was mostly on rubrics or the directions to be observed. This part of our training was seen as secondary to the more lofty theological seminars. In Homiletics, the professor would just assign us some topic and expect us to give a good sermon. Most of us couldn't. I'm embarrassed now to think of how poorly we did.

We were told to always begin a homily with something that would win the attention of the congregation. However, often the context was too ponderous and too dogmatic. Each sermon was to be based on expounding on the assigned scripture for that day. But we weren't adept in being imaginative and creative. Generally, we made use of doctrinal purity provided for us. This is what the Pope says; this is what the bishops say; this is what scripture says; this is what tradition says. It was a whole lot of indoctrination with little appeal to the heart.

By contrast, today, homilies are much more appealing. They can be more personally interpretive than just dogmatic and can emphasize practical spirituality.

I'll never forget the first time I had to get up in front of my classmates and practice a sermon. It was awful. I had no confidence in myself. I was too stilted and uptight. I didn't feel relaxed. I felt confused and unable to bring much feeling to it.

I had grown intellectually and spiritually during these years, but not as much emotionally. I hadn't experienced some of the things that other boys and young men my age had outside of the seminary. I was inexperienced. I was somewhat immature emotionally.

In part, this had to do with my personality and my entrance into the seminary at an early age. Where some of the other students were more outgoing, I was very serious and shy. My sense of security, such as it was, came not so much from feeling confident in myself, but from strong ideological convictions. This sustained me and compensated for the emotional vacuum in my life.

This inexperience would hurt me later when I became a priest and discovered that there was a big world outside of my confined one. I never had a choice of experiencing the fullness of life as I was growing up, so how could I give homilies that were supposed to touch people emotionally when I, myself, lacked so many normal human experiences. I was emotionally stifled. Seminary life was highly intellectual and disciplined, but it lacked humanistic qualities, at least for me.

I felt like a fish out of water. Why I didn't know. The contrast between home and seminary was too sharp. Rationally and in faith, I saw the meaning of my present life but it lacked exuberant emotional support.

We were so sheltered. You never met girls, for example. I knew even before going off to the seminary that I liked girls. But in the seminary, we were shielded from contact with them. Despite the more current sexual scandals in the Church, mostly involving pedophilia and homosexual encounters with young men, I was not aware during my seminary years of such abuses. However, this doesn't mean that such abuses did not take place. It just means that I didn't know of them. No classes were offered in the spirituality and psychology of sexuality. The focus was primarily on the morality of sex, what was permitted, and what was forbidden. I had to think all this through by myself.

I accepted the Church's requirement of celibacy for priests. However, if celibacy were optional when I decided to study for the priesthood, I probably would have chosen to be a married priest. I still had normal feelings about girls. I remember that when I had my tonsils taken out at Queen of Angels Hospital in L.A. being surrounded for the first time by all of these young attractive nurses. My feelings went off in all sorts of directions. Later, after my seminary training when I went off to Catholic University in Washington, D.C., I encountered, for the first time as a young adult, a coeducational setting. All of a sudden, I was amongst all of these attractive girls.

One strongpoint of my theological studies involved my singing with our choir. The choir of seminarians was known as "The Padre Choristers." We were educated and directed by Father Owen da Silva who had also been our director at St. Anthony's Seminary. We sang for the Sunday parish Masses in the Mission. People came from far and wide to be inspired by our church music, especially our singing of Gregorian chants in Latin. The chants were very moving and inspirational. I, myself, was a second bass with a pretty good voice, and, I felt very moved by this traditional music.

Especially moving was the Holy Week liturgy that included our chanting, and that was profoundly filled with deep human affection. The memory of those days lingers within me. The chanting of the Lamentations of Tenebrae (Darkness) on the Wednesday, Thursday, and Friday evenings of Holy Week was incredibly stirring. At the end of each Lamentation we would sing "Jerusalem, Jerusalem, return to the Lord thy God." And the singing on Good Friday of the "Seven Last Words of Jesus" on the cross moved me deeply. I grew in my understanding of the sacrificial love of Jesus and of that of many others whom I knew, such as my mother.

†

Despite some of the limitations at Mission Santa Barbara, I did feel that I was continuing to grow spiritually. In a way, the seminary was giving me some idea, though in need of updating, of what I was to preach as I would try to "save the world." Through my studying and my reading, I felt that my experiencing of a personal relationship with God was advancing. It was more positive than it had been before. All this made me more and more anxious to complete the process of becoming a Franciscan priest.

As I came closer to ordination, I felt more justified in my choice of the priesthood. Instead of any feeling that I was doing this because I had to, I now did it because I wanted to. I was free in this decision. I looked forward to using all of this knowledge and spiritual growth once I was out of the constraints of seminary life. I had this burning anticipation. The future – my future – was closer and closer. I was now feeling less depressed and instead happier because the end of my seminary years was at hand. I felt that I was becoming equipped for my task.

However, in this journey toward the priesthood, one of the disappointments I received, at least at that moment, was that by my third year of theology, I was selected to be sent to do more graduate work after my ordination and the completion of my fourth year of theology at the Mission. I had been a very good student and that's why Father Alfred Boeddeker, who was in charge of the students, chose me. The intent was to prepare me to become a Franciscan seminary professor of Theology.

But I didn't want to do further studies. I thought that I knew enough to be an effective priest. I enjoyed the intellectual life, but what I wanted the most was to be assigned to do parish work. I wanted to get to work as a priest in the community among the people. That's why I had joined the Order.

Yet I came to recognize the same challenge of earlier years: trust in God's mysterious ways. If I trust God even though my life isn't just quite what I would want, eventually I'll be better off. In giving of myself, I'll receive more in return. Again, this is the paradox that I had been wrestling with during my seminary years: self-denial leads to self-fulfillment.

My going on to more studies would in fact better prepare me – intellectually and spiritually – for the profound changes that the Church would undergo later in the 1960s as a result of the reforms of Vatican Council II. The winds of change were already beginning to blow and my continuing academic life introduced me to some of these stirrings. If I hadn't accepted Father Alfred's decision – and I had no choice anyway – I might have resisted Vatican II. I could have become an ultra-conservative priest, a fundamentalist. But I didn't and in retrospect I owe this to the decision of my superiors.

†

Finally, the blessed day came when I was officially ordained a priest. This came at the end of my third year at the Theological Seminary. At the end of my first year, I had taken my final vows as a Franciscan. Then I received a series of orders (minor and major) preparatory to the priesthood. Each one was a sort of rite of passage leading to my ultimate ordination as a priest.

Aside from the retreat before ordination, I didn't have enough quiet time to prepare. There was so much to do, including the sending out of invitations to family and friends, arrangements for my first Mass, etc. and just the whole formality of the ceremony. On the appointed day, the Mission was packed with friars, the relatives and friends of those of us who were being ordained.

Fortunately for me, on this occasion, my mother and Jim, who was now on his feet financially, were able to attend. Ray was still in the service, but his wife, Nell, attended. Ray had married while in the service. Jim had also married and his wife, June, was present. Both sisters-in-law became dear friends of mine. I regarded them as sisters.

The whole ceremony included the Mass in Latin, of course, and was presided over by Bishop Joseph T. McGucken, one of the auxiliary bishops of the Los Angeles Archdiocese. Later, he became bishop of Sacramento and then San Francisco.

As part of the ritual, we candidates for the priesthood prostrated ourselves in front of the altar as a sign of humble pleading before God. Finally, Bishop McGucken laid his hands on me and formally proclaimed me to be a priest of Christ. I felt both numb and elated. It was overwhelming. After eleven long years of study and of coming of age, I had finally reached my goal. I was a priest – a Franciscan priest. It was June 3 of 1945 and the war, at least in Europe, was coming to an end.

I had such a sense of attainment that my feelings do not allow for adequate explanation. I was glad that I had made the decision to become a priest. The fulfillment of a dream. Mission accomplished, the arrival at the top of a mountain after a long and difficult climb, winning a game when all seemed lost. The joy was numbing.

What a joy it was for me to have my family celebrating with me after these many years of very little contact. I felt as if I had returned from a long vacation to resume my life with family and relatives. I just picked up where I had left off. I was closer to them now than when I lived with them before leaving to go to the seminary. I was even more at home with them. I cherished my ties with them all the more. As I learned in my education, I received much more in return than I had ever given. It was the experience of the hundredfold that Jesus speaks of in the gospels, when one loses all to respond to a calling from God.

My first Low Mass (as it was called then) was celebrated in the chapel of St. Anthony's Seminary the following day – the very site of the beginning of my lengthy journey.

But I didn't have much time to dwell on this momentous event. I received a two-week vacation that included scheduling my first High Mass (as it was called) before a congregation in my hometown of Sacramento. This was a special occasion.

I chose to say Mass in my mother's parish of St. Mary's in our Italian-American neighborhood. The small church was packed with family, relatives, and old friends. Even some of the nuns who had taught me attended.

I felt very happy. It finally came to be! I was humble in accepting my new responsibilities as a priest, but at the same time, I couldn't help but be proud that I had finally accomplished my goal.

I celebrated the Mass, but I didn't give the homily. This would have been awkward since I was the special guest of honor in a sense. Indeed, a good friend of Jim's, Father Brendan Mitchel, a Franciscan, delivered the sermon. He was also a Sacramento native and that made it special. I don't remember everything he said, but it included some nice words about me and my family. For this, I was very grateful. After Mass, my mother hosted a very nice reception at Jim's house where there was much to eat and drink. It was a typical Italian celebration with accompanying Italian music.

The following Sunday, we went to one of my uncle's ranches outside of Sacramento for another big dinner and celebration. I attended this occasion and others during these two weeks wearing my brown Franciscan robe. I was proud of it. It was my "uniform." It told people that I was a Franciscan priest.

Needless to say, I was the center of attention and placed on a pedestal. In those days, this is how Catholics felt about priests. You might say that we were spoiled.

One might ask "how reconcile this with Franciscan humility?" Through the years I have reflected on what true humility is. Humility is truth, the truth about God, the truth about myself, the truth about others. I try to integrate true humility and justifiable pride, who I am, what I can do and who God is and what God can and desires to do in and through me. I am to be humbly proud or proudly humble. I am to live for God and for others. As Richard McBrien expresses it "humility is openness to God's call….The antithesis of humility is self-centeredness and closed mindedness. One who is consumed with self-interest, with advancing one's own goals and ambitions is not likely to hear the call of God." St. Paul puts it this way: "I can do great things in Him who strengthens me." Again, my education and my vision give meaning and direction to my heart and my emotional life.

Those two weeks back home after so many years of absence were very special and they passed much too quickly.

I now felt like I could take a deep breath. I had made it and was very glad about it. It was all worthwhile. The wait was over. I could relax. I was totally comfortable in my choice.

I was also happy because my mother showed pride and excitement in my accomplishment. She seemed much more reconciled now to my vocation. My mother didn't say much. Like me, she kept her affectionate feelings to herself. But I could "read" her well. She was very happy within herself and pleased that her son was happy. Our ties were even closer than when I was at home with her in my early years. It was the realization of what I came to understand in my priestly life: "born of mother to be born of God." My whole family was very accepting. This part of my journey ended well.

3

Go East, Young Man

Now in contact with people of different faiths and walks of life I became aware of what lay hidden deep within my self. I knew that I had a long way to go to 'be all things to all people,' as St. Paul says.

— Fr. Virgil Cordano

After two "exalted" weeks in Sacramento, I returned to Santa Barbara. That summer, and during my fourth and final year of my theological studies, I helped out in different parishes. My status was now that of a "simplex" priest. I still couldn't do everything a regular priest could. I could say Mass, but could not hear confession (reconciliation) or anoint the sick. I couldn't even deliver homilies. All of these privileges awaited the termination of my last year when I would be given full privileges as a priest. But I was very happy in presiding at Mass that summer and during the year in Santa Maria, Oxnard, and Ventura.

My fourth year at Mission Theological was anti-climatic for me. As far as I was concerned, I had already reached my objective of being ordained. At the same time, this year of study was a bit difficult in that the focus was on marriage and sexual morality. These topics were reserved until the end when supposedly we were more mature to deal with them. Moreover, since we would soon be dealing with parishioners and hearing confessions, the belief was that dealing with these subjects later rather than earlier in our training was more appropriate.

However, looking back, I would disagree with this approach. The fact was that as seminarians we had been too sheltered from real life and hence our own personal, including sexual, development and understanding had been retarded. It would have been better for us to study such issues earlier to assist us in our own emotional and psychological maturity. What was lacking was education in the psychological and spiritual aspects of sexuality.

In any event, we went through that year anticipating our first assignments as priests after our graduation. We all took a final examination called in Latin the <u>cura animarum</u> that means the care of souls examination. If passed, you were now a fully active priest with all the privileges of administering all the sacraments. I passed and awaited my first priestly assignment. There was no ceremony attached to this graduation and that was just as fine for me.

Ordination was not just a privilege for me. I wanted to serve others. At the time, I thought I was well prepared for priestly ministry. I had sufficient education.

My anticipation, however, met with disappointment. I patiently waited while my fellow young priests got their assignments. Some went to teach in our Franciscan high schools; some went into parish work; and some left for work in our missions in Third World, or what we call today "developing" countries. Much to my regret and even sadness, I received none of these assignments. I had been told in my second year of theology that I was to go to higher studies. But that was temporarily delayed.

"Father Virgil," my superior told me, "we need you to stay here and fill in for a year while Father Silvano is engaged in other ministries. We need you to teach his courses. You're one of our best students and we feel confident you can teach these theology classes."

While this sounded like a compliment and a choice assignment, I didn't take it as such. I wanted to do parish work not teach theology students. All these years, I had looked forward to working in a parish and being part of "saving the world." Parish ministry was my idea of being a priest – hearing confessions, caring for the sick and the dying, helping the poor, preaching, and, in general, ministering to lay Catholics. After many years in a classroom (12 years in the seminary), I longed to be in contact with people of all ages and walks of life. I was person-centered. I did not become a priest to be a teacher.

Instead, I was ordered to stay and teach other seminarians. Although disappointed, I accepted the challenge. And it was a challenge: to teach the students of the classes just behind me.

That summer of 1946, I used the time in part to prepare for the classes I would teach. But fortunately, I was also given another task. There was a need for a chaplain at Mary's Help Hospital in San Francisco and I was sent there for the summer. I was delighted. I took my books with me so that I could prepare for my teaching while at the same time working at the hospital. Although I was as green as could be in experiences outside of the seminary, I looked forward to being a hospital chaplain.

I still remember my excitement and nervousness when I got my first sick call in the hospital. Still another anxious moment was when one of the Sisters who ran the hospital asked me if I would give a talk to the student nurses. I had never done such a thing and, on top of this, I had never been in a room alone with young ladies. I was totally inexperienced and immature in such matters. Here were all these young attractive nurses and I didn't know what to say and how to act with them. I got through it, but I hate to think of what I said. I didn't have any of the usual common life experiences to share with them or to be able to interact with them.

I wasn't surprised that I would be attracted to girls my age. This was to be expected. In keeping with my then limited understanding of sexuality, I knew that sex in itself is good, being God's own creation. The problem was that in my secluded seminary years, I never mingled with young ladies or even saw much of them. As if making up for "lost time," I had to deal with a rush of sexual feelings. My gradual emotional experience and competency had been delayed. The normal male feelings were felt. But given my decisive commitment to the priesthood and the related celibacy requirements, I felt that I would never leave the priesthood to marry, though the natural desire was ever present. The road to the priest-hood had asked of me much and I would continue the journey. Yet, I still wished that celibacy were optional.

I came to enjoy my stay at the hospital. It helped me to mature and to enlarge my horizons. I moved about taking care of the religious needs of the sick. I said daily Mass for the Sisters and others who attended. I heard confessions. I administered the anointing of the sick (then called "extreme unction") and Communion to the bed-ridden. All this gave me experiences in pastoral activities. I was the only priest assigned to the hospital so I was always busy and on call seven days a week. When I had some time off, I enjoyed walking the streets of San Francisco and enjoying the beautiful sights of the city.

†

At the end of the summer, I returned to Santa Barbara to begin my first stint at teaching. I moved from being a student to being up in front of the class. I taught biblical studies. I enjoyed the classes especially because I was able to take advantage of new developments in the understanding of the Bible. Although it would be over a decade before these changes would become more concretized in the reforms of Vatican II, these new influences were already becoming visible in 1946.

We began to understand, for example, the human dimensions of the Bible. It wasn't just the Word of God, but also the word of human authors. Scripture had to be seen within the prevailing cultures of those times. We began to study literary forms, literary genres, history, and anthropology. It was the beginning of an academic revolution within the Church. Biblical scholars and other theologians – not many but some – were looking for new ways of expressing the faith. God spoke through human authors. That's a very important principle in both theology and spirituality. The only God we have is the God who reveals Himself in human manifestations. This is the incarnational principle. The divine is contacted only through humans. That's the basic principle. You just don't believe in God. You believe in the human expression of God. God is found in the person of Jesus and in all human experiences.

I was beginning to see that all of life is sacramental. A sacrament is meant to be a visible sign of an invisible grace or divine presence – "a reality imbued with the hidden presence of God." I could slowly (at that time) get beyond the dichotomy or split between nature and grace, the divine and the human. I was coming to see and welcome the infinite in the finite, the spiritual in the material, the eternal in the historical. We have a graced existence. In truly human love is the hidden love of God.

The story of the Bible kept telling me that God acts and speaks through all human events and persons. Only through human experience can I experience the mystery of God. I and others are to be channels or mediators of the active presence of God in the world. I don't just believe in God, I believe in the human manifestation of God. I have ever been mindful of the statement by a certain author "nothing human is foreign to me." It has served my theology and spirituality well. God says the same. Nothing human should be foreign to me because all of creation is not foreign to God. The word of God is filtered, channeled through the minds and experiences of Moses, Isaiah, Jesus, and others.

Through my reading and now through my teaching, I more and more began to absorb this view of life. It was similar to my earlier belief in the active presence of God in every moment. Teaching biblical studies really impressed this on me. To teach the Bible, I had to understand the historical and cultural contexts of scripture. I had to know what was going on at the time, as today I have to recognize what is happening in my modern culture. The unlimited – God – is in the limited – humans – in their particular cultural settings. Jesus was a human, a Jew, and a Galilean. In a way, God limited Himself in coming into the world through his son, Jesus. This has always been the profound mystery in Christianity, especially in Jesus' life of suffering and dying. The sacred is right there at the core of the profane. I saw that more clearly through my teaching as well as in the reality of my spirituality. Jesus embraced the human reality of his time. I was to embrace and celebrate the concrete reality of my life, even when it was not to my liking. I saw the need for a spirituality of reality.

Besides biblical studies, I also taught homiletics and liturgy. Teaching homiletics was like the blind leading the blind since I had very little experience at this time in delivery of sermons. Fortunately, the class was very small.

In my classes, I mostly lectured and answered questions. The process was not commendable in retrospect. There was very little dialogue with the students. I lectured and they memorized. I should have known better, but I was a creature of my own traditional training. To assist the students, I handed out an outline with notes so that they could better follow my lectures.

On the whole, I didn't enjoy this experience. I really didn't want to be a professor. I wanted to be in a parish. Still, slowly I was beginning to see the importance and need for further academic learning.

One thing I did enjoy was no longer being a student. I liked now being part of the priestly faculty and brotherly community and having more personal interaction with the older and more experienced Franciscans. Among other things, I could now eat with the priests at their table. I was able now to do more things. I felt myself more relaxed and liberated. I was advancing in the experiential aspect of being a priest. I said Mass daily in the Mission church or at the nearby convent of the Poor Clare Sisters as well as heard confessions. I also had a larger room in the better part of the house.

Moreover, I could even now go out to movies, ballgames, or to people's homes. Although I had this liberty, I actually didn't make much use of it at this time. For one, I was too busy preparing for my classes, and, also, I didn't know too many people in Santa Barbara at that time.

Hearing confessions for the first time was quite an experience. It was humbling to listen to people confessing their sins and a challenge to be able to counsel them about their lives. Here again, the lack of human experiences as practiced in the world outside of the seminary put me in a disadvantaged position. How could I understand people's experiences and sins when I, myself, had been so sheltered from what they were experiencing? All I could do was to try and understand. One way that helped was for me to realize that I had my own sins and weaknesses and that there was much that priests and penitents had in common. I began to acknowledge my own version of the sins and challenges of others.

In my youth, my sins were similar to those spoken to me in the confessional. I have come to know and accept my own shadow (this dark underside of myself). I have the potential – and at times the temptation – to commit the same sins others have confessed to me. I have ever been accepting of my weaknesses, knowing and believing in God's forgiveness. In a way, there are two classes of persons: those who admit their weaknesses and those who don't. I rejoice in knowing that God accepts me as I am. When I am at my worst, God can show up at His/Her best.

But still, it wasn't always easy to advise others. There were often different issues to ponder. At this time, the pressure was all on the priest with respect to offering counsel and forgiveness. The person confessed and I listened and absolved.

I have been affected greatly by what I have come to know in the confessional. Maybe I have benefited more from the confessional than the penitents who revealed their inner selves to me. They told me more than I told them. In listening to others, I have come to listen to my own inner self. I have my version of what others confess to. I grew in appreciation of my faith and in gratitude to a loving and forgiving God. I felt closer to my penitents than to people whose deeper self I have never come to know. Our common mortality unites us. Also, I have grown in empathy and compassion for those who carry the burden of self-displeasure and self-condemnation.

Today, things are different. For one, we no longer speak of "confession" but of the Sacrament of Reconciliation. This is more of an open conversation between the penitent and the priest. It is more dialogue and less of a monologue, a celebration of God's loving forgiveness more than just a listing of sins. But this would come later.

In the meantime, as I began to hear confessions I came more and more to understand something about the human spirit and about the interiority of people. This was a new kind of education for me. It related to the psychology, emotions, joys, and challenges of being a Christian, or better, of just being human.

But all this involved difficulties and challenges that the seminary had not prepared me for. Doctrinally, I was prepared. Psychologically, I was not. Human psychology had not been part of our curriculum. Instead, every-thing came from the top and the stress was on conformity to the Church's doctrines. I understood texts but not people even my own deep self.

That may have been all right within the seminary, but outside of it, I was not fully at home. I had to learn to deal with lay people through trial and error. I had to teach myself through study and experience a deeper understanding of human nature and most of this was just by beginning to interact with people including hearing their confessions and the stories of their lives. I learned that most of us live in the shadows. We live between the good and the bad, the beautiful and the ugly. We are all com-plex and our decision-making is equally complex. A priest cannot afford to be exclusively dogmatic in dealing with other people. He has to under-stand their shadows and meet individual people right where they are.

In my secluded life in the seminary I came to know myself in the quiet of prayer and in time alone with myself as I faced up to what was stirring deep within the core of my being. Also, my relationship with the different members of my class awakened me to my strengths and weak-nesses. Now in contact with lay people of different backgrounds, I became aware of what lay hidden deep within my self. I knew that I had a long way to go to "be all things to all people," as St. Paul says. I still had much interior "homework" to do. With the prophet Jeremiah, I could lament "the human heart! Who can understand it?"

I think I improved in "hearing confessions" more so than in delivering a homily. I still lacked confidence in speaking publicly. I felt theologically prepared but not experienced enough in the human condition to be able to effectively tie together scripture and human experiences. I wrote my sermons out and either memorized them or read portions of them. In time, I just referred to notes. I still do or at least have an outline so I won't get stuck or just ramble. There's nothing worse than getting stuck in the "lettuce patch" which is really the "let us patch." Let us say our prayers, let us attend Mass, etc., etc.

"Let us, let us," which really means that we're stuck and can't remember where to go from here to there. That's embarrassing. I wouldn't give any of these early sermons again. They weren't very good. But at least I was trying and learning.

That second part of 1946 really gave me an introduction to some of what it meant to no longer be a seminarian and now to be a full-fledged priest. I was growing but more changes lay ahead.

†

While I was preparing to teach the second semester beginning in January, 1947, I received another surprise when one day Father Boeddeker came to see me in my room.

"Father Virgil," he said, "Father Silvano is returning from leave and will take over the classes you taught in the fall. You're being sent to Catholic University in Washington, D.C. to begin work on your doctorate in theology. We expect that after that, you will go to Rome for more additional advanced work. This is a wonderful opportunity for you."

A wonderful opportunity? At the moment, I didn't see it that way. I knew that they had targeted me for graduate work, but, even as I listened to Father Alfred, I felt more disappointment than elated. I liked intellectual work, but I really just wanted to be a parish priest. Why couldn't this happen? Of course, I had no choice in the matter.

"Yes, Father," I forced myself to reply. "I understand. I'll start getting ready."

Again, I had to leave for the unknown, away from what I had become accustomed to. I was leaving another "home." I would feel alone once more, though not as intensely as when I first left my family for the seminary. My earlier experiences and my reading and reflection upon the necessity of detachment supported me. I had to trust what was different and new.

Since I had also worked through my separation from my family, I didn't feel anything similar on this occasion. I was now a priest and my family and I would always be close. I would return to California. Also, I would be making new friends. I would never feel homesick again.

So there I was. It was January 1947, which meant that I would be starting my STD (Doctor of Sacred Theology) work in the middle of the academic year. I had three days to pack. I got on the train and was on my way across the country. This was a huge change for me. I had never been out of California and never lived in a big city. I also had never encountered a really cold climate. It was freezing all the way to Washington. I stopped in Chicago and stayed at one of the Franciscan monasteries for a few days. It was zero degrees there. When I finally got to Washington, I saw my first snowfall.

I checked into the Franciscan monastery in the northeast part of the city where Catholic University is located. The monastery at 1400 Quincy Street was about a fifteen-minute walk from the campus. I walked there in the morning; walked back for lunch; walked again in the afternoon for classes; and then walked back home afterward. I did this sunshine, rain, or snow walking in my Franciscan habit although, fortunately, not in my sandals when it rained or snowed. At least, I was getting plenty of exercise. All along the way, I passed by other monasteries or residencies belonging to other Catholic orders such as the Jesuits, Dominicans, and Oblates of St. Joseph, and others. I never had the comfort of an automobile ride.

One nice thing about living in the monastery was that I met Franciscans from all over the country and, in fact, from all over the world.

The main purpose of the monastery was to raise funds for the Holy Land and to train Franciscans to serve there. I, along with a few others, lived there as guests.

My education began with a second semester. I had to take the second part of what were really yearlong courses. That meant that I would have to take the first semester later in the next fall. In my first year the classes involved an overview of theology such as Systematic Theology, Moral Theology, and Canon Law. The students were primarily other priests and a few advanced seminarians from different religious orders.

I found my coming into a class in midstream to be very difficult. For the first time, I began to have academic problems. I had always done well in classes, but here I felt handicapped because I was behind the other students. Somehow I struggled through it, but it didn't make me feel very good.

If those classes that semester proved to be tough, I knew that other more rigorous ones lay ahead of me. For one, I would have to take Hebrew the following academic year. I had mastered Latin in seminary but knew little Hebrew. Learning Hebrew in depth was a whole new ballgame. I decided to get a head start by taking a class in Hebrew that summer.

However, it wasn't offered during the summer at Catholic University. I checked around and learned that I could enroll in a Hebrew class at the University of Chicago. The problem was that in order for me to enroll in a non-Catholic university, I had to get permission from my Provincial in Oakland. This was more difficult than I imagined. They didn't want any Franciscan attending a non-Catholic campus. The Provincial wrote back and refused my request.

However, in one of my very few cases of questioning my superiors – this reflected how panicked I was about learning Hebrew – I wrote back that if I couldn't take this summer class in Hebrew, then I would have to be recalled back to California and be given another assignment.

To my surprise, this little display of opposition worked. In a few days, another letter from the Provincial arrived: permission granted.

In Chicago, I stayed at our Franciscan monastery, St. Augustine's, on the south side. Each morning, I boarded a streetcar and transferred to another to get to the campus. Despite the hot Chicago summer, I had to go to classes dressed in my black suit with Roman collar. This made the heat even more stifling, but this was the requirement for a Franciscan attending public events or functions or, in my case, classes outside of the monastery. Within the monastery, I wore my Franciscan habit.

On Sundays, the Franciscan superior sent me to a neighbor diocesan parish to help out with the Masses. I was assigned the 12 noon and 1 o'clock Masses. In those days we had to abstain from food and drink, even water, from midnight on. At 2 P.M., when I finished saying my second Mass, I left the altar "soaking wet" and experiencing a good-sized headache. Breakfast followed and I then returned to the Franciscan monastery, where I rested after the very tiring two Masses. The joy of the summer was my life with a very welcoming and fraternal group of friars at St. Augustine Friary.

However, my experience at the university was not as pleasant. To make matters more difficult, after I enrolled in the Hebrew class, I discovered that it was an advanced one. I had wanted to study basic Hebrew. I had no choice but to struggle with this class all summer. I could never quite master verbs and sentence-structure in Hebrew. This was all a very humbling experience. In the seminary, I had always been on top of my studies. Now I was lost and frustrated. But I did learn some Hebrew. It was a relief to return to Washington for the new semester.

During the 1947-48 academic year, I resumed my theology classes, which were actually the first parts of the classes I had started that January. I found them to be easier and less stressful. What did stress me were the additional classes in Scripture that I had to take while, at the same time, I had to finish the second semester of my first year at Catholic University in Theology. I had classes in Hebrew, Aramaic, Syriac, and Greek so that I would be able to read the original languages of the Bible. It was very demanding but necessary. I understood this, but it was still hard.

In some of my classes there was only one other student, an Australian

Franciscan. Our main professor was a Jesuit, a pleasant priest, but he seemed more concerned with linguistics than with other aspects of biblical studies. He'd give us a whole chapter of Ezekiel and expect us to explain the construction of each sentence. This was painful since we were just beginners in studying Semitic languages.

I wasn't happy during this semester. The subject matter was not to my liking. And, after having been very successful in earlier studies, I sensed that I was not that good a learner in this new field. I feared failure or, better, mediocrity. I lost a lot of weight (all of my walking back and forth from the monastery probably had something to do with this as well) and I began to have trouble with my eyes because of my personal tension. Slowly and with difficulty I became more proficient in both Hebrew and Greek, although not as good as some of the other students.

But life in Washington was not all studying. In return for my room and board at the monastery, I had to help out there as well. I had to say Mass and, more importantly, be on duty for confessions and counseling. Unlike today, this was a time when many Catholics would go to confession very often. So each Saturday, the usual day set aside for confessions, the monastery was crowded with confessors. For some reason more lay people as well as other priests, nuns, and seminarians chose to come to our church rather than to other churches. I once asked someone from one of the other religious houses why this was so. "Because you Franciscans forgive sins that nobody else forgives," he replied. What this person meant was that we were known to be kind and understanding and not harsh in hearing confessions.

Hearing confessions included those of other priests. This was new to me. Ordinarily, a newly ordained priest such as myself would not be allowed to hear the confession of another priest for at least five years. It was felt that you needed more experience before you could really advise in confessions of other priests. But due to the demand at the monastery, this rule of thumb was set aside, and I and other young priests heard these confessions.

As a result, I came to know many of the problems faced by other priests. Some were difficult to deal with since I was so inexperienced, but it was quite an education. I came to see what the challenges in the priesthood would be for me. Again, as in all confessions, God spoke to me about myself as I listened to and came to know what went on deep within priestly hearts. My ties to other priests were strengthened. We were a family, a community.

I learned very much about our human condition in hearing the confessions of some lay people as well. One day a lady came with a very serious personal problem. I helped her the best I could and she returned regularly to confess to me. We actually became good friends and I got to know her and her husband and their ten children quite well. At Christmas and Easter, they'd invite me to their home. This became a kind of home away from home. The parents have died, but I remain a good friend of the children. I also made friends of other lay people in Washington.

Washington, D.C., of course, was an exciting city with much history. I took advantage of this and did as much sightseeing as possible. I went to all of the usual spots: the White House, the Capitol, the Washington and Lincoln Memorials, and many others. In January 1949, since I was still there, I even attended the inauguration of President Harry Truman after his election the previous year. I stood out in the bitter cold with thousands of others and saw him take the oath of office and deliver his inauguration speech. I vividly remember standing in black suit and Roman collar some distance from the steps of Congress. A gentleman on seeing me said, "Ah, Rome!" Surprised, the only thing I could think of saying was "Yes, Rome. I'm a Catholic priest and an American citizen." Off he went and I watched Truman sworn in as President of the United States.

Later that spring, I got a further introduction to official Washington when to my surprise I was asked along with other Franciscans to participate in a ceremony at Statuary Hall in the Capitol rotunda to mark the 200th anniversary of the departure of Fr. Junipero Serra from Spain to the

Americas. His statue is part of the pantheon of heroes in the hall. Of course, it was Fr. Serra who traveled to California and established the mission system there.

One of the Congressional representatives from California asked that one of the Franciscans say a few words at the ceremony.

"Fr. Virgil, you're from California," one of my fellow Franciscans said, "why don't you speak."

I didn't really want to but I felt I had no choice. I agonized at writing my comments as well as having to brush up on the history of Fr. Serra. It was not a good speech, and, as I look back on it now, it had too many generalities and incorrect statements on my part. For example, I regrettably referred to the Indians whom Fr. Serra converted as "pagans." I would never say that today, but we in the Church at that time still possessed a more traditional Eurocentric and non-ecumenical view of other cultures. Fortunately, we began to move away from this perspective as a result of Vatican II a few years later. My speech unfortunately was also influenced by the Cold War politics of the period. I noted that if it had not been for the Spanish conquest of California and for Fr. Serra converting California to Christianity, it is possible that Russia would have expanded into this area, and then in 1949 we would have had to confront our Communist enemy at our borders. But all of this is in hindsight. At the moment, I was thrilled at being part of this impressive public ceremony at the Capitol of the United States. I was even more excited when my speech was printed in the *Congressional Record*.

Of course, Fr. Serra has more recently become a controversial figure since he is being considered for canonization as a saint in the Church. Some here in the United States, in particular certain Native Americans, are vehemently opposed to this. They counter that Fr. Serra was part of a violent and destructive conquest and oppression of the California Indians. I am sensitive to these feelings today, although I believe that they don't consider Fr. Serra in his proper historical context. In my opinion, if it hadn't been for the friars such as Fr. Serra, the Spanish presence would have been worse. It was the Church that in most cases protected the Indians and tried to integrate them into the new Spanish and later Mexican systems. Without the padres, I wonder what some of the Spanish soldiers would have done to them. Fr. Serra loved the Indians. Even so when Pope John Paul II visited California a few years ago, he personally asked forgiveness for the way the Indians had been treated by people of European descent, including some in the Church. On the other hand, he praised Fr. Serra for being heroic. He gave up everything for his faith. This was my view of Fr. Serra in 1949 when I spoke at the Capitol, and I still feel the same today.

But, at the same time, I echo the Pope's stress on forgiveness. Some time after the Pope's visit to California, I also wrote the following concerning the need to acknowledge injustices that the Church may have played a role in with respect to the Native Americans and about, in general, the concept of forgiveness:

> Without the admission of injustice and the offer and acceptance of forgiveness there is little hope for peace. We are peoples of differing religions, cultures, and ethnic roots. All of us occasionally fail others and ourselves. Who among us will cast the first stone? Today we have only to look at the Middle East, the centuries of cruelty in Yugoslavia, the violence in our cities, our personal biases, discrimination and defamation. Isn't it strange that all claim to be right and that no one is wrong? Forgiveness is the way to heal past hurts, to be transformed into a family of brothers and sisters, children of the same God, although He/She is understood differently.

Entering into a bigger world was very beneficial for me. I gained new experiences and insights into everyday living apart from life within the monastery. I was still pretty green, young, and innocent, but the experiences of this new world helped me better understand myself and others. I began to expand my emotional, intellectual, and social life. Again and again I came to know more about my true self. Because of this new awareness, I began to read and reflect more on the self, subjectivity, experiences.

My spirituality needed more psychological study. As I listened more to my inner self and had others share themselves with me, I had to delve into the psychological world and my theology justified the new interest. God meets us and deals with us as we are. Who really am I? My person and not merely my achievements. I developed a special interest in the study of the self, especially its desires. Today bookstores abound in studies and biographical accounts of human interiority.

Throughout all of this, I never once questioned my vocation as a priest. I knew I was going to stay with it. I had no temptation to leave. I was in for better or worse. When you sacrifice as much as I did to become a priest, you feel committed. And I viewed my ministry as vital for myself and others.

After one year of study at Catholic University, I received what is called a Licentiate (STL – a Licentiate in Sacred Theology) that is something like a Master's degree in Theology. For this I also had to pass an oral exam, an overview of theology.

†

The next two years, I worked on my STD in Theology with an emphasis on Scripture also at Catholic University. I had been told that after the first year, I might be sent to study in Rome. But this didn't happen. Conditions were still pretty bad in postwar Italy, so my superiors felt that it was best that I stay in Washington.

I did but I didn't enjoy most of my work. It was down right unpleasant. It wasn't what I had expected. Biblical studies, for example, was primarily linguistics. The teaching and the classes were very poorly done. I couldn't get enthusiastic. I tolerated the experiences. I looked forward toward the summers that meant returning to Santa Barbara and a visit with my family in Sacramento.

In the meantime, I grew experientially. I continued to meet new people. I heard more confessions, counseled many people, and learned more about human reality in this way. All this led to better self understanding and a better view of the human condition. The mystery of the human person fascinated me and not merely the mystery of God. I came to know and experience God in and through my human reality. Also other persons became for me revealers of God. To extend John's Gospel, the Word, or God's self-revelation became flesh also in us. All life is sacramental, a hinting of the invisible God.

Part of my discomfort during these years in Washington was that I knew by then that I was doomed to be a teacher and a professor in the Franciscan Order. Instead, I just wanted to be a parish priest. But this wasn't in the cards. I had no choice. I was just told what I had to do. You couldn't complain. There was no dialogue. But I had learned to obey. And time would show that the decisions of my superiors was for me a wise one.

In looking back, I have come to see that the decision by my superiors turned out to be a blessing for me. I hate to think what would have happened to me if I hadn't gotten this advanced education. Maybe I would have gone into parish work inadequately prepared. I wouldn't have been accepting of the changes that Vatican II inaugurated in the 1960s. Because of my graduate work and my experiences in Washington, I understood the need for change and renewal associated with Vatican II. I was better able to handle the changes. Some of the other priests seemingly couldn't. They remained committed to the old ideas of the priesthood and Church.

Despite my anguish, I did my graduate work. I was lucky and fortunate for this opportunity. It's the old principle that if you trust in God's mysterious ways, and practice patience, as St. Paul said, everything turns out for the better. For those who love God and surrender to God, everything turns out for the good. When you live by faith and trust that you're doing God's will, God rewards you for it.

Sometimes I think that if I hadn't become a priest that I would have stayed home, gotten an education, maybe in business, joined my brother, Jim, in real estate, but all of this without much instruction in my faith. I wonder where I'd be spiritually.

Graduate work was not my original choice, but God was right. I came to see that true growth costs. As St. John of the Cross noted, you go through all of these dark nights of self-emptying and surrendering to God. I was coming to better understand the paradox of life. You lose your life but you save it. You give but you gain more in return. I was experiencing all of this in Washington, especially in my studies, but since I had learned discipline early in life as well as obedience and dutifulness, I persisted and hopefully went my way.

After I completed my course work for my doctorate, I now moved on to my dissertation. I could choose any scriptural topic I wanted. I decided to focus on the theme of "unforgivable sin" in Matthew 12, 31-32, Mark 3, 28-29, and Luke 12, 10. This had always fascinated me. How can you explain that while God forgives all sins, there is still the seeming exception of the unforgivable sin linked to blasphemy against the Holy Spirit. "The sin against the Holy Spirit will never be forgiven!" It didn't make sense. It was inconsistent and an apparent contradiction, or what?

I started to research the topic in the broader context of the Bible and its times. I spent a few months working on it and had written a third of it when I was ordered to return to Santa Barbara in 1950. One part of me welcomed going back, but another wanted to remain and finish the thesis. Again, I had no choice. I took a leave from my dissertation work and returned to California.

I was assigned to be the new spiritual director of the students at Mission Theological Seminary. These, of course, were the seminarians who had completed their college at Mission San Luis Rey. I served in this capacity from 1950 to 1955. My official title was Master of Clerics or in Latin *Magister Clericorum*. Part of my duties was to be a spiritual advisor as well as to teach some classes. I taught Bible, homiletics, and liturgy. But being a spiritual director was a misnomer. My main role was to enforce the rules and regulations of the school, give weekly talks on spirituality, and eventually with the others on the faculty to decide on who would be ordained. I was the enforcer, a kind of religious cop. But I was not well prepared for this important task.

I didn't enjoy enforcing discipline. It was unpleasant. But I had to do it. If someone didn't properly do an exercise or an assignment, I had to correct him. When I encountered someone who I thought was bucking me, I probably reacted too quickly. I didn't like what I did, but I was serious about it. I became known as the authoritarian or bad guy because I was more a disciplinarian than a spiritual director. Human nature being what it is, I wasn't too popular. But I was probably admired for my fidelity to religious life as then lived.

It was never easy to deal with the more serious disciplinary cases. Fortunately, these cases didn't just fall on me. All of the faculty participated by voting on the students. Actually, each year after many faculty meetings, we voted on every student as to whether they should continue or be dismissed from the seminary. We discussed each case and then voted by secret ballot. In cases with serious issues, we deliberated more and often slept on the case and then voted later.

Some cases were particularly difficult because they could go either way. The basis for not allowing someone to continue involved character, behavior, attitude, and academic performance. We were especially concerned about those students who might be rebellious and non-obedient. This wasn't easy because in some cases we had very little depth of knowledge of the true person. We did our best. However, some were advanced who, in retrospect, should not have. They later left the priesthood.

After voting not to continue a student, we then had to decide who was to inform him. Since I was the spiritual director or enforcer of the rules, it usually fell on me. I hated to do this. In one case, the father of the fellow being expelled came to see me.

"What's the problem, Father," he said to me. "My son is better than some of the priests I know. Why do you want to expel him?"

I couldn't really respond because our discussions were confidential. All I could tell a student or a parent was the general nature of the problem. But I couldn't go into specifics. All I could say was "Sorry, but I can't talk about this."

Or in some cases, another seminarian who we advanced would come to see me and say: "Why did you expel Mark? He's so much better than I am. You should have expelled me."

"I'm sorry. I'm sorry," I'd say. "I can't really talk about it. We did what we had to do."

Expelled students couldn't appeal. Our decisions were final. We sent our report to the Provincial in Oakland. He generally agreed with us. But all this was never pleasant. I did my job, but I looked forward to someone else doing it.

In those five years, I continued to grow academically and spiritually through my teaching, my reading, and my reflections on my experiences. I was putting into practice what I believed. One enjoyable new experience was that I now was getting to know more people in Santa Barbara. I was also becoming better known in town. Groups began to invite me to give a talk or an invocation. These initial community contacts would serve me well later when I became even more involved in community affairs.

During these five years, I tried to work on my dissertation but found it very difficult due to my responsibilities at the seminary. I would go to our library but there were always things coming up plus my own teaching that distracted me. So I finally requested permission to return to Catholic University so that I could finish the thesis. Permission was granted and I left for Washington in the summer of 1955.

†

This time I arranged to stay for awhile at the Academy of American Franciscan History in nearby Maryland. I helped out a bit there, but mostly concentrated on my dissertation. I had no time to spare since my leave was only for a year. If I didn't finish in this time, I felt that I would never complete my doctorate.

I still kept the same thesis topic on the concept of unforgivable sin. I titled the study "The Blasphemy Against the Holy Spirit." Besides resuming my research at Catholic University, I also spent some time at St. Bonaventure University in upstate New York researching and writing.

To research my subject, I mainly focused on the original Greek of the specific passages in the gospels of Matthew, Mark, and Luke that concerned "unforgivable sin." I also read a number of books and articles on attitudes about forgiveness in Hebrew 6, 4-6 and 1 John 5, 16-17. Most of these were in English, but a few were in German and French that I wrestled with in understanding.

I was intrigued by the seeming contradiction between these texts and others that tell of God's willingness to forgive all sins. Yet the one exception seemed to be blasphemy against the Holy Spirit. Was this a contradiction or was there a logical consistency? I would have to understand the literary genre and thought process of the time.

As I researched this problem and thought about it, I came to study in depth biblical teaching on eschatology, "the last things," the future. The biblical texts suggest that sin against the Holy Spirit will never be forgiven in this world or the next. The implication here is that this is the eternal sin for which there is a final judgment. This brings you into eschatology, that is the concern for the end of time and what happens at the moment of death and the next world as perceived in those days. "Eschatology" comes from the Greek meaning the final stage in the final era. So I researched biblical eschatology and what different authors say about differing eschatologies. In the Bible you have different eschatologies or different ways of understanding the future and the final judgment.

One idea that I focused on to help explain the seeming contradiction I was concerned with had to do with what is called "realized eschatology." In popular language, this refers to the idea that the final judgment, your final judgment, is already anticipated in a present judgment. In a sense, your fate is decided here and now. We are in final times. The Messiah has come! There is no other. If you take a stand against God and the Holy Spirit, for example, you are condemned now, or better, you condemn yourself. This present condemnation is in anticipation of the final condemnation. The final judgment was already pronounced upon you at the present time. This is "realized eschatology." By contrast, whoever believes in the Lord is saved now. The future is the outcome of earlier present decisions.

The key to the contradiction is that you decide your own fate in the present. What Jesus was pointing out in these New Testament passages was that there were some, like those who believed that Jesus was an emissary from the devil, who would never accept the Holy Spirit or be open to what the Spirit was revealing in the person of Jesus. They thus condemned themselves in this world. The final judgment would only confirm this. It's not that people can't change, but that some don't want to change. It's not that God doesn't forgive, but that some don't believe in this forgiveness. They remain in darkness. As such, they're not forgiven. If you don't recognize or admit your sin of blasphemy, you condemn yourself. You make it unforgivable, not God.

Jesus was trying to show just how serious the sin of self-blindness is. It's like saying you better change your mind before you're truly eternally condemned and lost forever. Even we today sometimes go to the extreme in saying "If you don't change, you're going to go to hell." The person might change. The intent is to effect change. Some people only behave through fear of punishment. A parent says "Johnny, do this or if not, you're going to get it." And sometimes this works. I know of some people who thought of committing suicide, but the fear of hell stopped them rather than the love of God. You first start with trying to get people to accept the Holy Spirit through love, but if that doesn't work, then you instill the fear of eternal damnation in them. Remember the hell and damnation talks of former priests who gave missions in our parishes!

Jesus' statement about "unforgivable sin" has to be qualified in the light of his full teaching on sin, forgiveness and related subjects, and against the background of the threatening speech of Hebrew prophets who intended to move listeners to repentance and a change of mind and heart. The pastoral purpose of the words of Jesus is in effect a warning against final unrepentance, the hardening of one's heart. However, the door to repentance is not closed to them. Jesus continues to speak of the universal mercy of God. With this pastoral purpose in mind, the threats spoken by Jesus may be regarded as words of mercy.

The above is a popularization of the more academic language I used in my thesis. They are some of the ideas that I expressed in my manuscript.

When I finished at the end of the 1955-56 academic year, I had to defend it. This involved going before a committee of three professors whom I had worked with and answering their questions. But unlike a dissertation defense today where you get quizzed only on the thesis, I had to deal with a variety of questions outside of my dissertation as well. These included, for example, possible questions on issues such as the Dead Sea Scrolls. The preparation for all this was taxing. All this raised my anxiety level. I was a ball of nerves on the day of my defense.

The chair of my committee, whose name I no longer remember, was a Precious Blood priest. He was very good to me. He was also a controversial professor. He was, like a few of my teachers in the seminary, beginning to reinterpret scripture from an advanced nontraditional perspective that included historical and literary analysis. Yet such an approach was not fully accepted yet and would not be until Vatican II a few years later. In fact, Catholic University was a very traditional and theologically conservative institution. It did not favor innovative much less revisionist studies. If you came up with an interpretation different from what was coming out of Rome, you were in trouble. There wasn't full academic freedom.

All of this didn't really affect me. Despite some difficult questions, I passed my defense. It was more of a humbling experience than a stimulating exercise. But I was glad it was all over. Thank God! I now officially received my Doctor of Sacred Theology (STD). It wasn't called a Ph.D., but it was the equivalent.

As I look back on my dissertation now, I'm proud of it. I could have possibly done more research if I had had the time. But I didn't. My superiors gave me one year to finish so I felt pressured. Still, I think I did a good job. For its time, it was a unique study and I came up with a particular explanation on the concept of unforgivable sin that was somewhat different from the explanation given by others. I wouldn't necessarily call it revisionist, but it did reflect the stirrings in Catholic theological studies that would lead to significant changes in scriptural studies, moral theology, and systematic theology following upon Vatican II.

But I didn't dwell on this at the time. Getting my advanced degree had been hard for me. In the seminary, I had always been on top of everything. By contrast, at Catholic University I was always trying to catch up. I started late and then finished late because of the five year interval when I had to return to Santa Barbara. I'm surprised I got through. I wouldn't wish my experience on anybody.

I celebrated by going the very next day up to New York City. I had gotten a call from my brother Jim who was now quite financially successful in commercial real estate in Sacramento. He would go on to be a pioneer in the development of some of the very early shopping malls in northern California. Jim was in New York on business.

"George, what are you doing after your defense," Jim asked me on the phone.

"Nothing really. I'll be getting ready to return to Santa Barbara."

"Well, don't get too ready. How would you like to meet me in New York and go see the World Series? I have tickets for tomorrow's game."

Jim didn't have to say anything more. I loved baseball and had kept up with the major league teams throughout the seminary and beyond. I had never seen a major league ball game much less a World Series one, and the opportunity to see the Yankees and the Dodgers at Ebbetts Field in Brooklyn was a dream come true. I jumped at the chance. Jim and I had the time of our lives. What an incredible day. I'll always be grateful to my big brother for this.

María Cordano, Fr. Virgil's mother, early 1900s.

The future Fr. Virgil Cordano, age 1-2, Sacramento.

Age 3-4, Sacramento.

First Communion, Sacramento, 1924.

Top of the world, Sacramento, 1929.

Fifth grade, Cathedral School, Sacramento (front row, first on left).

Around 1936, Sacramento.

Playing soccer at Marymount School, 1990s.

Blessing Harley-Davidson bikers, 1990s.

Saying Mass, 2001.

Welcoming the new century.

4

THE WINDS OF CHANGE

As I look back on the period of the 1960s, I'm just amazed at how hectic, tense, special, painful, and historic this time was. So many things that
we had taken for granted – in both the religious and secular worlds –
were being unraveled.

– FR VIRGIL CORDANO

I returned to Santa Barbara in the fall of 1956 and resumed my teaching
position in the theological seminary. Fortunately, I did not have to serve
as spiritual director again. I taught the same classes I had done before. I
enjoyed this, but this almost placid existence wasn't to last for long.

Two years later, my superior appointed me as Rector or President of
The Mission Theological Seminary. I found this very amazing. This was the
same seminary where I had taken my final vows and was ordained a
Franciscan priest, and now, some thirteen years later, I became the head of
it. I didn't relish administrative duties, but I again had no choice. This was-
n't something you negotiated. You just accepted it and hoped for the best.

Being the Rector involved running the whole theological seminary. I
supervised the faculty and students, prepared the curriculum, chaired
faculty meetings, met with students, and did everything else to make sure
the school ran smoothly. If difficult decisions had to be made, I had to
make them in consultation with the faculty. I found administration taxing. I hated to do paperwork. But I had no choice.

One of the changes that I instituted after I became Rector was to make it possible for our students to study during the summer at public institutions without having to go through a lot of red tape in getting permission to do so. We offered no such classes in the summer in the seminary. We at first still preferred that they go to Catholic universities during the summer, but in time we let them go to public ones. Some, for example, started attending classes at the University of California, Santa Barbara. This began a close association between that campus, especially its new Department of Religious Studies, and our Mission Theological Seminary. I felt that we had to be in dialogue with all schools of theology and religious studies.

To add to my administrative load, that very same year I had to also replace the outgoing Guardian or Supervisor of Mission Santa Barbara. This would be the first of three stints as Guardian in my career. My official title was Father Guardian (*Custos* in Latin). As Father Guardian, I was in charge of administering the Mission property and all the personnel.

I felt like I was a chicken with two heads.

But to my surprise and anguish, this wasn't the end of my administrative burdens. A little while later, I was also appointed to what is called Prefect of Studies. This meant that I and my committee, in response to our Provincial, were in charge of assigning Franciscans to teach in all of our educational facilities throughout the Western Province of the Order. This included the schools in California, Oregon, Washington, and Arizona: high schools, minor seminary, novitiate, college, and the theological school.

We, in consultation with the principals of our schools, chose the teachers and professors for these institutions, what they were to teach, and approved or disapproved their requests for summer study. We had to know who could teach math, biology, Spanish, etc. in high school, college, and the various theological areas. This was a lot of work that involved traveling to different meetings and making many long distance calls. I worked with an advisory board that really helped. I couldn't have done all of this by myself.

The most pressing issue for me as Prefect was dealing with personnel changes in our schools. If a principal of one of our high schools needed someone to teach Spanish, we had to find such a teacher if available in one of our other schools or somewhere else. This was a time when our schools and all of the Catholic elementary and high schools were still taught predominantly by clergy and religious including the nuns. We had some lay teachers but not to the extent that we have today where few if any clergy teach at this level anymore.

Personnel needs were particularly acute in our high schools. We operated five high schools in the Western Province: Salem (Oregon), Oakland, Phoenix, Stockton, and Santa Barbara. Locally, we were in charge of Bishop García Diego High School until we turned it over to the diocese. We also staffed two minor seminaries: St. Anthony's in Santa Barbara and St. Francis in Troutdale, Oregon.

Besides my appointment as Prefect, I was also elected to the Franciscan governing board that met in Oakland and assigned all friars to their positions. We called this board the *definitorium*. The board along with the Provincial was in charge of the whole province. I served on it for three years. A board member was referred to as a *definitor*.

Through all of this administration, at one time holding down three jobs, I learned through trial and error. I had no formal training in administration, but I worked hard, although I didn't always please everyone or entertain much self-satisfaction.

†

This was certainly the case at the theological seminary. There's no question but that this was my biggest challenge. I still don't know how I survived ten years, from 1958 to 1968, being head of a school that began to experience traumatic changes.

These changes were linked to new winds blowing through the Church, inaugurated by the succession of Pope John XXIII in 1958 as head of the Church. Although already quite old and seen only as a transitional

Pope, in fact, John XXIII had every intention of shaking up the Church and bringing it into the modern world. To do this, he organized a convocation of all the bishops throughout the world to a council in Rome which met from 1962 to 1965. This came to be known as Vatican Council II. Vatican Council I had met in 1869-1870.

As I've noted, some of these changes were already being discussed in the 1940s and 1950s. New ideas about how to update theology and liturgy, the opening of the Church to greater involvement in the world, more dialogue within the Church, and a new relationship with other religions. All of this, however, began to pick up with the ascension of John XXIII. This updating came to referred to as *aggiornamento*.

If you read some of the Catholic journals and magazines in the late 1950s and early 1960s, you could sense a new thinking in scriptural studies, systematic theology, canon law, and moral theology. Pluralism and new expressions of the Catholic faith were needed to make the Church more relevant to modern times.

The new thinking of the bishops at this historic meeting finally opened the doors of change. It didn't mean that the old Church was being abandoned, but that it was being renewed: theologically, spiritually, culturally, and structurally. It was very much in tune with the turbulence of the 1960s that swept the world in reaction, in part, to the rigidness and dogmatism of the post World War II period. In this country, there were the civil rights movement led by Martin Luther King, Jr., a new youth culture, the anti-Vietnam war movement, the new role of women, the farm workers' struggle here in California led by César Chávez, as well as many other social movements. Internationally, it included many other professed expressions of change such as the anti-colonial movements for independence and national liberation. All of this was happening at the time of Vatican II. The Church could no longer afford to be aloof from the world.

Unfortunately, Pope John XXIII didn't live to see the results and conclusions of what he had unleashed. He died in 1963. Yet in this short period of his reign, he had changed the Church in a way that maybe had not happened since the Church's Counter-Reformation in response to the Protestant Reformation. His successor Pope Paul VI was more cautious, but he could not stem the new transformation of the Church.

Some of the changes were theological, institutional, and liturgical. Perhaps the best recognized changes involved liturgical ones. For example, Masses could now be said in English and other vernacular languages instead of Latin. The priest now faced the congregation rather than presiding with his back toward them. In addition, the laity was given more of a role in the liturgy of the Mass as lay ministers of Communion and lectors at Mass. Rather than their earlier more passive roles, the laity was given more active ones not only in the liturgy but also in administration.

For us in the theological seminary, the most immediate changes that appeared even while Vatican II was taking place, if not earlier, had to do with the need of renewal. Self-examination opened up for us, and for other religious orders as well as for the entire Church, what would prove to be difficult, but necessary, and in some cases painful changes or suggestions for change. We had no experience in questioning how we, at the local level, might operate as an Order since formerly all directions came from the top. Now a certain democratic opening was developing that caused much confusion because we really didn't know what we should be doing or how to go about it. The strong winds of change rushed in.

I was particularly affected by this due to my position as Rector. I believed that changes in the Church were long overdue, but I also believed that we couldn't just transform everything all at once. What should be changed and why? Others thought otherwise. They wanted an almost immediate complete transformation of how we governed ourselves in the seminary.

The results were serious divisions among our faculty and students. Some positioned themselves as liberals and, perhaps, even as radicals and unfairly labeled superiors, including myself, as conservatives. These self-proclaimed liberals wanted to radically change things. "We don't have to take directions from Rome anymore," they would say. "We can just do what we want and what is called for here and now."

What did they want to do? Some of the faculty, for example, wanted the students to have an equal voice with the faculty. The students agreed. I thought that this went too far. These discussions were held not just at faculty meetings, but also among the students. Some changes were needed on how we were to undergo renewal, but how far to go was difficult to determine. It was like pulling the cork out of a champagne bottle. The intoxicating drink began to fizz and spill out in all directions.

The proposed changes went beyond new forms of governance. Some wanted to revamp the traditional and rigorous schedule of our students that included early rising, silence at meals, a variety of daily prayers, confinement to the seminary, and other practices perceived to be too demanding, old-fashioned, and irrelevant. The curriculum was also challenged. This was influenced by the discussions at Vatican II that had to do with re-thinking Catholic theology to make it more relevant to contemporary life and open to new interpretations. Some of these ideas that had predated the Rome meetings now received greater advocacy during the Council.

Defining what our role as Franciscans today should be was not easy. How should we live the Franciscan life in modern times? How should we in the middle of the twentieth century emulate the life of St. Francis coming out of the thirteenth century? For example, should we wear our habits all of the time or not? How much should we get involved in nonreligious matters? What new structures and procedures should we accept? These were challenging questions and the answers were not easy or readily apparent. Changes had to be made. I had no doubt about this. It was a question of how much and how fast and which ones. It was confusing and very divisive.

No one seemed to know how to go about all of this. We had no clear and specific directions from our Provincial, only that we should fall in step with the concept of the renewal being promoted by John XXIII and the Council. Getting no directions from above, in a way, was already part of these changes. We were expected at the local level to begin to discuss what changes we felt were appropriate in our seminary. However, the problem was that we had no tradition or experience in self-rule and in discerning the true promptings of the Holy Spirit among the many diverse stirrings of human spirits.

Things became somewhat chaotic at the seminary. Some of the students, probably egged on by some of the faculty, began to change their schedules on their own. They refused to get up at the usual 4:40 A.M. for prayers at 5 A.M. They just wouldn't show up. Some of the faculty said "that's okay, it should be voluntary anyway." The whole issue of obedience and discipline and order was under siege. Some of the students went so far as to taunt me.

I found myself right in the middle of what amounted to a split in our faculty and among our students. It was like a teenager going through those difficult years of change, getting away from dependence, and coming to some independence. Were we mature enough to handle this, or should we be more reliant on Rome? There was no consensus.

But the issue of a liberal/conservative split was too simple a categorization. It was more complex. I had no problem with Vatican II. I supported the changes. The issue for me was how to define change. The Council, although it proposed changes in theological thinking, liturgical reforms, and new directions for the Church, did not say to us: "Here is what you have to do in your location or in your Order. You need to do so and so." I often pondered: what is essential and what might be changed in spiritual formation.

So we had broad directions but no specifics. And perhaps that was the way it should be as the Church now stressed less uniformity and centralization and more diversity and pluralism. But it didn't make it any easier for us.

I was for changes but not for hurried extreme changes like those proposed by some others on our faculty. I believed in more local governance, but we still needed to listen to Rome and its directives. We couldn't just do whatever we wanted either administratively or even theologically. This is actually what, in effect, some advocated.

One area where we had much tension and disagreement had to do with our evaluations of seminarians and our decision as to who were to be advanced to ordination and who were not. What were the agreed upon norms? Some of the faculty were quite liberal and permissive in their judgments. They favored advancing students over dismissing them. In their reaction against authority, they didn't want to exercise any. This was very much in keeping with the political temper of the times: question authority. But it wasn't that simple for me. I needed more assurances of the student's character and spirituality.

I would think that a candidate might be too immature or too rebellious and would never make a good priest. I felt that in this case we should delay his ordination or ask him to leave. Well, not everyone agreed. We had secret votes that often resulted in a split judgment. It was very burdensome. We were deciding a person's vocation. I tended to be cautious. Because of the immaturity of many of our students and the lack of harmony in the faculty, I recommended to higher authorities that we postpone the ordination for two or three years for some students. But this suggestion was not accepted. These questionable candidates kept on being ordained only to have a growing number of ordained priests leave after a few years in the priesthood.

Part of these tensions had to do with reconciling greater individuality in the Church that seemed to be coming out of Vatican II with the need for communal agreement. How much freedom of choice could we allow? It represented a historic problem: individualism vs. community. There's always a necessary tension between the individual person and what can be called the relational person: I vs. We. It's diversity in tension with unity. At one time, the Church overemphasized uniformity. Now, during this time of change, it was a question of how far to go in the other direction.

I was prepared to swing in part toward the new stress on individuality. But the path wasn't clear. We live in community. Some days there would be certain things that I favored, and, on other days, some that I didn't. It boiled down to my own judgment in relation to that of others. But I had no set norms. Who did? I didn't want the old exercise of authority, but I wanted a little more of agreed upon consensus. Also, the effects of all this on the spiritual growth of the seminarians concerned me. Again, it was the challenging issue of individualism and communal obligations.

†

As part of the uncertainty and questioning unleashed by Vatican II, the more radical Franciscans in the theological seminary urged that all of us should participate in sensitivity workshops. The first was held at our retreat center in Malibu sometime in the mid-sixties. There was little traditional spirituality involved in these sessions. It was meant, at least by the organizers, to let things hang out, to give expression to bottled-up emotions.

I'll never forget the first session that took place the evening of the first day. Some proceeded to openly criticize and attack their superiors, including me. All their anger was expressed. They felt that this was therapeutic. I was certainly supportive of the idea that we needed to integrate sound psychology into our seminary training, but this went much beyond that. The notion was that all emotions are to be given expression. Everyone should be heard, and one shouldn't be passive. Vatican II never specifically recommended sensitivity sessions, but its stress on openness seemed to have justified more attentiveness to the fully human education of religious and clergy.

Of course, sensitivity sessions and encounter groups were in vogue at this time in the secular world due to the countercultural movements of the 1960s. As a result, a number of religious people throughout the country got into such sessions where everybody spoke out and expressed their pent-up frustrations. This was a reaction to the pre-Vatican II imposed uniformity in the Church and the stifling of the thought and human needs of individuals.

In general, I didn't disagree with the idea of freer expressions within the Church, but what I didn't like was how such encounters deteriorated and became personally destructive. The "scattered pieces" were never put together again. That's what happened at Malibu. It was one thing to question authority and another to destroy all authority. Reforms were certainly needed in the Church, but not anarchy. Some wanted "freedom," but the boundaries were not defined. I believed that you couldn't have a religious order, such as ours, without some authority and communal responsibility. Each individual Franciscan just couldn't do his own thing. What kind of community would we be?

I found the whole exercise at Malibu to be very uncomfortable. I didn't say very much. What could I say? Everyone was being encouraged to be critical of one another. But I couldn't. I couldn't tell a person that I didn't like something about him. I could express my feelings before God in prayer, but in charity I couldn't be that critical of others.

My feelings didn't prevail, although they were shared by some. The more critical and outspoken Franciscans proceeded to tear into the rest of us.

"You're a hypocrite. You're a phony."

That's the kind of criticism that was regrettably used. It was destructive of ties among us. It was like a dam suddenly collapsing. All of these feelings came gushing out, and there was no direction to it. It just splattered in all directions without any ensuing new direction.

This went on for two or three days. Then, after we returned, the students here and the faculty at St. Anthony's had their own sensitivity sessions. All during this time the students at the Mission clamored for major changes. They wanted more freedom. They wanted equality with their professors. This may have been liberty for some, but it divided the community.

There was another sensitivity session held at La Jolla, but I didn't go. I had had enough. I longed for a more enlightened and balanced understanding of the tension between individuality and community. We didn't achieve it then, but more recent studies are providing such directives and religious life is better for the change.

Among other changes instigated by the "extremists" was the celebration of Mass for our students, not in the Mission or chapel, but in the student recreation lounge. They also introduced popular music into the liturgy featuring the Beatles, Bob Dylan, Joan Baez, and Peter, Paul and Mary. At the time of the homily, everyone commented, not just the officiating priest. Non-Catholics, mostly UCSB students, were welcomed to receive Communion. These innovations, such as Folk Masses, were coming into vogue. I didn't oppose some of them, although I knew that Cardinal McIntyre in Los Angeles did. What I didn't care for was the "in your face" attitude of the "extremists."

†

During the 1960s and into the early 1970s, I wore still another hat. I was appointed on three occasions by Franciscan headquarters in Rome to be what is called a Visitor General. This meant that I would represent the head of the Franciscan Order who is referred to as the Minister General. Being a Visitor General entails doing on-site inspections of different provinces and writing a report to our Rome office. Every three or six years each Franciscan province throughout the world had to be inspected by a Visitor General. He interviews the Franciscans about conditions and problems in their area as well as examines the administrative documents. The Visitor General further presides over the election of a new Provincial and governing bodies for these jurisdictions. The whole process could take up to three or four months or even more.

I was appointed as Visitor General to three provinces. One was in Australia and New Zealand. A second included a province with headquarters in lower Manhattan of New York City, the Immaculate Conception Province, that included more than New York. It included places along the East coast, in Canada, and even in Central America. My third area was not a province per se, but a group (called a Custody) of Lithuanian Franciscans who had been expelled from Communist-dominated Lithuania and had found refuge in the United States. Their head-quarters was in Kennebunkport, Maine, but they were also in Brooklyn and in Canada and a couple of other places. They regarded themselves as temporary exiles who would one day return to their home country. In the meantime, these Franciscans took care of the spiritual needs of the Lithuanian-speaking people in this country and Canada.

Of the places I visited, two particularly stand out for me. The first was my trip to Honduras, Guatemala, and El Salvador in Central America, part of the missionary work of the Immaculate Conception Province in New York. I spent about a month traveling through these countries and visiting our Franciscan priests and brothers there. They were English-speaking Franciscans from the United States who knew Spanish very well. I was impressed with their heroism in giving up the comforts of life in our country to labor among the poor in Central America. They worked with Franciscans from Spain and a few other countries. In all, there were about thirty Franciscans spread throughout the three countries.

What saddened me the most was the poverty of the people to whom the Franciscans ministered. I saw kids hungry, naked, and with distend-ed bellies. Workers were lucky to get a dollar a day. There were homes with little or no sanitation. These were not only poor people but oppressed ones. All three countries were ruled by a small number of very wealthy and powerful families supported by brutal military groups armed by the United States.

On top of this, Central America was earthquake country, and these natural disasters only added to the misery of the people. On one occasion when I was in Guatemala, an earthquake struck. We all ran out of the building we were in at the time. It was not one of those massive destruc-tive quakes, but enough to scare me and everyone else. Everywhere you went in Central America, you could see ruined buildings and homes resulting from earlier earthquakes or neglect.

I was also impressed by the cultural differences between life in Central America and in the United States. I'm sure the people in these poor countries couldn't help but contrast their poverty and misery with that of the richness of the United States, which they got a glimpse of through American films and television programs dubbed into Spanish. I'm sure they felt envious. "Look how poor we are and how rich you are," they must have thought.

But despite the poverty, there were those who were working for positive social changes, including our Franciscans and other groups within the Catholic Church in Central America. What I saw was certainly a response to Vatican Council II that had called on the Church to reassess its role in the modern world, especially in doing even more to assist the poor and the oppressed.

In Latin America and elsewhere this social and economic inequality gave rise to what is called Liberation Theology. Liberation Theology is a social and theological movement that emerged principally, but not exclusively, in Latin America in the late 1960s. It was social ethics guided by Christian revelation in response to a political and economic condition. Maybe some Marxist language was used, but there was no adherence to Marxist doctrine. Conceptualized by Latin American clergy and lay people, and in keeping with a long tradition of Catholic social doctrine, the Church preached a "preferential option for the poor." It challenged all in the Church to side not with the rich and the powerful, including the military, but rather with the people. It was a way of reminding the Church of its original roots as a Church of the poor and of Jesus' message of serving the poor. It was a dynamic and inspirational movement that was sweeping the Latin American churches when I visited Central America.

Our Franciscans, followers of St. Francis who cared for the poor, embraced Liberation Theology. They took up the cause of the poor even though it was risky to do so. Liberationists within the Church were often accused of being Communists by the authorities, and some were even persecuted. When I visited Honduras, the poorest of the three Central American countries that I visited, I went to a district called Olancho. An American Franciscan served as the bishop of that area. He spoke Spanish fluently.

It was a poor province and he had only six to eight priests to minister to thousands. He told me that he was accused of being a Communist because he sided with the poor. In fact, the government and military had placed a $10,000 price on his head for anyone who would kill him. I can't remember his name anymore, but I admired his courage and commitment. He lived a very poor life himself. Eventually, he did leave Honduras because of these threats on his life. He would have preferred to stay, but his Superior ordered him out. Unfortunately, later two of his priests were arrested by the military and killed. Such tragedies would only escalate during the next two decades as the Central American wars intensified.

Part of my report was to note this oppression of our Franciscan Order in Central America. Because our priests were asking for economic and social changes in order to meet the needs of the poor, the right wing in these countries opposed them and falsely considered them subversives. The Church hierarchies, although sometimes caught in the middle, in general supported the Franciscans and other Liberationists. Some of the hierarchy later themselves became Liberationists, such as Archbishop Oscar Romero of El Salvador who was brutally murdered in 1980 by the repressive Salvadoran military.

In my report, I observed the type of work among the poor that our Franciscans were doing. They went out to the villages of the rural areas, to minister the sacraments, say Mass, bless marriages, teach the villagers, young and old, and to do what they could to improve the economic condition of the people.

In addition, they dispensed food and clothing sent by Catholics in the United States to the poor. They set up schools and tried to alleviate the illiteracy of the rural *campesinos*. I was struck by how they tried to do something more than just have the people say their prayers. They tried to empower the people so that they would struggle for social and economic change.

I thought that what my fellow Franciscans were doing was right and just. I had a positive reaction to Liberation Theology. I always and still do believe that the role of the Church has to go beyond meeting only spiritual needs. Inspired by faith, it must also confront the economic and social problems of the people especially the poor and oppressed. This is what Jesus did, and that's what our Franciscans were doing in Central America and elsewhere.

I could see how in this context, the Church could not counsel the people to passively accept their lot. They were not to be deprived of basic liberties by the rich and the military. Liberation Theology had its roots in the tradition of the Church always coming out strong on issues of social justice. God wants more than the salvation of souls or the spiritual growth of individuals. He wants all the needs of the human person to be met, and these are more than just purely spiritual.

There were, of course, some within the Church who were uneasy about Liberation Theology. They thought it was too Marxist due to the stress on class conflict and combating economic injustice. They'd prefer sticking to what they would interpret only as Christian principles. Some of these concerns originated in Rome. In fact, often the views of the Vatican and local Latin American bishops differed concerning Liberation Theology.

But to me, the discourse on whether or not Liberation Theology was too Marxist should not halt what the Franciscans were doing. Christianity was not to be isolated from concerns for the poverty and oppression of the region. Whether you called it Marxism or something else, the Church had to address, and still does, gross economic inequities and lack of a voice for the poor. This is a Christian obligation.

Part of this controversy had to do with the direct participation of priests in politics to which the Vatican was opposed. Rome wanted priests in Latin America and elsewhere to just concentrate on the spirituality of the people, or just preach about social justice, but not engage in political action. The political world was the domain of the laity. But some of the clergy responded: "Unless we get into politics, there will be no changes for the poor."

I appreciated the concern that if priests openly enter politics, there may be a compromise in one's religious faith. The blend of politics and religion, state and church, as we're seeing in the Islamic world and even in our own country, can be quite problematic. On the other hand, in Third World countries, such as in Central America, the clergy sincerely believe that their faith commits them to involvement in working to alleviate the conditions that oppress the people that they minister to in these locations. They would counter that you can't, or shouldn't, divorce religion from human suffering. I agree. But the issue is how much engagement in political matters. Perhaps the social context determines that.

Since my visit, some forty years ago, we have fewer U.S. Franciscans in Central America. The Franciscans in the countries of Central American have formed their own province separate from the U.S. province.

If my Central American visit was a sobering one, my trip to Australia and New Zealand as Visitor General in 1965 was highly enjoyable. Of course, this in part had to do with the totally different socio-economic condition between Central American and Australia.

The Catholic population of Australia, along with other European descent people, lived in great part along the long coastline of the continent. Central Australia was not heavily populated at that time. I believe that there were only about fifteen million people in the whole country. Many of the Franciscans there were of Irish descent. Also, there were many Irish laity, descendants of earlier "convicts" sent by the English government. They had mixed feelings regarding the English. On the other hand, they were very friendly toward the United States and thankful that it had protected them from invasion by the Japanese during World War II. They revered General Douglas McArthur as an authentic hero for doing this.

The Franciscan Order in Australia and New Zealand was doing very good work. They were opening schools, doing parish work, organizing retreats, and all of the usual ministries associated with the priesthood and religious orders. One difference between them and what was happening in our Order based in the United States was that the effects and changes associated with Vatican II were just beginning to surface "down under." Still, I did pick up some stirrings and rumblings of change and of a growing diversity of opinion within the Order and the Church in both Australia and New Zealand. However, I could tell that renewal here would be more difficult, especially due to the very conservative bishops that I met. The bishops, like most of the laity, were of Irish background. Irish Catholics, here and elsewhere, tended to be much more conservative both theologically and institutionally. I thought that the Catholic Church in Australia and New Zealand would experience a tension in living Vatican II similar to what we were beginning to experience.

Besides meeting with the Franciscans and the bishops, I also had time to sightsee and learn about the customs of this area of the world. I noticed that Australians, for one, lived life at a slower pace than we in the United States. As a result, they enjoyed life more, I think. In the Franciscan monasteries, this slower pace was also evident. Influenced by the English, the Franciscans, for example, had to have their tea breaks often. Of course, we have our coffee breaks. After breakfast, you would pause later in the morning for tea. The main meal was around one, but then you had another tea break in the afternoon. After supper time around six o'clock, in some cases, you had tea around nine in the evening. It was certainly a most welcomed custom.

It was an enjoyable trip and my work was very meaningful. Perhaps the best part was making some new and good friends. I felt as much at home in the Franciscan friaries there as I did in California. On the way home, I stopped to visit our Santa Barbara missionaries in the Philippines, many of whom I had taught at Mission Santa Barbara. The Philippines, of course, represented another culture so different from life in the United States.

†

Back in Santa Barbara, I continued to teach in the theological seminary as well as at different periods serving as Father Guardian of the entire Franciscan operation at the Mission. In almost everything I did during this period, the challenge was how to implement Vatican II. As these changes began, such as the revised liturgy of the Mass and the greater emphasis on laity participation both in the liturgy and in Church affairs, I and others found ourselves more and more having to explain these changes and their meaning to lay groups.

I and one of my colleagues, Father Stanislaus (later John) Altman and a Sister of the Immaculate Heart Community organized some talks on Vatican II. They were well received except for a very few who disliked and even resisted the new changes, especially new expressions of doctrine. They felt that they were losing "their" Church and "their" Mass. They didn't want the Mass to be said in English; they still wanted it in Latin even though they couldn't understand it. At a theological level, they didn't understand Vatican II's insistence that relevancy in modern times called for changes in thought and practice. For some time we were undergoing a radical cultural revolution in the Church.

They also didn't like the acceptance of ecumenism and dialogue with other religions. Some seemingly went so far as to believe that you had to be a Catholic to be saved. They had their own limited understanding of Catholicism. They were very monolithic and simplistically dogmatic. They favored only one way of expressing the truth. They couldn't tolerate a more pluralistic Church. Maybe they would have to think too much. They represented a type of Catholic fundamentalism that Vatican II was rejecting. The fundamentalist's reaction was less a theological one and really more an emotional and psychological one. Vatican II threatened their sense of security. Everything had to be black and white. They wanted a Church in which everything was simplified; where there was a clear "right" and an easily defined "wrong." I wonder if they have ever come to know and experience what is essential in spirituality.

Some of these conservatives went so far as to write to Cardinal McIntyre in Los Angeles about what I and other Franciscans were teaching. The Cardinal wrote to our Franciscan Provincial, and I, in turn, explained myself to the Cardinal. Even though Cardinal McIntyre, himself, opposed many of the new reforms, he had to go along with them.

Nothing came of these complaints.

I did come to know of the names of the accusers. I thought that I should phone one of these persons and explain myself to her as charitably as I could. I did so while stating that she had misquoted me. She insisted that I was heretical. Since the mild approach was ineffective, I firmly told her that while I respected her view of Catholicism, she had not observed the procedure for dealing with diversity that was outlined in the Gospel. Matthew 18, 15-17 says, "If your brother/sister sins against you, go and tell him/her the fault between you and him/her alone... If he/she does not listen, take one or two others along with you... If he/she refuses to listen to them, tell the Church."

Then I went on to say, "You have skipped procedures one and two and have gone on to procedure three. I invite you to discuss the matter with me." But she insisted that I was wrong and refused to dialogue with me. In turn, I firmly cautioned her against failing to obey the directions of the Gospel that both of us were committed to observing. I have not heard of her or seen her since. Such persons are too serious about serious matters. And they don't smile much either.

Speaking of the Chancery office, an incident occurred that gave the archdiocese reason to question what was going on at our seminary. A friar of the faculty, on his own and without permission, married a priest and a religious sister who had not received dispensations from their vows. This Franciscan knew this, but married them anyway. He married them in the home of a family that I knew very well.

Upon returning from an educational meeting in the east, I got a call from the Chancery office telling me that they had a copy of this marriage license with the name of the officiating priest on it. The officials blamed me for permitting this. I had to tell them that I didn't know of it. In the end, the Franciscan priest had his faculties to function in the archdiocese nullified. However, this was at the same time that the theological seminary moved to Berkeley, and the priest went up with the faculty. Eventually, he left the Order and priesthood, renounced Christianity, and married outside of the Church.

This wasn't a surprise to me when I heard about it. I knew that given his grievances and disagreements with our Order and the Church that he would in time leave. Unfortunately, this was also the case with three other priests of my faculty who left the priesthood. Also, a larger number of the faculty at San Luis Rey left the Order and priesthood. All of these friars had their personal reasons to leave, and I respected that. These were challenging times for all of us. I had to acknowledge my own limitations. None of us had all the answers to questions and solutions to problems.

All of this, especially the divisions within our theological faculty, made my job as Rector very difficult. My authority was being challenged, and while I supported a greater openness in the seminary, I could not abrogate all of my responsibilities. Because I was seen, I guess, as an obstacle to change or at least some changes, my Superior eventually removed me in 1967 as Guardian, but not as Rector, for a year. I continued as Rector until the following year when the seminary moved to Berkeley, when I again became Guardian. It wasn't that my Superior disagreed with me or didn't like me. But after being in the midst of a lot of the turbulence, he believed it prudent to replace me as Guardian.

Fortunately, this coincided with the termination of the Theological Seminary in Santa Barbara. Because of the new changes resulting from Vatican II and the accompanying problems and stress, we were losing many recruits to the seminary as well as priests. We could no longer afford to keep the seminary open. Instead, it was deemed more economical, and perhaps in keeping with the spirit of the times, to transfer our students and faculty to the Graduate Theological Union in Berkeley. Here we would join with other religious orders such as the Dominicans and the Jesuits, as well as some of the mainline Protestant churches, in a more pluralistic and ecumenical theological school. I had no problems with this, and given the division we had suffered, I felt it was the right decision. We had no promising future for a theological seminary in Santa Barbara.

I could have joined the faculty at Berkeley, but since I already was having much difficulty with some of them, this didn't seem to make sense. I preferred to stay in Santa Barbara and do what I could in helping with the transition here. We continued to staff the Mission parish and we had to make use of buildings vacated by the departing seminary.

Still, I was hurt emotionally by my removal as Guardian as well as the turmoil in the seminary. Luckily, I had a meaningful spirituality. My relationship with God sustained me. I had to adjust to the change. Of course, I had no opportunity to argue my position. In fact, I was never asked to do so by higher authorities. Providentially all this was for my good. I would go on to be pastor of Santa Barbara Parish and to enlarge my horizons in being in charge of public relations for the Mission. As my earlier experiences had taught me, and as I came to understand much better later, there is something to be gained in every loss. I grew spiritually thanks to some very painful changes.

†

Fortunately, I had experiences and interests beyond the challenge of administration. One exciting aspect of the Vatican II years involved occasional visitors who had participated in or had some influence on the Council. One such person was the prominent European theologian Hans Kung. Some of them came to Santa Barbara at the invitation of the Department of Religious Studies at the University of California, Santa Barbara, one of the finest such departments in the nation. Kung, a priest himself, stayed with us at the Mission. He was a very brilliant fellow. His liberal theological views had influenced some of the reforms of Vatican II. While I might not have fully understood all of his ideas, still what I appreciated about him was that Kung's ideas were not just emotional expressions. They were well thought out and articulated. I was open to pluralism in theological expressions of God's revelation. I enjoyed listening to his lectures and reading his books. This was a far cry from the heightened emotionality of sensitivity sessions and the burdens of administration.

While I no longer recall specifically what he lectured on and what some of his ideas at the time were, I do have an impression of Kung as one of those liberal theologians who promoted greater diversity of thought within the Church to modify what many believed was rigid uniformity. He believed that the discourse in theology and Catholic beliefs should be more open and pluralistic. In theory, many of us agreed with him in holding that the one and same truth could be expressed in different ways. Over the years in changing times there have been new theological expressions of God's revelation.

This was an exciting time – theologically speaking. Besides Kung, there were many other insightful and critical theological voices that blossomed as a result of Vatican II. It was hard to keep up with all of this literature. I tried to read as much of it as possible although my many ministries limited my time for keeping up with the academic world. Still, it was a delight, and still is, for me to be caught up in new thought.

One writer that particularly impressed me, and who without doubt was the leading reform theologian of this time, was Karl Rahner. He was a Jesuit and a highly influential Catholic theologian. Desirous of making the Church relevant and relying on modern thought, Rahner created a theological anthropology that attempted to give new meaning to Church teaching. Other theologians whom I enjoyed reading at the time included Edward Schillebeeck, David Tracy, Bernard Lonergan, and modern Franciscan scholars. In biblical studies, I was influenced by, among others, Raymond Brown, John Meier, and Joseph Fitzmyer. I also read very much about new trends in spirituality and psychology. I tried to keep up with magazine articles in these fields. Often what I read would move me to pray what I experienced while in dialogue with God through the mediation of these many human authors. God speaks and inspires in and through dialogue with one another, including authors of books and articles.

I liked all of these different perspectives as opposed to the more uniform and rather dry theology that I had learned in the seminary. I was not personally prepared to be as revisionist as people such as Kung and

Rahner and others, but I still appreciated them. My field was more in biblical studies. I was not at their level as a theologian, but by reading their works and that of other Vatican II inspired ones, I entered into a dialogue with them. Likewise of late, there is a renewed study of the Franciscan intellectual tradition rooted in scholars such as St. Bonaventure and Blessed John Duns Scotus.

One particularly controversial visitor at the Mission was Bishop James Pike an iconoclastic Episcopalian bishop who was one of the leading critics of the U.S. role in Vietnam. He was also quite critical of his own church. I believe he had been invited to speak at UCSB. He spoke a number of times to our faculty and students. One of our radical priests invited him to con-celebrate Mass at the Mission. I knew that this was not proper because Pike was not Catholic. However, I had to keep this place going and didn't want more trouble and conflict, so I looked the other way. Sometimes you have to weigh what is best for the common good beyond your own personal feelings.

A breath of fresh air compared to Bishop Pike were the times César Chávez, the inspirational and deeply spiritual leader of the farm workers' movement in California, chose to come for retreats and rest at St. Anthony's Seminary and the Mission. He loved Santa Barbara and several times graced us with his presence. We as Franciscans, in turn, supported him and his struggle. Some of the Franciscans in the San Joaquin Valley actually joined in the effort to unionize and bring dignity to the mostly Mexican and Filipino farm workers.

César would stay at St. Anthony's and would talk with our students. He was a very humble person and I admired him. Some of the growers charged him with being a Communist, but we didn't believe that. He was a sincere and very Catholic man. He was a true reformer. I didn't know him very well because I was so busy then, but we always exchanged greetings and small talk.

†

As I look back on this period of the 1960s, I'm just amazed at how hectic, tense, special, painful, and historic this time was. So many things that we had taken for granted – in both the religious and secular worlds – were being unraveled.

Personally, although I gained much more than I lost, I had to move beyond old securities to new securities or, maybe I can say, few securities beyond the support I got from my relationship with God. I had to make many painful adjustments while being very much alone and at times feeling that I received little support. I knew that I had to keep from falling into self-pity. I am grateful that I came to have less and less exaggerated assurances. Though my convictions were strong, I had to admit that I might be wrong. I recall hearing a Catholic priest psychologist say that it was acceptable to have strong convictions while having to admit that one could possibly be wrong. My education guided me in finding spiritual meaning in all my experiences. I often wonder what I would have done if I were not supported by my education in theology and spirituality.

One very good example of this within the Church was the issue of birth control. The Church had never supported the use of artificial birth control, but the Sixties witnessed the so-called sexual revolution to a large degree influenced by the availability of the "pill." Lay Catholics were caught between the Church's position and their personal and family views on pregnancy and family size. The Church was forced to respond.

In the mid-sixties, Pope Paul VI formed a special commission on birth control to advise him on this very troubling issue for him and the Church. After careful and lengthy deliberations, the commission in 1967, by a majority, came out for accepting artificial birth control under certain conditions. The Pope reflected for a long time and finally in his encyclical *Humane Vitae* rejected the commission's report.

The Pope's decision unleashed an avalanche of criticism and protest by many lay Catholics as well as some clerics. This was a big turning point. For many, it seemed to represent a conservative backlash against the reform spirit of Vatican II. For some, especially Catholic young women, this was a defining moment. For this reason and many others, some left the Church, including some nuns and even some priests.

I, personally, was disappointed at the Pope's decision. However, I would never get up and preach against it. But I dealt with the issue in a pastoral and sympathetic manner. I felt torn, especially as I heard the confessions of many women and men who had good human reasons to practice birth control.

On the other hand, I also saw the need for some objective norm in the purpose of sex. Catholic moral theologians were and are still divided on this issue. For some time there has been in the Church's teaching on moral behavior a tension between what might be called, on the one hand, universal ever-binding objective law rooted in natural law and, on the other, subjectively circumstantial norms of morality. It is between an act-centered biological view of sex and a person-centered view that takes into consideration the circumstances of a particular person. One view sees the purpose of sex as procreation (life-giving), while the other sees it as an expression of personal love (love-making). For a long time the Church had insisted on the primacy of the procreative purpose of sex. Sex as an expression of love was viewed as secondary. But Vatican II stated that both purposes are equal without any priority. However, the two purposes cannot be separated, and, therefore, artificial birth control is forbidden. In disagreement, others would give consideration to the proportionality of values and make a decision that favors the greater personal value.

Birth control to this day remains a divisive issue in the Church. Its official position is still against artificial birth control. However, it's clear that many lay Catholics practice birth control through artificial means. The Church's stance is still a rigid one, yet otherwise today the Church's view of sex is much more positive than it was in earlier times.

Is there a norm or directive for sexual activity that is both universally applicable and considerate of personal circumstances? I, as a priest, try to live the tension between holding on to something normative while listening to someone who tells me: "Father, the doctor says if I get pregnant again, I could die." Or "Father, I can't afford to get pregnant again. We're already suffering economically."

Of course, there is the so-called rhythm method that the Church approves of. Some persons trust it and others don't. I go from case to case, keeping the Church's teaching in mind, but being compassionate toward people who in conscience find the implementation of this ideal too demanding and too harmful.

Another difficult issue for me early in my ministry was the issue of divorce and remarriage. The Church's traditional position is that it does not recognize divorce when the marriage is truly valid. When there is sufficient evidence that the marriage when entered into was not valid, the Church grants an annulment. Marriage is sacred and cannot be legally ended. Divorced Catholics can still remain in the Church but cannot receive Communion. Now in the wake of Vatican II, some divorced Catholics desire and actually receive Communion.

As with birth control, I, officially as a Catholic priest, cannot publicly speak out against the Church's directive. However, I and many priests offer Holy Communion to whomever approaches the altar.

If, because of issues such as birth control and divorce and other personal reasons, some adults began to leave the Church, so too did many young Catholics who had their reasons for ceasing to practice the Catholic faith. There are no simple, clear explanations for this exodus. As part of the general rebelliousness of many young people in the Sixties, many young Catholics became alienated and abandoned the Church. But it wasn't just the Church they were reacting to. Some youth were likewise opposing all authority including that of their parents. More and more young people stopped going to church. Some young women, feminists, believed the Church to be too patriarchal. Authority didn't seem to matter to many youth. By contrast, when I was a youngster, you went to church because you were obligated to do so. It wasn't a choice. It was a discipline you learned very early in life. You just went ahead and did it and, hopefully, later freely accepted membership in the Church.

Now in the Sixties, many youth viewed going to church a personal choice and not a personal obligation. No one was going to tell them what to do. Many wouldn't listen to any authority figure. Yes, we had witnessed a radical cultural and revolutionary change. Here in Santa Barbara, for example, the students at UCSB burned down the Bank of America in Isla Vista in 1970.

I tried to be understanding of our youth, although ministry to the youth is not my specialty. I sympathized with many of their feelings for greater freedom and subjectivity, and listened attentively to what stirred within them. I tried my best to educate them in appreciation of the blessings of our rich spiritual tradition that speaks to the true desire of their hearts. This was just one more of the challenges we faced in these troubled times. Fortunately, many young Catholics remained in the Church or came back to it in later life. This doesn't mean that they accept all of the Church's teachings, such as on birth control, but they still value much else in the Church and feel a vacuum without it. They were and are selective in what they believe and practice. Modern times presents a big challenge to young people.

But it wasn't only young people who were rebelling. Many adult lay people began to speak their minds and demanded being heard by a patriarchal authoritarianism. Many believed that they were stifled by a controlling male celibate clergy. Their voices were in keeping with the spirit of Vatican II that encouraged greater lay participation in Church affairs. Out of this came the concept of "We are Church." It isn't just the priests who speak for the Church, but all Catholics are the Church. God also speaks through the laity. It was a question of how the laity would use their newly recognized "authority" in the Church and relate to the Church's traditional authority. Through education in theology and spirituality, they are winning a hearing by decision makers in the Church.

Although some of the laity had difficulty in responding to this new relationship, many others welcomed it as being long overdue. They began to speak their minds and to offer alternative proposals to authoritarian figures. They wanted to be involved in a number of ways: the role of laity in the liturgy; they wanted a financial accounting of the diocese and the parish; they wanted the Church to be less secretive and autonomous. Above all, they wanted dialogue between clergy and laity. This was especially the case with many women who wished that their voices be heard.

I had no problems with these issues, and, later when I became pastor, I encouraged lay participation. I invited an already established lay parish council to continue to dialogue with me, as prompted by the spirit of Vatican II. I understood that the old structure where the pastor and his priests ruled supreme was ending. We now had to adjust to a more sharing relationship with our congregations. Some in the Church adjusted well to this, others less so. I could see that some bishops and priests rejected and still reject these changes. They continue to make decisions without adequate lay consultation. But they are more and more a minority as the impetus for reform increases.

These changes particularly affected women, both lay and religious. Women have always been marginalized in the Church, but Vatican II was seen as an empowerment of their role. I saw this especially among religious women. In the Sixties, I taught at both the Immaculate Heart novitiate in Montecito and the Religious of the Sacred Heart of Mary novitiate in Santa Barbara. The latter was located next to the present day Marymount School above the Mission. These were the training schools for young women wishing to be religious sisters. I taught theology and scripture at both places, while also being one of the confessors for the Immaculate Heart community. Others of my Franciscan colleagues likewise taught at both places.

The spirit of reform was also welcomed by women in religious orders. They enacted changes within their orders and in their relationships with the rest of the Church. They wanted more freedom and independence to run their own affairs, including being involved in community issues such as civil rights and other political and social issues. They did not want to be restricted to teaching in the schools.

Unfortunately, the Immaculate Heart of Mary Sisters ran into stiff opposition from Cardinal McIntyre, Archbishop of Los Angeles. He opposed the major reforms proposed by the Sisters. After coming to a deadlock in dialogue, while a few remained in the Order, the majority obtained dispensations from their vows and re-grouped as The Immaculate Heart Community in 1970. The whole story, well documented, is told by Anita M. Caspary in her book *Witness to Integrity*. Membership became open to men and women, single or married, from all Christian denominations. Interestingly, in the year 2000, thirty years after Cardinal McIntyre broke the ties of the Immaculate Heart Community with the Catholic Church, Cardinal Roger Mahony in his public apology for the sins of the California Catholic Church acknowledged the "unfortunate dispute" between his predecessors and the Immaculate Heart Community. He apologized to those "who felt hurt and rejection by the Church during those years."

We Franciscans sympathized with the Sisters and supported them. Some accused us of encouraging this split by what we taught in their novitiate. But we had nothing to do with it. Rather, the Sisters made their own decisions after much dialogue with the Church and prayerful reflection.

But this rupture was symptomatic of what was happening elsewhere as well. This period saw a huge drop in the number of religious in the Church. The inability or the slowness of the male hierarchy to accept a new relationship with these women religious is largely responsible for this loss. It was part of the fallout of Vatican II.

†

While Vatican II for me characterized so much of the 1960s and following years, there were other major social, cultural, and political changes.

The times were exciting and promising. For the first time a Catholic was elected President of the United States: John F. Kennedy. I was quite pleased with this. I was not Irish like Kennedy, but we shared the same faith. I felt that after so much anti-Catholic sentiment in the country, Americans had finally overcome this bias. This was a great time to have a Catholic in the White House. It was a wonderful time to be a Catholic. How would Kennedy be both President and Catholic?

Then came that awful day: November 22, 1963. Like most other Americans on that tragic occasion, I'll never forget where I was when I heard the news. I was driving back from teaching the novices at the Immaculate Heart novitiate in Montecito. It was around eleven in the morning. I turned on the car radio and the first words I heard were: "...we're going back to Dallas to get a further report on the President's condition." I knew by the grave tone of the reporter's voice that something terrible had happened. Within a few minutes, I learned that he had been shot and possibly killed.

I got back to the Mission just in time to hear the confirmation of President Kennedy's death. I and my fellow Franciscans watched television for the next few hours. I don't remember doing anything else. We were all in a state of numbness and disbelief. How could such a tragedy befall our nation? What would happen now? There was sadness and quiet. I easily cried. It was one of the saddest moments in my whole life.

We, of course, prayed for our fallen Catholic leader. Somehow we organized a prayer service later that afternoon or early evening in the Mission. A large number of people attended, even on such a short notice. We held a second service the following day. In the meantime, we watched more television. You couldn't help but be moved by the images of the funeral. I remember especially how dignified and in control Jacqueline Kennedy was. And then that memorable sight of her son – little John John – saluting his father as the casket passed by. These are images and memories that are burned inside of you. You never forget them and they serve as a compass for the rest of your life.

Tragically, a few years later, in 1968, Robert Kennedy was also assassinated just a couple of months after Dr. Martin Luther King was killed for his beliefs. The nation again suffered the loss of two great and inspiring men. A couple of days after the Kennedy assassination, I was asked to speak at a large memorial service for him at UCSB. I gladly accepted because I was a great admirer of Robert Kennedy. Campbell Hall, the largest lecture hall on the campus, was filled to capacity. It was therapeutic for me to write my eulogy. In part, here is what I said:

> "I have cried over the death of Robert Kennedy. I have felt deep revulsion over the blackness of the crime. I have been anxious about the moral health of my country. And now, as I believe I am expected to, I wish to view this national tragedy in the context of religious faith. I hope that what I say is confirmatory of and complementary to what is being said by others about this Senator's political and social achievements, for I speak of a faith that is not divorced from political ambition and social involvement, but a faith that calls for such ambition and involvement. I find a close analogy, or better, an intimate link between this man's public life and the challenge issued by his God and my God and, I hope, the God of all who would listen to their true selves and meet the demands of life with others. This message of faith gives me hope, which I sorely need at this time, and I wish to share with you.
>
> "Today we repent of our ill-treatment of this prophet. We pray that God will rid our hearts of evil thoughts and of hatred, for from the heart, as Christ has said, comes murder. And, then, may we be attentive to what St. Francis of Assisi often said to his followers: 'Let us now begin, for up to now we have done nothing.' Robert Kennedy would want us to move ahead. Let us go forth – together."

The 1960s, of course, was one of the great periods of civil rights struggles. I admired Dr. Martin Luther King, Jr. and what he stood for, especially nonviolence and full rights for all Americans. We at the Mission and in our seminaries were now much more aware of political and social issues. We were no longer as sheltered as before. Vatican II called on the Church to involve itself in the modern world. We accepted that call.

Our priests and students, for example, began to become involved in civil rights issues. They went to UCSB and participated in teach-ins, conferences, and demonstrations on civil rights. We encouraged this connection with the university. This included close ties with Professor Walter Capps who through the Department of Religious Studies was doing exciting work bringing the campus and the community together to discuss and act on the great social issues facing the country. Walter was one of the most sincere and honest individuals I have ever met. He personified integrity. It was my privilege to get to know him and his wonderful wife, Lois, and their closely-knit family. Walter used to come often to the Mission to talk to our students. He was a Lutheran by birth from the Midwest, but he was quite at ease with Catholic spirituality, and he and his family often attended Mass at the Mission. Walter also used to take his students on retreat up at Big Sur at the Camaldolese Monastery.

Such connections with the university and the community meant that we at the Mission were coming out of the ghetto setting, characteristic of the pre-Vatican II years. I encouraged our priests and students to have ties with the campus and with community groups. I had become convinced by then that you're really not educated unless you get beyond your own parochial mind and open yourself to everyone and everything in life. God is present to all persons, in all their experiences. We as religious persons have to be open to all that is human as is God. That's because God is the creator of all that is human and is more concerned than we are. God is present in all human activities including political and social issues and struggles. God is not confined to a church.

The Church's increased involvement in social issues in the 1960s reflected the new way of linking the divine and the secular. Earth and Heaven, the natural and the supernatural, nature and grace, the human and the divine are intimately linked. Generally speaking, before Vatican II quite often human nature was viewed as self-enclosed, and grace (God's Self-Gift) appeared as extrinsic to human life. It was one of the many dualisms of the times.

But Vatican II began to change this perspective. Grace is now viewed as an integral dimension of human nature. Although conceptually distinct from grace, everything that is natural is graced by God's personal presence. The sphere of the natural is not only good but carries within itself the offer of a personal encounter with God.

We speak of grace building on nature and grace working through nature. Through all that is creaturely and human we are in touch with God. Or we can say that all of life is Sacramental, "a reality imbued with the hidden presence of God" (Pope Paul VI). Not only the seven sacraments but all of creation is a visible sign of an invisible divine presence. All reality is sacred. And more than this, God acts in and through all of human reality: persons, events, places, human experiences. God channels saving, healing grace through all that is creaturely. We are privileged to be cooperators in the fulfillment of God's plan for creation.

When our priests and students became involved in civil rights and other pressing social issues, they weren't acting apart from God and the sacred because God was present there as well. This was a new emphasis in theological thought that helped bring the Church more into the world.

As we priests and religious in the Church became more involved in social issues in the Sixties, the question of the Vietnam war also affected us. Catholics were just as split on the merits of U.S. intervention in that conflict as all other Americans. At the beginning, when we began to first send military assistance to the South Vietnam government against the nationalist and Communist insurgents and then American combat troops, I thought that we were doing a good deed. I thought that most Americans in the early 1960s also believed this. We were going in there to help fight against Communism.

However, as the war progressed and it became more and more an American war with increased American casualties, I, along with many others, began to change our minds. I began to question just what we were doing in Vietnam because the intent became murkier and murkier as the war progressed. We were allegedly fighting for freedom while, at the same time, supporting a repressive South Vietnamese military government. It didn't seem to make sense.

On the other hand, I wasn't too keen on the large, unregulated demonstrations against the war that in some cases erupted into violence. I believe in speaking up, but I don't think you fight fire with fire. I don't believe in breaking the law to fight injustice. I believe that Jesus and St. Francis would never do that. Not all agreed. Maybe I was too optimistic of the good results of respectful discussion within the law.

My more cautious views weren't necessarily shared by some of the other Franciscans in Santa Barbara. Some of them, along with some of our students, were strongly against the war and participated in local and national demonstrations against U.S. policies. Some of our priests began to speak out against the conflict in their Sunday homilies, and the congregation gave evidence of political division. The focus was on the concept of a "just war" that had been developed centuries before in the early days of the Church. Many concluded that in the case of Vietnam, the "just war" concept did not apply.

I didn't necessarily disagree. Some today go even further and believe that no war can be justified. For example, who decides what is "just"? I didn't speak out on this issue publicly, but privately, in the case of Vietnam, I could no longer justify it.

The reaction to these homilies on Vietnam led to splits in our congregation. Conservative Catholics supported the war and resented priests becoming involved in this issue. They thought it was bringing politics into religion. They had, and many still do, an exaggerated understanding of the separation of politics and religion. Many complained to me and other Franciscans about this. Of course, more liberal Catholics, especially younger ones, endorsed these views against the war. Many of them opposed the war and were concerned about their draft status.

Vietnam, as well as so many of the other social issues of that period, only added to the turmoil and painful changes we were experiencing in the Church. I can't think of another era in my life as a Franciscan when I felt so much tension and anguish. Exciting new things were happening both inside and outside the Church, while, at the same time, much conflict was also occurring. To quote Charles Dickens' famous line: "It was the best of times; it was the worst of times."

†

One issue associated with Vatican II that I fully embraced concerned ecumenism and interfaith relationships. In the Catholic Church the ecumenical movement sought to unite the many differing Christian churches. The term has been extended to the issue of interfaith dialogue and collaboration among all religions. For Catholics, the main issue has been and remains just how is the Church necessary for salvation. Does not God will and provide for the salvation of all people?

After all, Christianity is only 2,000 years old. Before that God loved all those Assyrians, Babylonians, Jews, etc. They didn't have the sacrament of baptism or anything like that. Abraham wasn't baptized and neither was St. Joseph. At every moment in everyone's life – irrespective of religion or no religion – God is present in each person offering sufficient grace for salvation.

Ecumenism, which comes from the Greek word meaning worldwide, encourages interfaith dialogue. This dialogue doesn't mean that you give up your particular faith. In fact, you can still believe that your faith is the best way for you to achieve salvation. But it does not mean that you restrict God's saving grace to your own religion.

What Vatican II said was that what saves you is being a member of God's kingdom that speaks of being right with God which is the purpose of religious truth. The Church is ordered to and serves the kingdom. A number of people may be in the Catholic Church but not necessarily in the kingdom. Others may not be in the Church or any formal religious group and yet may be in the kingdom. A Buddhist, for example, may be closer to God than some Catholic or Christian. Having said that, the Catholic Church still believes that the best doctrinal expression of salvation is that of the Catholic/Christian experience and that Jesus and the

Church play a vital and necessary role in the salvation of all. But all of this still invites respectful dialogue among different religions and continuing theological study.

What is important to stress in ecumenical dialogue is that everyone can be saved. The issue is spirituality, personal growth, and interior personal transformation. This is what saves you, aided by religious practices. With that understood, I still believe that the Catholic Church, for me, is a better means to salvation. I am aided by the Catholic traditions as others believe in and value their traditions.

I had no trouble accepting ecumenism and the clearer concept of universal salvation. My only regret is that this was not highlighted in my seminary years. There was very little talk about ecumenism then. It was more the Catholic Church against all other religions. What is the true religion? This lack of ecumenism actually went further back. I cannot recall believing that only Catholics went to Heaven. However, some Catholics believed this and perhaps still do. In the seminary, little if anything was said about other religions and the salvation of all. Yet we have to be open to all religions. Else we would be like persons concerned only with being good Americans without being interested in the United Nations and what goes on among various countries. Recent theological study has become more and more interfaith.

My response was to try to discover and talk about what unites us with other faiths, rather than what divides us, while respecting what separates us in theology and practices. This calls for dialogue. Ecumenism also can lead to greater charity and support among all peoples. You're further challenged through dialogue with persons of other faiths to critique your own faith as well as to deepen it. I find that I'm a better Catholic, and my faith is deepened in and through dialogue with non-Catholics, and I hope the same is true of a Protestant, a Jew, a Hindu, a Moslem, and a Buddhist, etc. Ecumenism opens us to a universal charity and support. Religious differences are no excuses for persecution and wars.

Ecumenism is not just some trendy thing invented by Vatican II. It has deep roots in the Bible. In the Old Testament, for example, the Jews spoke of the day when all nations would come together in Jerusalem. There would be a union between Jews and Gentiles. In the New Testament, Jesus told his disciples to go out and preach to the whole world. We tend to forget that everybody, irrespective of his/her faith or no faith, is made in the image and likeness of God. God loves everyone and everyone has the same destiny. God provides for everyone's fulfillment of the goal of life.

One of the other important changes that resulted from the Church's focus on ecumenism is that conversion is viewed differently. The traditional form of conversion involved proselytizing non-Catholics in the hope of converting them to the Catholic Church. Yes, we Catholics believe that in some way salvation is linked to Jesus and the Church. But this now has been nuanced. What saves is a change of heart and not just changing from one religion to another. I've had people come to me and say:

"Father, I was a Catholic, but I became a Protestant [or Pentecostal] because I never experienced God that much as a Catholic. Now I feel closer to God and I'm a better person."

I can't argue with that. It saddens me that such was not their experience in the Church. If I'm a Catholic and yet come to believe sincerely that I can better enter the kingdom of God in another religion, then I have an obligation to accept membership in that other church. But, I will also tell someone who feels this way:

"Give me a chance to show you how you can in fact find the same thing or a better means for growth in the Catholic Church."

Many people have the wrong impression that the Church is merely the Pope, ecclesiastical and aristocratic institutions, doctrinal and moral statements telling people what is wrong. Certainly all of this is part of the Church. However, the Church, before all else, also possesses a rich tradition of spirituality. What is important above all is having the right loving relationship with God. Membership in the Church should promote your personal growth. Many, however, experience their growth in other faiths.

I personally believe that, for me, the best means for spirituality and salvation is in the Church. That's why I'm a Catholic.

This doesn't mean that the Church after Vatican II has ceased to bring the good news to all people in sending missionaries to non-Christian parts of the world. However, even here Vatican II made important changes. It promoted what is called "inculturation."

We have to accept humankind's changing historical and cultural conditions, its cultural pluralism. The Church is not tied exclusively to any one race or culture. The Christian message must be open to re-expression in a new culture. God in Jesus Christ revealed a divine message in a way meaningful to the culture of Jesus' time. The spirit of God is active in every culture, its institutions, and thought patterns. The Christian message is countercultural (critical of what is false in a culture), challenging, and transforming where necessary, but also in need of reappropriation in terms of the culture. How might our tradition be better heard and lived in our present day U.S. culture? I often ponder: what can and must the Church do to be more relevant in modern times?

In the past, too many missionaries were not respectful of the native cultures and attempted to impose an understanding of Christianity that was foreign to these cultures. They also failed to recognize the possibilities for salvation in the native religions since they went with the idea that unless one became a Catholic, you could never be saved. They may not have articulated that view in this way, but for all practical purposes many acted in this way.

After Vatican II, this type of missionary endeavor began to change due to the concept of inculturation. This means adapting Christianity to an individual culture and not identifying with only one culture. Inculturation involves having respect for native religions and cultures and entering into a dialogue with them. The Church still believes in making converts, but not by stripping them of their native cultures and by destroying their native customs and ways of thought. We're recognizing more and more the efficacy of other religions. I wouldn't call anyone today a "pagan." Ecumenism and inculturation inspire us to accept religious and cultural variations.

Ecumenism welcomes diversity and pluralism. But it can only succeed with education and understanding. Often those who reject ecumenism are those who are insecure about their own faith. They also are simplistic about religion. It's much easier to deal with simplicity than with complexity. We are reminded of how often we hear a husband or wife say to the spouse "why can't you see it my way." There's always a tension between diversity and unity. Some are too insistent on uniformity in religion. They can't handle diversity and fail to recognize that God is at work in many differing ways.

I was somewhat open to ecumenism even before Vatican II, but the contacts with other churches and synagogues locally in Santa Barbara hadn't been effectively made. The Council provided the impetus to do so. Out of the theological seminary we initiated a number of meetings, conferences, and lectures that brought together Catholics and Protestants. One of the first Protestant groups that we initiated a dialogue with were the Lutherans, who, theologically and liturgically, are close to Catholics. As part of this dialogue, I preached in one of the local Lutheran churches and, in turn, I had a Lutheran minister preach at one of the Masses at the Mission.

I also started going to a number of other non-Catholic services, including some Jewish ones. These contacts were very useful and helped promote greater understanding. I never detected any suspicion or hostility. The Protestants had already done their ecumenical work among themselves, but they were pleased to see the Catholics participate. At first, they maybe thought that we'd be standoffish and insist that one had to be a Catholic to be saved. But when they saw that we no longer did so, they relaxed and welcomed us.

Besides the theological discussions, ecumenism in Santa Barbara led to greater cooperation among the different faiths with respect to social issues such as civil rights, poverty, social justice, and a range of community problems. We didn't organize a formal interdenominational association, but we did form a gathering of clergy, one that is still active.

Ecumenism and inter-religious relationships have come to be a very major part of my own spirituality. A few years ago, I expressed some of this in an opinion piece I wrote for the *Santa Barbara News-Press* about how Christmas can be an occasion for us to think beyond our Christian faith. I reminded my readers that the true meaning of Christmas that applies to people of all faiths is the goodness of human life. There is something profoundly good about being a person in a loving exchange with other persons. People are at their best in reaching out to others and being concerned for those in need.

I concluded my piece by writing:

"And may we who claim to believe in the true God and are members of religious organizations rethink just who our God is. May we grow in respect of people of all faiths and persons who have no explicit ties to religion but often are more considerate, gracious and God-like than we are.

"There is a way we can be true to our own religious beliefs and at the same time welcome the religious, ethnic and racial differences among us. In this way we may remove some of the scandal given by those who, with the falsely presumed approval of God, hate and vilify others.

"Each one of us might ask him or herself, who is my God? Isn't my God the God of all persons?

"'Whoever loves God must also love brother and sister.' (1 John 4:21) Is God for all or just for some? Is God working through all or just through some?"

†

In all, the 1960s, highlighted by Vatican II, represented a major transforming period for the Church and for me personally. I look back on these years and ask myself "how did we survive all of this turmoil and change?" We did but it wasn't easy. In some ways, we were flying by the seat of our pants. Some wanted more changes; some wanted less. I often felt myself caught in the middle. I wanted change, but it wasn't easy to decide what changes were for the better. I can't say that I was right or wrong. What is essential and what is secondary? What promotes true growth and serves ministry? I can see now forty years later, and in light of the recent scandals in the Church, that we probably should have made more changes, especially with respect to accountability on the part of the hierarchy, the greater role of the laity in decision-making, and changes in the Church's insistence on celibacy. Of course, it's always easier to see things in hindsight. Some are calling now for a new Vatican III and perhaps they are right.

The years beginning in the 1950s and 1960s effected major changes in my outlook and also my personal activity. I was favored by a fast growing variety of tasks and the blessing of highly diversified contacts with organizations and friends. I gradually moved beyond my earlier smaller world into what I like to call my "expanding horizons." I have more easily lived the integration of the often separated worlds of the divine and the human, heaven and earth, grace and nature. I sensed that I was collaborating with God in all human interests. I began to see spiritual meaning in all my experiences. I read books of all kinds, became interested in all that was typically American, if there is such a thing, and mingled with people of all walks of life. More and more persons shared their views and experiences with me. Much to my surprise, our deepest experiences were similar if not the same.

I tried to keep in step with what Vatican Council II stated in its Pastoral Constitution on the Church in the Modern World: "The joys and hopes, the grief and anguish of the people of our time, especially those who are poor or afflicted, are the joys and hopes, the grief and anguish of the followers of Christ as well. Nothing that is genuinely human fails to find an echo in their hearts....They cherish a feeling of deep solidarity with the human race and its history....In every age the Church carries the responsibility of reading the signs of the times and of interpreting them in the light of the Gospel....In languages intelligible to every generation, it should be able to answer the ever recurring questions which people ask about the meaning of this present life and that of the life to come, and how one is related to the other."

I wonder if the Catholic Church today, especially its leaders, is reading the signs of the times correctly. Are we open to inculturating the good insights and values of our American culture? There may be a gulf between our modern expression of what is essential in Christian faith and American culture. Are we so concerned with what many consider to be the rigidity of liturgical laws and doctrinal uniformity that we are failing to give consideration to a healthy pluralism in the Church? Are we engaging in true and sincere dialogue with other faiths? Are we in the United States really knowledgeable of and encouraged to live our rich and varied Catholic traditions of spirituality and mysticism? Why are New Age and other spiritualities so much more popular?

5

COMMUNITY PRIEST

My spirituality ever reminds me, awakens me to the inclusiveness of God, who is actively present in the lives of all persons and all human events.
— FR. VIRGIL CORDANO

In the early 1960s, I assumed still another role within the Mission complex. I became the Director of Community Relations for the Old Mission. This was not a new position. I replaced another Franciscan, Fr. Noel Moholy in this capacity. Moreover, community relations were not something totally new to me. Prior to my appointment, I had already been making contacts in the Santa Barbara community, although not to the extent that I would in this new position. Little did I know that I would hold on to this responsibility for over forty years. I'm still the head of community relations at age 86.

At first I viewed this new position as just another task. Also, I felt somewhat awkward not knowing what to say or how to respond to new faces and situations. But in time I began to welcome this new responsibility as a blessing. As I opened out to expanding horizons, I became better acquainted with a world much broader than my small area of concern. I was inspired by the goodness of others and their commitment and service to our community. I likewise should involve myself in matters other than those of formal religion. My spirituality ever reminds me, awakens me to the inclusiveness of God who is actively present in all personal and human events. All my relationships provided opportunities to give more and more. And I had to face up to the truth about myself, my strengths, weaknesses, and limitations. There is always more to know and more to do.

My responsibilities in this new assignment were and are to represent the Old Mission or the Santa Barbara Mission to the public. Not just to the Catholic community, but to everyone. I explained what the Mission was all about, its history, and what it represented, and its value to the community, especially as a living historical institution. I was to go out and meet the public and make myself available for talks and invocations. Above all, I was to uphold the good name of the Mission and to improve relations with the city of Santa Barbara and with visitors.

So besides my other work in both the Mission and the theological seminary, I now had to reserve time to go out and meet more people in the community. I did this both on an individual level and with groups. Some of these organizations included the Red Cross, St. Francis Hospital, Marymount School, Old Spanish Days Fiesta, Santa Barbara Historical Society, I Madonari Festival (a chalk-sketching event in front of the Mission), and Hospice of Santa Barbara. I attended various civic meetings or was invited to them. I gave invocations or blessings if some of these groups requested them. I also got involved in the Jewish Anti-Defamation League and worked closely with some of the Jewish leaders in the community. For a long time I gave the blessing at the Anti-Defamation League's annual meeting.

But there's no question that the most visible public role that I played, and continue to do so, is my work with the annual Santa Barbara Fiesta. My relationship with the Fiesta actually goes back even further. As a seminary student here and later as a young priest, I used to attend and even participate in some of the Fiesta activities. I have always enjoyed Fiesta that is celebrated every first week in August. I feel that it helps to develop a sense of community spirit and brings attention to the wonderful and historical Hispanic roots of Santa Barbara.

However, when I was appointed to the Fiesta Board of Directors around 1961, I, of course, became even more involved. To this day, I'm still serving on the Board. It meets once a month to prepare for the annual Fiesta activities including the big parade along the waterfront and up State Street, the main downtown avenue. The history of Fiesta goes way back. It started in 1924 and it has been continuous ever since with the exception of 1925 when the big earthquake led to its cancellation that year.

My biggest role in the Fiesta has been to organize and to be the Master of Ceremonies for what is called the Fiesta Pequena or the small fiesta. It has become anything but small. It actually officially opens Fiesta week. It is held on a Wednesday in the early evening in front of the Mission and includes various Spanish flamenco and Mexican folkloric dancing and some singing groups, and they all represent Spanish/Mexican culture. The Fiesta Pequena also has a long history and, in fact, another Franciscan was in charge of it until I took it over in 1961. Holding the start of the Fiesta at the Mission not only underscores the historical dimensions of the pageant, but it also is a way of asking God's blessing on it.

The Fiesta Pequena's structure has remained pretty much the same over the years, with some differences. In the earlier days, the theological students would actually participate. They would put together a little play depicting some historical event in Santa Barbara's Spanish/Mexican and early California past. One that I remember had to do with the wedding witnessed by Richard Henry Dana and mentioned in his famous 1839 book *Two Years Before the Mast*. Dana, who was from New England, made a voyage with one of the Yankee clipper ships that traded along the California coast at that time in what was called the hide and tallow trade. The New England merchants traded manufactured items with the Spanish/Mexican rancheros for the cattle hides and the tallow or fat from the cattle used to make candles.

The students also served as announcers for the parade. They'd announce the particular floats and contingents as they passed by a certain location. When I was in charge of the students in the 1950s, I was involved in all of these activities as well. That actually brought me into contact with many civic leaders before I became the head of community relations for the Mission.

Much earlier, we also had a firework display. The fireworks would be shot over the tower of the Mission. However, this got to be a fire hazard. We used to station some of our students with hoses just in case some sparks might threaten the surrounding heavily wooded Mission Canyon. In time, the Fire Department didn't allow us to display any fireworks.

Organizing the Fiesta Pequena with a committee was my responsibility, and still is, and it is a lot of work. It's a year-round task. I not only serve as Master of Ceremonies, which is actually the easiest part of my job, but I and my committee also help organize all of the show. We have to audition and then select the dancing groups. This isn't easy. We've made mistakes. We've selected some who have bombed! Then they wanted to return the following year and we had to tell them: "Sorry, we can't take you again." But it was hard to say this after we had initially invited them. In the early days, it all fell on me to select the dancers. Now, I have a committee that relieves me of some of the pressure.

Part of the pressure comes from the fact that over the years a number of dance studios specializing in Spanish and Mexican dances have sprung up in Santa Barbara. They all aim to participate in the Fiesta not only at the Mission, but in other venues during that week such as at the sunken gardens at the courthouse. This gives the studios a great amount of publicity that results in more students.

So a kind of political game is played. Each studio asserts some pressure not only to be selected for Fiesta Pequena, but to achieve an advantageous position in the schedule. They don't want to go on too early when the audience is just settling in and they certainly don't want to go on too late when some of the audience is beginning to leave. They want to go on just right in the middle when they have a capacity crowd to dance in front of. It was all very competitive but of late this has lessened.

Then, of course, sometimes we have to deal with temperamental artists. This is not so much the boys and girls who dance, but their instructors and even in some cases their parents. Everyone thinks that their group and their daughter or son is the best.

The selection of the Spirit of Fiesta from one of the studios adds to the competition. The Spirit of Fiesta is the young dancer, usually a girl, who is picked to be the princess of the entire Fiesta week. There's also a Junior Spirit of Fiesta who is selected from among the younger competitors. The Spirit of Fiesta gets to lead the big parade. The Junior Spirit gets to lead the children's parade. Fortunately, I didn't have to be involved in these selections. There is a contest and a committee does the selections. In almost all cases, the competitors are girls, but I remember once a boy dancer was chosen Junior Spirit. He was very talented. I've known many of these girls and boys over the years. Many, of course, are now grown up. I've since officiated at the weddings of many of them and baptized their children.

My job as organizer of the Fiesta Pequena was made more complicated when we would have the Governors of California in attendance. They didn't necessarily come every year, but often enough so that I had further work on arrangements for them, such as where they and their entourage would sit as well as introducing them. Governors who attended included Earl Warren, Goodwin Knight, and Edmund "Pat" Brown in the late 1950s and early 1960s. Ronald Reagan came only once. Security was an issue during Reagan's tenure of office. The tradition ended when Jerry Brown was Governor in the 1970s. He never attended.

One funny story that I heard from my predecessor before I took over had to do with Governor Knight who enjoyed the Fiesta Pequena in the 1950s. After the dancing was over, he and his wife attended a Noche de Gala or gala night at the Coral Casino right across from the fashionable Biltmore Hotel in elegant Montecito.

Late that evening, the Governor's wife said that it would be nice to go back to see the Mission with no people around. So she and the Governor and their group, accompanied by my Franciscan predecessor, went back up. However, by then the Mission was closed since it was around midnight. So they were out in front talking, not realizing that some of the friars were asleep in the front corridor where they could hear the Governor's entourage. One of the brothers was awakened by all of this commotion and opened a window and yelled out, "Folks, the party's over. Go home!"

My predecessor recalled how red-faced he became at this and how he had no alternative but to tell the Governor and his wife: "Well, I guess we'd better leave."

Part of the Fiesta is the big parade. At times, I've participated in the parade by being asked to be on one of the floats. I once was Honorary Marshall of the parade. It's fun to be on a float. I'm riding along, waving to all of the people, many of whom are tourists so they don't know me at all. But then someone calls out, "Hey, Father Virgil!" I gladly wave back even more animatedly.

Sometimes I've been asked to be part of the radio and later television coverage of the parade. I was what is called a color commentator. With the help of a text, I'd identify the floats and say something about them. This was not easy because the names had to be pronounced correctly and at the proper time. "Here comes this float sponsored by such and such and on it are such and such persons."

Thursdays of Fiesta week the Misa del Presidente (Mass of the President – the Fiesta President) is celebrated in the Mission Church. Early Mission music is sung, and a reception in the garden follows. I give the homily at the Mass, usually speaking of spiritual themes that are inclusive of both Catholics and people of other religions. Also as a member of the Board, I am expected to attend the other events of the Fiesta.

I love Fiesta. For me, it's been a wonderful way of meeting many people and feeling very much a part of the Santa Barbara community. It's an occasion for me to get outside of my own limited Catholic circle and to be open to a universe of people. That's actually what catholic means anyway, to be universal.

For me, Fiesta is community. It brings people together who otherwise might not be together. It unites people. We all like to eat and drink. We get beyond church and ethnicity that separates us. One of my guiding principles is focusing on what unites us while still respecting diversity –

community and diversity.

Fiesta has embodied this principle. For the most part, it's been successful. Here and there, there's been some disturbance. During the period of the Chicano Movement of the late 1960s and early 1970s, when a new generation of Mexican Americans proudly called themselves Chicanos, asserting their drive for civil rights and ethnic pride, there were some problems. This, in particular, involved the Casa de la Raza, the principal Chicano community center in Santa Barbara, and Fiesta organizers. The Casa felt that Fiesta was stressing too much the Spanish heritage of the city to the detriment of the Chicano or Mexican one.

I don't think there was a full meeting of the minds then, but in time both sides recognized that what was being celebrated was in fact both the Spanish and the Mexican history of Santa Barbara. In fact, La Casa has become a big supporter of Fiesta, and it raises a lot of money through its food booth.

†

Besides my participating in Fiesta, I've also, as director of community relations, been involved with many other events and groups. For example, each year for some time now, I've blessed a group called Los Rancheros Visitadores or the Visiting Ranchers who revived the old tradition of neighboring ranchers keeping in touch with each other and enjoying life in the wide open spaces. This is a group of horsemen who keep their beautiful horses in this area, especially in the lovely Santa Ynez Valley. I knew about them even when I was in the seminary. As seminarians we used to sing for them.

Every first Saturday in May, they would come to Mission Santa Barbara to be blessed, even though most were not Catholics, but it was a tradition they kept, more symbolic than religious. After I was put in charge of community relations, I blessed them. This way, I came to know many of these excellent horsemen over the years. These included some Hollywood stars such as Leo Carrillo and Art Linkletter. They would ride their horses right up to the front of the Mission. That's where I'd bless them.

Although I have varied over the years my blessings, here is a sample of part of one of them:

> "My prayer is that as you move from place to place, event to event, moment to moment, that you find time to reflect on your own personal inner journeys. With open spaces before you, may you with open minds and all embracing hearts discover more about yourselves and those who travel with you. In a spiritual sense may all the roads ahead of you be safe. May you not be disappointed by delays, detours, occasional breakdowns, misdirections and personal stormy weather. In time and with patience may you come to your intended destination of personal wholeness and mutually respectful and supportive relationships. May you believe that wherever you go and whatever you experience, God goes with you. And we pause to remember those who have completed their journeys on earth. Amen."

In later years, with more traffic, it became difficult for them to ride their horses into town so I started driving to the Santa Ynez Valley where I would do the blessing. After my blessing, they would ride to Mission Santa Ynez where the Capuchin Franciscans would give them another blessing.

I still bless the Rancheros Visitadores, and the event has become international, with some of the riders coming from Mexico, Australia, and England as well as from other parts of the United States.

One particular blessing I'll never forget was in 1989, and on this occasion the blessing was in the Santa Ynez Valley. As I began my prayer, to my surprise and that of the assembled Rancheros and others, two male streakers – completely naked – ran in front of me. I have no idea who they were and why they did this. The assembled crowd roared with laughter at this incident. I waited for the laughter to die down, and then with the timing of a stand-up comic, I said:

> "I have a word from the Lord for those two gentleman: 'Repent, for your end is in sight.'"

As part of my community activities, I also got to know many of the prominent leaders in Santa Barbara. Many of them became good friends. One such person was Tom Storke, the publisher of the *Santa Barbara News-Press*. I first got to know Tom in the 1950s. He and Pearl Chase were the two most influential people in town. Tom, besides publishing the paper, also had served earlier as U.S. Senator from California. Tom knew all of the powerful politicians in the state. Due to Tom's influence, California governors such as Earl Warren, Goodwin Knight, and Edmund "Pat" Brown in the fifties and early sixties would often come down for Fiesta.

Tom was a wholly political person in mind and heart. Civic society was his great love. He was always trying to improve the city and to make it a better place to live. He, himself, was a native of Santa Barbara. In fact, his mother was of Spanish/Mexican descent from one of the pioneering families of Santa Barbara. He also did a lot for the University of California, Santa Barbara. I believe that he, before all others, brought the University of California to Santa Barbara. He contributed to many programs, and to acknowledge this, the university named the central tower and square Storke Plaza.

Tom had much to say about the direction of Santa Barbara. He particularly promoted what he considered to be the city's most prominent characteristics: its natural beauty and the continuation of Spanish culture and architecture. He worked closely with Pearl Chase on this. Chase was more the ecological of the two, while Tom provided the political know-how to get things accomplished. Together, they fashioned contemporary Santa Barbara. The Mission, of course, was part of the image of Santa Barbara that they promoted. In general, Tom believed that we were operating the Mission in a way that complemented his image of the city. He would always participate in our Fiesta Pequena and Misa del Presidente.

Tom was baptized a Catholic, but never raised in the Catholic faith. He and I became quite good friends. He used to like having me stop by his house on Santa Barbara Street, not far from the Mission, to have a drink with him around five in the afternoon. We'd do this at least once a month and he would hold court talking about life in general and what he thought about Santa Barbara and the Mission. He would also invite me from time to time to dinner with other key people in town including those he hosted at his ranch during the Rancheros celebration.

In our conversations, Tom did most of the talking. He wanted to know more about my religion, the world of Franciscans, and all that was beyond his pale of interest. I didn't find it easy to explain to him my own personal pursuits. I think, or I wish to think, that I helped him open out to the world of the spirit and the importance of faith in a better world.

There is no question but Tom was the most prominent and influential of the movers and shakers in Santa Barbara. He was a kingmaker in local and even state politics. Above all, he wanted to protect the image of Santa Barbara as a beautiful, wholesome, and friendly community. He didn't like friction and division. I remember in the late 1950s or early 1960s when a local chapter of the John Birch Society, a highly conservative and even reactionary group, surfaced in town, Tom publicly took a stand against them and pretty much eliminated any influence they might have. There was no question but that Tom was the most powerful person in Santa Barbara.

When Francis Minturn "Duke" Sedgwick, a prominent artist and friend of mine, died, I had a funeral service for him. I composed a special liturgy for him. Tom attended and later told me, "Padre, when I die, I want a service just like this. Will you do it for me?"

"Of course," I told him. Not too long afterwards, Tom also died in 1971. He was 95 years old. I organized the service in the Mission. Because Tom was not a practicing Catholic, I didn't think it appropriate and meaningful to have the traditional funeral Mass. Instead, as I had done for Sedgwick, I put together a special liturgy without the Mass for Tom. As part of this service, I called Chief Justice Earl Warren of the U.S. Supreme Court and convinced him to come and say some words about Tom's political importance. The Chief Justice, who had been Governor of California in the 1940s and knew Tom very well, was kind enough to come. I also had the new editor and publisher of the *Santa Barbara News-Press*, Stuart Taylor, speak about Tom's journalistic contributions. Finally, I had the Chancellor of UCSB, Dr. Vernon Cheadle, address Tom's contributions to the university. I talked about Tom's faith and his love for the Mission. In this way, we had four aspects of the man celebrated interspersed with music sung by our seminary students.

In my funeral homily, I had these words to say about Tom:

"The most profound reason for the celebration of the achievements of this great man in the Mission is the religious belief that God Himself assigned Tom Storke the task of building up the city of man [and women]. The nobility of this task is recognized by the Church. The greatest human achievement is to be faithful to the task given by God for the good of fellowmen. To build the city of man is to build the city of God. God enters into man's making of man and his fashioning of his earthly dwelling place. The cause of God is the cause of men [and women]. Tom fulfilled his God-given role in life.

"We thank God for this man who was so near and dear to us and who has now been taken from us. We thank God for Tom's many and enduring achievements. We thank God for the friendship that went out from him and made him a person others could love while he was with us on earth. We pray that nothing of Tom's life and work will be lost, but that it will be of benefit to this city, state, county, and the world, that all he held sacred may be respected by those who follow him, and that everything in which he was great may continue to mean much to us now that he is dead."

Years later in 1993, I was very humbled to receive a *Santa Barbara News-Press* Lifetime Achievement Award that was established in honor of Tom Storke and given to those who carried on his legacy of community service. I wasn't sure I deserved this award, but in memory of my friendship with Tom, I accepted it.

In retrospect, I think what attracted me to Tom Storke and what I most admired in him was his sense of civic responsibility, his commitment to Santa Barbara, his shrewd practical wisdom, his "know how," his personal interest in the persons he met, including me. Although he probably was not aware of what God asked of him, he fulfilled his calling or vocation in life. Everyone has a vocation, clergy and laity alike. I have come to appreciate more and more the importance of the roles that laity perform outside of formal religion. Again, God works through all persons in all walks of life. Not just Heaven but earth also is dear to the heart of God. The common good must be served.

As I noted, Pearl Chase was still another giant in Santa Barbara. More than any one person including Tom Storke, she was responsible for Santa Barbara's unique Spanish or neo-Spanish image. She had arrived sometime in the early twentieth-century and following the disastrous earthquake in 1925 which destroyed much of downtown, Pearl took it upon herself to redo the city in Spanish style with red-tile roofs and all. She was Santa Barbara's unofficial Minister of Architecture and Landscape. She just had all of this energy and drive and a real love for her adopted city.

Pearl was responsible for the beautification of Santa Barbara. She made all of the decisions regarding anything that had to do with the city's external appearance. She was *numero uno*. If it weren't for her, Santa Barbara wouldn't have the distinctiveness it possesses. She was fully involved in all aspects of the community. She belonged to or had contacts with every civic group in town. She organized plantings all over the area. If an area was out of order, she'd suggest planting trees or flowers and cleaning up the neighborhood.

I got to know Pearl fairly well, although not as well as Storke. Our paths would cross quite often. Like Storke, she also was very interested in the Mission's appearance. If she felt something was not right, she was not afraid to tell me so. Once, she noticed that in the front area of the Mission, we had an old sundial. It didn't go back to the Spanish colonial days, but it was old.

"Father Virgil," Pearl told me, "I think that sundial should be removed. It isn't in keeping with the Mission's history."

Needless to say, I had it removed and put inside the grounds. Pearl could come on strong, not in an abrasive way, but in a genuinely concerned one. When she talked, you listened.

Every year there is a luncheon remembering her and honoring a present-day citizen.

Still another important figure in the community that I came to know was the artist Francis Minturn Sedgwick, or "Duke," as he was called. He was a sculptor and did various statues around town including the big one of the horseman that stands in the Earl Warren Show Grounds. When it was finished, there was a big dedication attended by all of the major civic officials. I was honored when Duke asked me to bless the statue. Besides being an artist, he also owned a lot of land up in the backcountry, most of which he later donated to UCSB. He was a strong promoter of the Fiesta, and that's how I got to know him. We hit it off right away. He would invite me to his ranch for Sunday dinner, where he also entertained various other people. He always insisted that I appear in my Franciscan habit, which I did to please him. We became dear friends.

Duke told me his whole life story. I listened attentively since I thought that he had never bared his soul that much with anyone else. I learned of his dreams and hopes, his searching and his struggle. Perhaps the artistic and reflective person has more insight into the human heart than the person who just gets things done and fails to ask "is that all there is?" Duke and I, much to my surprise, easily bonded.

Later while he was battling cancer, he approached me to get permission to do a statue of St. Francis in the quadrangle next to our chapel. I felt honored and got the Mission to approve it. Duke had had somewhat of a painful family life. Two of his sons committed suicide. He wanted to do a statue that expressed his suffering and as a way of identifying with St. Francis whose name he shared.

He depicted St. Francis in joyful agony receiving the stigmata, the five wounds, looking up to God for help. The image, the face, however, is that of Duke Sedgwick. It is Duke pleading with God for the souls of his sons.

Every time I pass by the statue, I think of Duke and say a little prayer for him.

When he died in 1967 after a long battle with cancer, I organized, as mentioned, his funeral service. Here is part of what I had to say of Duke:

"I knew of his work throughout the early years of our occasional meetings. Then during the last months of his life – if not earlier – it became evident to me that the divine sculptor was fashioning him, a man of clay, into a work of beauty. Together in time we came to see that the most meaningful activity on earth is the building of a human edifice, a spiritual creation. The great and noble work of art is the person. The world is a workshop in which we are to perfect the masterpiece that our lives must become. This work of art is not molded from material clay nor carved out of stone but it is extracted from the clay of one's own flesh and the sentiments and deeds of a lifetime."

†

In the midst of all of these community and Mission activities, in 1970 I celebrated my Silver Anniversary as a Franciscan priest. I couldn't believe that I had served twenty-five years already. The time had seemed to go so fast.

A lot of people attended the festivity. My family came down including my mother and my brothers, Jim and Ray with their families. Many civic leaders and friends joined us. All together there were about 800 people. I had no idea that I knew so many especially here in Santa Barbara. We had a Mass and a wonderful friend, Mary Mazzia, did all of the cooking for the reception. She would also do the same twenty-five years later for my Golden Anniversary. As part of the celebration, I was very honored that a resolution was passed by the California State Senate, introduced by our local State Senator Robert J. Lagomarsino, that commended me on my anniversary and, in particular, called attention to my spiritual and civic contributions to Santa Barbara and to the state of California.

After the first twenty-five years, I felt that I now more truly understood the meaning of being a Franciscan priest – of giving to others and of being humble. I felt grateful that I didn't leave during those difficult seminary years. I felt justified that I had made the right decision. I knew more than ever that this was my calling in life. Never once had I seriously doubted this. I saw the tremendous potential for good in it. This included caring for people and focusing on the purpose and goal of life: to serve God and others. There is nothing more important given my belief that we live forever and that there is a loving God who shares divine life with us. Nothing is more important than spiritual growth. That's the whole purpose of life. That's why I became a Franciscan priest. I'm still growing.

But my special memory of my Silver Anniversary is seeing my mother and how proud she was of me. By then, she had accepted my becoming a priest and understood why she had to give up her fifteen-year-old son to the Church. It had hurt her very much. It had hurt me very much, also, being away from my mother and brothers. But now, she was very pleased at what I had become and the work I was doing here in Santa Barbara. But deep down, I was still her little boy and she was my mother.

Three years later in 1973, my mother died. She was 87 years old. It was a heavy, lamentable loss. I was very close to her. She wasn't one of those demonstrative Italians, but I noticed amongst my brothers and myself a tremendous affection for her. In a way, her death was the culmination of the emotional and psychological break I had made when I left home. There was a period between 1939 and 1945 when I saw her only once. However, after I was ordained I truly enjoyed being with her. I used to go home and drive her around, visiting all of the relatives. She had been living in a house that Jim, who was by now a wealthy developer, had built for her. She was totally dependent on him and Ray. When I visited her, she used to love to show me off. I saw her death as part of my spiritual journey that began when I first left home to tell all of the good news of life forever with God, family, and all of creation.

When she died, I was on one of those assignments to Central America. She had been in relatively good health. However, she had a fall in front of her home and broke her hip. She died a couple of weeks later. When she fell, I was still in New York preparing to go to Central America. Jim called and told me about her fall.

"Shall I come home?" I asked him.

"No," Jim said, "I don't think she's in any danger. But give me your itinerary so I know where you'll be in case I have to call you."

"Are you sure I shouldn't come home? I can go to Guatemala from Sacramento."

"No, she'll be okay."

So I went down to Guatemala. I was out in the country visiting the American Franciscan missionaries. One day I went into Guatemala City for lunch. When I got to the Franciscan house there, they had a message from Jim that mother had died. A bit later, Jim called back and gave me the details.

My mother was the type of person who didn't believe much in doctors. After her fall, she knew that she'd be crippled the rest of her life. She'd never walk again. Jim felt that she just gave up. That day, Ray's wife, Nell, had been at the hospital and had helped Mother with her lunch. Nell thought that she was fine and went home. Nobody was with her when she died. She just dropped her head and died. She didn't want to be a burden to anybody. She must have figured that there was no point in living anymore. She would have felt terrible to be totally dependent upon others.

The Franciscans in Guatemala City arranged for me to get a flight that night to California. My younger brother, Ray, picked me up in San Francisco and drove me to Sacramento. I arrived on a Friday morning, and we had the rosary that night and the Mass on Saturday. I said both the rosary and the Mass at my mother's church, the new St. Mary's on 58th Street. The original St. Mary's was on 7th and T streets, traditionally the Italian church in Sacramento. Many people attended the funeral, relatives and friends. As I mention in the Prologue, my mother was the most important person in my life. Her death was the saddest moment in my life. I pray for her now as I know she prays for me.

We buried Mother at St. Mary's cemetery where my father was buried as well as my brother, Phil, who had died about a year before my mother. He died of a heart attack or stroke. Phil when very young had contracted a disease accompanied by a very high fever. Without any available antibiotic, Phil remained handicapped intellectually and emotionally throughout his life. He could not hold down a job, but was well provided for by Jim. Phil was a good companion for my mother and was loved by all of us for his childlikeness. My brother Andrew, who had died shortly before I was born, was buried in the older Catholic cemetery.

†

Into the 1970s, I also took up other responsibilities outside of the Mission. One of these was becoming the chaplain of the Marymount School. I assumed this role in 1972 and still have that honor. I was asked to do this because I not only was by now pretty well known in town, but also I had been teaching in the novitiate of the Religious of the Sacred Heart of Mary (RSHM), the community in charge of Marymount. The novitiate was in Santa Barbara on Tremonto Road just above the location of Marymount in the hills of the well-to-do Riviera area of the city. I was a good friend of the Sisters and still am.

Marymount had started in 1938. Originally only girls attended both the elementary and high schools. It was also a boarding school then. When I became chaplain, only girls still attended. It was a small school, as it is today, with no more than about 200 students, though today it is well over that number. A few years later, after I became associated with the school, the Sisters, due to shortage of numbers, sold the school to a lay board. It now operates as an independent Catholic school open to children of all faiths and is coed. It is an elementary and middle school.

Marymount further became quite an expensive school due to higher tuitions to pay the lay teachers who took over such as Dr. Dolores Pollock who became the principal until her recent retirement in 2002. But at the same time, Marymount offered an attractive educational environment. The classes were small and so students received much individual attention. It's been a very positive and joyful school. I've always seen it as an example of the best of a Catholic education, even though the majority of students have been non-Catholics. This shift from Catholics to non-Catholics was also reflected in the teachers, many of whom were not Catholics, including Dr. Pollock.

This shift in the religious orientation of the student body led to Marymount creating a two-course system in teaching religion. One course was for Catholic students and the other for non-Catholics. At times the two classes were combined and the result has been a more ecumenical approach to religious instruction. I was involved in some of these changes, because for awhile I also served on the Board of Trustees.

The change in the religious background of the student body at Marymount did raise, and still does, the issue of whether an independent school such as Marymount with a Catholic orientation can effectively remain Catholic in a theological and spiritual sense. I think that it can and does remain Catholic. However, it is not Catholicism in the traditional sense, but in a more ecumenical one. I supported this change in religious instruction because it fit in with my own developing ecumenism out of Vatican II. What was happening at the school reinforced my belief that you can find a common denominator among all religions. You can be ecumenical and still be true to the Catholic tradition. The religion class at Marymount became a model for interfaith dialogue. It was and is good for the students, both Catholic and non-Catholic, to learn from one another about their religious faiths and practices. As our Catholic elementary schools, high schools, and even colleges become more religiously mixed, it is even more important to stress and implement ecumenical religious approaches and curriculum.

This religious diversification can be seen in the religious services at

Marymount. I always appreciate and enjoy them, especially when the youngsters come up to Communion. To the Catholic students, I give Communion. To the non-Catholics, who come up with their arms crossed, I give them a blessing. No one is made to feel isolated or ashamed. Everyone participates. Some of the non-liturgical celebrations sometimes include a Protestant minister, a rabbi, a Muslim, etc.

Marymount has succeeded largely because through its expensive tuition, it can sustain itself. This, unfortunately, has not been as much the case with our parochial schools affiliated with the Church. Many of these schools, in Santa Barbara and elsewhere, have had serious financial problems. While they charge tuition, it can't be very high or else parents, both middle and working class, would find it difficult if not prohibitive for their children to attend. We also are having problems hiring and retaining good teachers and principals because we can't pay them enough. This is an issue that needs to receive serious attention. Vouchers would help, but that is a hotly debated political issue.

Parochial schools are changing but there will always be a need for some form of Catholic education. I support retaining parochial schools because it's important for Catholic youth to learn more about their religion. However, to me the main teachers of religion are not the schools but the parents. And if not, this is the way it should be. I would even go one step further and argue that the real need is not so much the religious education of children but of adults. How many Catholic mothers and fathers have an understanding of their faith beyond that of an eight or nine year old?

The religious education of adults is today even more important due to secularization of our society as well as increasing religiously mixed marriages. In these instances, you wonder how effective a Catholic upbringing a child can have. Parochial schools to some extent fill the gap. Religious education programs in our parishes for public school students, to another degree, helps although enrollments in these programs are not what they should be. Parents will enroll their elementary school children in these classes to prepare them for their First Communion, but after that often you don't see them. You might see them later for Confirmation but not as many. The next time may be when they get married, if they marry in the Church. I'm disappointed that we don't seem to have a better way of educating our children at whatever level in the Catholic faith.

I think the way to change this is by putting more stress on education or re-educating our adult laity in their faith. This will involve both theological and spiritual formation or re-formation. I believe that adults are the key to educating our children about their religion. This doesn't mean turning parents into theologians, although I favor the theological education of adults. It does mean, however, teaching our parents in greater depths about some of the mysteries of our faith and about Catholic doctrine on a range of issues such as spirituality, the role of the laity, marriage, and sexual matters. Unless parents are well educated on these issues, how can they in turn teach their children?

How we go about educating the adults is another matter. For several years I've organized classes on spirituality for adults, and this is one way. Adults, themselves, are anxious to learn more about their faith. At the Graduate School of Theology at Berkeley where we have a Franciscan presence, the majority of the students now are lay Catholics and not seminarians. I think, too, given the moral crisis that the Church, as I write, is undergoing due to the sexual scandals exposed in 2002, that one result of all of this will be the laity insisting on a greater involvement in decision-making in their parishes. This may result, hopefully, in the laity learning more about the theology of their Church and exercising more authority.

The laity need to deepen their understanding of the Catholic faith if they are to meet the challenge of ecumenism. As we engage in more interfaith dialogue with our non-Catholic neighbors, it is extremely important that we participate in these discussions and contacts enlightened and secure in our faith and in our religious beliefs. This calls for a certain amount of study. Unless people of all religions are educated about their beliefs, not only are they a hindrance to the growth of their own religions, but it makes interfaith dialogue very difficult. To me, there is no contradiction in being

Catholic and being ecumenical. In fact, if you're not ecumenical, you're not Catholic. If you're not ecumenical, you're not truly Jewish or Protestant or Muslim. God is active in all religions and expressions of belief. Your own faith will be strengthened if you have a good religious education and enter into dialogue with non-Catholics. You become more Catholic because you're challenged to clarify and justify your Catholicity.

†

Of course, all of this is an ideal scenario. The fact of the matter is that today, at least for European-origin Catholics in the United States, there is a crisis of Catholic identity. I'm not as sure about Latino Catholics since many are recent immigrants, and although they seem to identify strongly with the Church, I wonder how well educated they are about their faith. However, I suspect that more acculturated Latinos may also face a Catholic identity crisis. We've always had such an identity crisis in a largely Protestant country such as the United States. Yet through the years, as Catholics have assimilated or acculturated more, I believe the crisis has deepened.

The reason for all this has to do with historical and socio-economic changes. In an earlier period, most Euro-Catholics were isolated and hence possessed a "ghetto religion." To be a Catholic was a way of creating a sense of community in a hostile American environment. The same was true of ethnic identity. Ethnicity and Catholicism combined as a self-defense mechanism. When I was a kid in Sacramento, my whole neighborhood was mostly Italian and Catholic. That isn't true today. With greater mobility, acculturation, and ethnic diversity, there is the problem of religious identity. The increased intermarriage of ethnic groups adds to the ambivalence of identity. If you're not well educated in your Catholic faith and don't have strong Catholic convictions beyond what your mother and father or parish priest taught you, you're going to weaken in your Catholic convictions. This only reinforces the critical need today for Catholic adult education at the college level and beyond.

The greater ethnic diversification and ethnic intermixing, of course, has given rise to many more interfaith marriages. Over the years, I've married many couples where one of the persons is not a Catholic. In some cases, the Catholic party, to boot, is not a very strong Catholic. On the other hand, the non-Catholic may possess a stronger faith. Eventually, the person whose religious belief is stronger is going to persuade the other to change. The challenge in such marriages is what faith the children will be brought up in? This is a difficult issue.

In the past, the Church insisted that the non-Catholic agree that the children be raised Catholic since the marriage took place in the Church. However, since Vatican II, we don't put as much pressure on non-Catholics. On the contrary, we put the pressure now on the Catholic party. In order to get a dispensation to marry a non-Catholic, the Catholic has to sign a written agreement in which he or she promises to raise the children Catholic. The non-Catholic is to respect the obligation of the Catholic partner. But this is no guarantee. It's quite possible that both parties are really not certain just what they will do about the religious education of their children.

Adding to the crisis in Catholic identity has been the increased numbers of divorces. Of the many marriages I've performed, I don't know how many have ended in divorce. People that divorce don't come and tell me. I'm always surprised that some marriages continue and others don't. I can recall thinking that a certain couple wouldn't make it, and yet they have. Then there are those who I think are a perfect couple, only to learn a few years later that they have divorced. You can never tell. Who can predict the evolution of love? Some people get off to a good start, and then after fifteen or twenty-five years, the man or woman no longer loves the other. What is love? How many people are up to a lasting commitment in the midst of fluctuating sexual attractions and mores? If two people as individuals don't grow over the years, why continue the relationship? The relationship is as good as the two, as individuals, mature. It's like a soup. It's as good as its ingredients.

The Church still is strongly opposed to divorce and does not grant divorces nor sanctions them. However, the reality is that more and more Catholics are simply not paying attention to the Church's teachings on divorce and are getting civil divorces.

Besides increased divorce rates among Catholics helping to create a Catholic identity crisis, there has also over the last few decades been an increase in annulments. An annulment is an official Church recognition of the invalidity of the earlier marriage at the time of the wedding. The Church gives consideration to an annulment when a marriage does not have all that is essentially required for a valid marriage or when certain nullifying irregularities are present. We can't keep up with annulments. There is a large waiting list for annulments in the Archdiocese of Los Angeles. There aren't enough people to work on these cases. Still many of them are granted. Although the Church retains its high ideals for married couples, still it recognizes through annulments the limitations of a person's good intentions and his or her inability to make a life-long commitment.

Some of the most common grounds for annulments include couples not wanting to have children. On the other hand, I have encountered couples already with children who seek an annulment. Another is the immaturity of one of the parties or in some cases both. Some people are too immature to make a life commitment. Then there are other psychological and even biological grounds for annulments.

I've always had mixed feelings about the breaking up of marriages. I want couples to have the commitment, discipline, maturity, selflessness, and patience to make marriage work. On the other hand, I can see that some marriage relations are miserable and even destructive. They have to separate. Some people can be very heroic in tolerating a bad situation. Others just can't and may even end up having to see a psychiatrist for reasons of health. I can understand and sympathize with those in such situations.

In fact, over the years, I find myself becoming more and more not a priest but a psychologist, in counseling married couples who are having difficulties. Sometimes marriage counselors send couples to me, as if I could do any better. The sad thing is that most don't come in soon enough. They have small difficulties at first, but these build up and up. By the time they come to see me, the bond is no longer there.

In any event, all of these things – intermarriages, divorces, annulments – when combined with greater secularization, greater social and economic mobility, and the end of "ghetto Catholicism," all have to one degree or another contributed, in my opinion, to a Catholic identity crisis in this country. The recent sex scandals in the Church have only added to this crisis. The loss of trust in the Church leads to a weakening in some cases of one's faith itself. Not in all cases, but in many. How all this will be resolved is open to question.

†

Thanks to my assignments, the things I have been asked to do, the many persons I have come to know, and my understanding of a God who cares for all, I feel close to St. Paul's motto: "Be all things to all people." The God I believe in is a God who deals differently with different persons. So I look beyond all labeling to be open to all. What matters the most in life is the kind of person I am coming to be. I am aided in this regard by my particular way of life, while I accept and even support others in their personal development. To love is to affirm and promote the other even though different from me. I try to join God in His/Her interest in and care for all of creation.

6

The Good Pastor and Challenging Times

Although I welcome my membership in the institutionalized Church, it is
my faith in God active in the Church that above all else sustains me.

— FR. VIRGIL CORDANO

In 1976, I was appointed pastor of the Old Mission Church. I was recommended as pastor by my Franciscan Order and the Archdiocese of Los
Angeles officially approved me. This meant that I was now in charge of
the parish. It was one more hat that I wore as a Franciscan. This wasn't
totally a new change for me. In my previous positions at the Mission, I
had always helped out in the parish. I had done a lot of pastoral work
along with the theological teaching I was doing. I was also accustomed to
administration as Rector (President) of the theological school and
Superior of the Old Mission. What was different was that this was the first
time I was actually in charge of the administration of a parish and dealing with such things as arranging for the Masses and the liturgy, including the music to be performed at each service, hiring new help, balancing
the books, etc. Making these kinds of particular decisions was new for
me. I was used to making decisions but not of this type. Little did I know
that I would be pastor for some 18 years until 1994.

As pastor, I didn't attempt to introduce too many changes although I
did propose some. My main intent was to involve the laity much more in
ministry. This, of course, came from the impetus of Vatican Council II.

Along these lines, I organized laity discussion groups. I arranged for the creation of a large number of small groups in the parish. Originally we started with between 15 to 20 small groups. Each group focused on a particular topic or set of topics. We had several groups in order to keep the number in each one down to a manageable size, where constructive dialogue could take place. This was a structural way of listening to the laity. The idea was that each group would meet, and then the leaders of each group would come together and jointly present to me, as pastor, various recommendations for changes or improvements within the parish. It was a way of facilitating dialogue and consultation with pastors who in the past, unfortunately, had been too authoritarian. It was an exercise, to some extent, in democratic procedures within the parish.

I tried meeting with each group, but there were so many that this wasn't always possible. Sometimes I would be asked to attend a particular group meeting because it had questions for me. Some groups were more involved in theological or spiritual issues, and I would go and explain certain things. Others were more involved in the practical side of the Church, such as what times should Masses be scheduled. Or they might suggest different types of music to be used in the liturgy. Still others felt that the Mission wasn't doing enough for the young people. Some felt that we should be working on more social justice issues, such as assisting the poor. I appreciated all of these types of suggestions, and some I accepted. Others, in light of the whole picture of the parish, I decided not to make the changes. In the end, of course, we still had a kind of top-down structure, since I was responsible for making the ultimate decisions.

But on the whole, it was an amicable relationship between me and the discussion groups. Issues in liturgy and music were the most difficult. On one occasion, one group wanted a change in the choir director while another wanted to get rid of the organist. This split often mirrored the division between the choir director and the organist themselves. Both often clashed as to the music to be performed at different Masses.

Members of the choir took sides. Some wanted me to dismiss the choir director, while others wanted me to let the organist go. I listened to both sides at one meeting for several hours, well into the late evening. Both sides were very strong in their arguments. Finally, I suggested that both of them resign in order to clear the deck. Fortunately, they did, and I hired a new director and organist.

Besides liturgical issues, some of the groups focused more on theological and spiritual ones, using the Bible as a basis for discussion. These were my favorite. I liked listening to the laity, their interpretations of the Bible, and their spiritual interests. The theological basis for listening to all is that God speaks to and through everyone. So if I want to know the Word of God, it isn't just what the Pope says or what the bishops and priests say, although they have a certain primacy and make decisions after listening to all. But you also have to listen to the laity. If you do not listen to all, you do not hear God fully. This is what Vatican II meant by stressing that all Catholics, clergy and laity, represent the Church. We are all Church.

This broad approach to the meaning of Church also reinforced my own strong ecumenical views. God speaks and acts through all religions and through all persons. So in a way, you have to listen to all of creation if you want to know the fullness of what God has to say. No one church, no one group, has a justifiable solitary claim on receiving the fullness of God's message. All of creation is a word from God.

The way these Bible classes worked was that they would take a scriptural reading or a passage from the Bible, or in some cases from a theological text, and use that as the basis for their discussion. They often favored using the scriptural reading for the coming Sunday. This way, they would get even more out of my homily or that of the other priests.

We still have some of these groups, but not as many as we used to during the time I was pastor. But it's important, still, to hear the voice of the laity, especially now with the Church and the hierarchy under such pressures and scrutiny due to the recent sexual abuse scandals. In this context, the role of the laity, in my opinion, becomes even more important in reforming the Church. The hierarchy cannot reform itself without the involvement of all in the Church. Part of the problem is that during the last couple of decades, there's been a regression in the concept of all Catholics representing the Church. There's been an unfortunate sliding back to a more hierarchical structure beginning with the Vatican. The Vatican during this time has become too autonomous, and there's not enough dialogue. Some within the Church have charged that two very important principles that came out of Vatican II have been reinterpreted by the present Vatican administration. These are the principles of subsidiarity and collegiality. Simply stated, in subsidiarity you allow a lower group, to some extent, to settle its own affairs. In the strict sense, collegiality refers to the interaction and collaboration between the Pope and bishops and among the bishops. This spirit of participation, dialogue, communion, and co-responsibility should be lived among all the members of the Church. Some say, and I agree, that these principles are not being fully implemented today in the Church.

As pastor, I also had to be involved in the finances of the parish. This wasn't a particular problem during my tenure because our parishioners were very generous in their Sunday contributions. Because the Franciscans manage the parish for the Archdiocese of Los Angeles, the Order does not subsidize the parish. So the parish is totally reliant on the Sunday collections and donations for services. The money collected goes to the Archdiocese which keeps 10% of it as a tax, but returns the rest to the parish to pay for the services it provides, including the salaries of the parish priests and some rental for the use of the Mission.

†

During some of my years as pastor, I also took on a part-time teaching responsibility at the Archdiocesan St. John's Seminary in Camarillo. St. John's had both a college and a theological seminary. My seminar was in the theological seminary. I was asked by the seminary to teach two classes on Johannine Literature. This includes the Gospel of St. John, the three letters of John, and the Book of Revelation or Apocalypse by John. I wasn't exactly an expert in this area, but I was trained sufficiently in scriptural studies to be able to teach the class. I taught this class for about three or four years.

I enjoyed the experience at St. John's, although it was different from my previous teaching of Franciscan seminarians in Santa Barbara. At St. John's these were young men in their twenties and early thirties who were training to be diocesan priests and not Franciscans or members of another religious order. I also found that by the 1980s life in the seminary had significantly changed. It was more informal and relaxed and had less of the strict discipline that had certainly characterized my seminary years and continued to some extent in our Franciscan theological seminary until it moved to Berkeley.

I was at the same time surprised that in theology and spirituality, some of the students at St. John's were more conservative than in earlier times. Some seminarians reflected a post-Vatican II mentality and the conservatism of the Vatican. They were not necessarily supportive of all of the reforms of Vatican II. Some even expressed a hope of returning to some of the pre-Vatican II traditions and liturgy. Some were very much into the charismatic movement. They questioned some of the new thought. The faculty, however, were well educated in new trends and healthily progressive.

On the other hand, the students weren't passive as my generation of seminarians had been. They were quite outspoken in their views. The Anglo seminarians at that time still represented the majority of students. But today the Latino and Asian students outnumber the Anglos. Also the seminarians are fewer and older than they were in my seminary years.

But even though I differed in certain theological and spiritual views from some of the students, I still enjoyed teaching the class on Johannine Literature. I introduced them to some of the key concepts in understanding not only the writings of St. John, but of the other New Testament writers.

Most of my time was given to explaining the gospel of John in itself and in comparison with the synoptic gospels of Mark, Matthew, and Luke. Modern scholarship has identified three stages in the formation of the gospels: stage one: the historical life of Jesus, 28-30 AD; stage two: the diversified re-interpretation of the traditions of the life and teachings of Jesus in the early Church, 30-70 AD; and stage three: the written gospels of Mark (circa 70 AD), Matthew and Luke (in the 80s AD), and John (in the 90s AD). This means then, that by the time of the writing of the gospels the words and deeds of Jesus had undergone a certain amount of progressive theological interpretation and adaptation in various churches. The result is a theologized life of Jesus that is a mixture of historical facts, oral traditions, and theology.

It's very hard to identify what is historical. One can imagine in those days, without the means of communication that we have today, and without a highly unified Church, the different interpretations of Jesus that abounded. One church or one community of Christians would give their interpretation of Jesus and others would give theirs without necessarily being in contact with one another.

A classic example of these differing interpretations in the early Church is that we have two versions of the "Our Father" prayer as well as two versions of the Sermon on the Mount. Luke has "blessed are the poor" while Matthew has "blessed are the poor in spirit." What exactly did Jesus say? We really don't know. Then you have eight beatitudes attributed to the Sermon on the Mount in Matthew but only four beatitudes in Luke plus four "woes."

Scholars don't agree in their search for the historical Jesus. The extreme liberal position is that the gospels are predominantly theology or interpretations and not history. The other extreme – call it conservative – is that the gospels are in fact totally historical and that what they depict actually occurred in that way. Then you have an in between position or moderate one that suggests a blending of both history and theology, which is the one the majority and I accept.

In the particular case of John, it's not clear whether the author of the Gospel is John, the apostle of Jesus, or the Beloved Disciple, or even another John. What is clear is that "Johannine" expresses the belief of a community of believers differing somewhat from the communities of Mark, Matthew, and Luke. Each of the gospels represent not so much individuals but communities.

What makes John's gospel different from the others is the greater emphasis on the divinity of Jesus not excluding what he says about His humanity. In John, Jesus knows it all. In the other gospels, Jesus appears more like us in our struggles and searching. For example, on the cross, Jesus, according to Matthew and Mark, cries out his anguish: "My God, my God, why have you forsaken me?" He appears to be very weak and vulnerable. But not so in John. In his gospel, Jesus is ready to die and he seems in control of his own crucifixion and death. He has no agony in the garden and on the cross he doesn't cry out. He is divine, the Son of God. However, this is not to say that John denies Jesus' humanity, but only that he privileges the divine more than the other gospels.

There are many more intricacies in teaching about the New Testament and in particular the gospel of John. The important thing that I stressed to my students was that you have to understand the gospels both in historical terms and in literary ones. By historical, I mean that it's important to place them in their historical periods and try to understand the specific historical meanings and not take the gospels literally. There are historical references in the gospels that have to be interpreted in light of their times and not given undue symbolism. Many of the long talks of Jesus in John (for example John 14-17) are expressions of the theology of the Johannine community.

By the same token, we have to understand the literary genre of the gospels and the Bible. There are certain fictional elements in the Bible that should not be taken literally as fundamental Christians do (for example, Genesis 1-11 and the way the world was created, the Adam and Eve story). We look for the meaning of what might be historical or purely symbolic. At least, that's how I taught my classes at both the Franciscan and Diocesan seminaries. But there is heightened diversity of thought among scholars.

What is said about the gospels is true of the whole Bible. The Bible is an inspired divine-human record-in-writing of a people's developing experience of a God who reveals Himself and will in an ongoing history, in various ways, to men and women according to God's loving divine plan, and also in keeping with a people's humanness (their times, needs, questions, limited capacities, culture, self-understanding). It is the word of God expressed in human words. Human persons record their human experience of the divine, the transcendent. Many ongoing traditions are reinterpreted again and again and point toward a fuller future meaning. God's earlier revelation is ever being transmitted and reinterpreted.

†

Pastoral work also involved performing some of the basic duties of a priest, such as ministering the sacraments and being a listening counselor. One such activity that I particularly enjoyed, and still do, involves baptizing infants. The sacrament of baptism symbolizes and effects new life. There's a statement in the Bible made on the occasion of John the Baptist's circumcision. The neighborhood wondered: "what will this child be?" (Luke 1:66). I often think of this passage when performing baptisms. Here's another person, another child, another personality, another individual. How will this child grow? What will he or she become? I'm fascinated with the anticipation of the child becoming an adult and making her or his own contributions to society. I've actually lived long enough now that children that I've baptized, I've also later married, and then baptized their children, and even grandchildren!

Although the ritual of baptism – pouring water on the forehead of those baptized – has not changed over the years since I became a priest, the interpretation of this sacrament has. Earlier, the emphasis was on the individual beginning to share in God's life. This is very true! But today we also celebrate the welcoming of a new member into the Church. The shift is from the individualistic to the communal aspect of baptism. One enters into the Church. Therefore, parents and godparents must receive instruction in the full meaning of baptism since they are to see to the spiritual growth of the child in the community of the Church. Baptism is a wonderful sacrament. It tells of the beginning and continuance of a person's growth with others in the love of God and of neighbor.

Then, of course, we celebrate in funerals the death and new life of one baptized. I've certainly presided over many funerals in my life, including some of my loved ones. Yet, I always link baptisms and funerals. I've said many times in my funeral homilies that death is the way to the perfection of life in Heaven. Instead of looking at death as only the cessation of human life, which is true, we should also view it as the beginning of full life with God. We so live in this world to eventually come into the fully experienced presence of God. So I always stress that funerals are the celebration of both a person's life on earth, whether it be a few years or many, and also the individual's new life with God in Heaven. Life continues. In fact, as has been said, the only way to get to Heaven is to die to a limited life on earth. We leave this world to enter fully into God's world. There's no other way. Loss gives way to gain.

The focus should be positive: an arrival preceded by a departure. If you want to get somewhere, you have to move beyond where you are. If I want to move to Los Angeles from Santa Barbara, I have to say goodbye to Santa Barbara. Every movement forward implies a death or a loss or a leaving behind. Every "hello" to what is new follows upon a "goodbye" to what has been. That's the Christian pattern of death and resurrection. To enter more fully into newness of life, we deny ourselves what is false to our true selves. Jesus says "If you want to save your life, lose it." The whole pattern of dying in order to live, or of giving in order to receive, is paradoxical and characteristic of all of life. This is what I celebrate at a funeral, at Mass, and as a necessary pattern in our spiritual journey.

One of the most meaningful moments in priestly ministry is to be present to those who have to face physical death. I've been asked on panels discussing death and dying "what do you do and say to one who is dying?" The approach has to be different in each case. I have to be very reflective and prayerful. I try to come to know where the person truly is in his/her faith or lack of explicit faith. I have to meet people where they are, as God touches every individual right where he/she is. Each person is in his/her unique place. Some people want to face up to death while others do not.

If I know that the person is aware of his/her condition and desires to discuss it, I tactfully dialogue with the person. If they refuse to face up to the critical situation, I speak to them about what they are willing to discuss. I offer them the sacrament of "the anointing of the sick" with an explanation that you don't have to be actually dying to receive the sacrament. It is not "the last rites" or "extreme unction." God through the sacrament offers the strength, courage, and trust they need. The whole Church prays with and for them, the communal aspect of the sacrament. But again, different approaches for different people.

If they are unconscious and possibly can still hear me, I lean over and speak phrases like "don't be afraid, surrender and accept what you experience, you're not alone, you have nothing to fear. God is with you. Your family is with you. You are loved," and similar phrases.

Ministering to the sick is very trying when the patient is suffering heavy pain. Many find it very difficult to accept their suffering, so much so that they or others may desire to deliberately end their life. The Church is opposed to euthanasia. Life is a gift from God and it's not for us to terminate it. From a practical viewpoint, who is going to decide on the cessation of life? Who is going to pull the plug and when? Who is going to "play God?" If a person is very sick, he or she may say, "Oh, I'd just as soon die." But that statement may not necessarily be expressive of their better judgment. In practice, it's very hard, if not impossible, to come up with norms that would be truly just regarding the deprivation of someone's life.

While euthanasia amounts to terminating life, certain conditions justify the removal of extraordinary life supports. The Church has no problem with this. In fact, we as Franciscans all sign documents in which we say that we don't want the use of extraordinary or disproportionate means to keep us alive. Just let us die. We don't want to be kept alive as a vegetable. But this is different from euthanasia. Here we are just letting nature run its course.

The Church's opposition to euthanasia is for the same reason as it is also opposed to capital punishment. We are pro-life. In past times, the Church permitted the use of capital punishment. Now the Church is officially opposed to it as well as abortion. Besides, is capital punishment truly preventive of crime?

†

One of the highlights while I was pastor was the visit by Queen Elizabeth of England in 1983. She and Prince Philip were visiting President Reagan at his ranch in the Santa Barbara area and the Reagan's arranged for the royal party to visit the Mission. I was informed months in advance due to security precautions. I was interviewed by both American and British Secret Service agents for security reasons. I had to provide them with my background, my social security number, and details about how many people lived in the Mission complex. I also had to show them around the grounds. They wanted to know who else I planned to invite to meet with the Queen. I told them that I was planning on inviting a good number. But they limited me to thirty. I had to provide the Secret Service with the social security numbers of all of them so that they could also be checked out. I was likewise planning on having our choir sing for the visit. The agents wanted the same information about all the choir members. All this detail impressed on me how careful the Secret Service was in plotting out a visit of this kind that would involve not only the royal couple but Nancy Reagan and some other public officials as well.

"Is there anyone in the area that you think might cause any trouble, Father?" they further asked of me.

"Well, there is an emotionally sick person who lives just across from the Mission. While I don't think he would do any harm, he's liable to embarrass us."

They took his name down and checked on him.

The day of the visit, March 1, found me extremely anxious. I was so concerned that everything would go right and that I would make no mistakes. My anxiety was not helped when I awoke to a cold, rainy, and bitter day. It was one of the worst days we've ever had. My anxiety level went up even higher when two or three hours before the scheduled arrival, the electricity went out throughout the Mission. This didn't make dealing with the Secret Service and the British Secret Service, who had also arrived, any easier either. One of our Franciscans got caught in an elevator of the Mission for over an hour. Fortunately, the lights went back on shortly before the royal visit.

There were Secret Service, both American and British, all over the Mission and in the surrounding area. There were even some up in the Mission tower next to the statue of St. Barbara. I could see that they were armed.

Just before the entourage arrived, I had already been instructed by the Secret Service to wait for the Queen at the foot of the Mission. There were people gathered across on the Mission grounds. In fact, I caught sight of that fellow who I thought might cause some trouble, but next to him was someone whom I gathered was an agent. I had also been instructed on the proper protocol upon greeting the Queen. I was not to extend my hand. In fact, I was told that I couldn't touch the Queen at all. The only occasion would be if she extended her hand. The same applied to Prince Philip. I was also to address her as "Your Highness." Upon greeting her, I was to tell her what we were going to do. I had been told that her visit would last no more than half an hour.

The tension mounted as I saw her car and her entourage approach the Mission and drive right up to the Mission stairs where I was. As she stepped out, I, in my Franciscan robe and with an umbrella to protect me and her from the rain, greeted her, "Welcome to the Santa Barbara Mission, Your Highness."

As instructed, I didn't extend my hand and neither did she. Frankly, I was relieved that she didn't since the agents had been pretty firm about not touching the Queen. She was followed by Prince Philip and Nancy Reagan, both of whom also didn't extent their hands in greeting.

"Your Highness, I'm going to give you a tour of the Mission, beginning with the old church and then some of the rest of the Mission, including our archives where we've arranged for an exhibit that I think you'll enjoy."

She didn't say anything but just followed me. There were various other officials, both American and British, who accompanied us on the tour including, of course, many Secret Service agents. We went into the church where, as we entered, our choir began to sing. They had been practicing old Spanish songs that went back to the original ones sung by the Indians under the direction of the padres. They sang beautifully as I took the Queen through the church, explaining various details and the history of the Mission.

On exiting the church through the side entrance, we went into the inner garden where we had arranged for her to plant a tree. We did this quickly because it was raining quite hard. Unfortunately, the tree she planted died a few months later. Someone had selected a tree that does not easily survive in Santa Barbara. I felt like saying later, but I didn't, "Why didn't we get the right type of tree?" We then went down the inner corridor and into our archival library. It has a lot of documentation concerning early British explorations along the California coast, such as the voyage of Sir Francis Drake. Our archivist, Fr. Virgilio Biasiol, O.F.M., arranged a nice display about the British in early California. The Queen and Prince Philip expressed much interest in this and looked carefully at the documents.

As we left the archives library, I introduced them to one of our Franciscan brothers, Brother Oswald Masters, who was a British subject who had lived in the United States for many years. In fact, he was quite old and not in very good health, but we thought the Queen would be delighted to meet him as he would meeting her. She brightened up with a beautiful smile upon meeting Brother Oswald. He, of course, was equally delighted and very much moved.

During our tour, the Queen didn't have any questions. Neither for that matter did Prince Philip who always walked behind her. Nancy Reagan didn't say anything either. I found out later that the Queen on such visits doesn't like to say much so that she won't be quoted. I found her very reticent but most gracious.

Our visit to the archives and the inner garden ended our tour and her visit to the Mission. I escorted her back to the front of the Mission where her motorcade awaited her. She thanked me as did the Prince and Mrs. Reagan. They were gone as fast as they had arrived. I don't think the visit lasted more than thirty minutes. From the Mission, she went to the Santa Barbara courthouse for a big reception with local leaders and dignitaries.

I found her, to my surprise, very down to earth. There was no pomp and ceremony about her. She was a very simple and humble person but elegant. She was like a good friend. She was very much at ease and made me feel likewise.

As soon as the Queen left, I was surrounded by the news media, including reporters from *Time* and *Newsweek*, who wanted to know what the Queen had said to me. But there was nothing I could say. She hadn't really said anything. It was just purely a very short social visit. The reporters were quite disappointed.

Actually, with tongue in cheek, when people ask about my discussion with the Queen, I go on to say that she took me aside and asked if I would consider becoming an Episcopalian priest. I would receive more pay and enjoy having a wife as a companion. I pondered the offer. The pay would certainly go for the upkeep of a wife and family, but I graciously turned down her offer.

I was relieved. The visit had gone according to schedule and there were no mishaps. The next day turned out to be a glorious sunny one in contrast to the dismal weather on the day of the Queen's visit. I have many pictures of the event.

Still, I had been a ball of nerves on this occasion. I was afraid that I would say the wrong thing, and that it would reflect on the Mission, Santa Barbara, the Catholic Church, and even God would be displeased!

†

One of the pleasant events while I was pastor was the celebration of the 200th anniversary of the Santa Barbara Mission in 1986. Of course, we have so many big celebrations at the Mission that it is not easy to properly evaluate them all. However, the 200th anniversary of the Mission was particularly memorable. It symbolized the long presence of the Catholic faith in the Santa Barbara area and in California as a whole beginning with the Spanish friars up to contemporary Franciscans. To commemorate this event, we organized a Mass and a dinner for various civic officials. We also published a very attractive history of the Mission entitled *Mission Santa Barbara: Queen of the Missions – A Bicentennial Celebration*. In the preface, I in particular stressed what I believed to be the importance of this event:

> "For 200 years this 10th of 21 missions has been blessed in serving the needs of differing people in a variety of ways. Like a queen surrounded by a royal court of kneeling hills, praying seas, protecting islands, red-tiled roofs, and trees and flowers of all colors, she has been many things over the years: a wellspring of Christian Indian life, a home for Franciscan friars, a seminary for aspirants to the Franciscan Order, a school for the laity, a parish church, a place of spiritual renewal, and an Archive-Library rich in recorded memories of her noble past. Those who stand before her admire her mingling of Hispanic, Roman, Grecian and Moorish architecture. Those who walk through her doors contemplate her works of art and discover rest and hope in prayer."

The 200th anniversary of the Mission in a way allowed me as pastor to stress the interconnectedness between religion and civic life. The Mission, and this is true for other still active missions in California as well as elsewhere in the Southwest, has both a religious and a civic function. As a church, it provides a variety of religious and spiritual services to its parishioners and visitors. However, because it's also a historical landmark, it functions as a kind of living museum with many community and civic programs. The Mission is a historical site and a big tourist attraction. It is the pride of Santa Barbara. Many people come here for Mass, not so much to go to just another church, but to an historic mission. There's an attraction that people sense about the 21 missions in California. People come here both from other parts of town as well as from out of town. This civic responsibility, rather than taxing me as pastor, only made my job even more enjoyable. I, of course, had already been serving as Director of Public Relations for the Mission for some time and I continued to do so even while I was pastor.

I welcomed the opportunity for a civic celebration because the Mission is more than just a Catholic Church. I'm glad to let people know that religion is not to be separated from the rest of life. Religion cannot be divorced from family, marriage, political, or civic affairs. God cannot be limited to formal religion. Yes, there's a distinction to be made between the sacred and the profane, the divine and the human. However, God is the creator also of the human and has concern for all of life including civic life. I continue to speak of God's presence in all of creation. God's not just present in the Church. God attends every human event such as sports, entertainment, social (at every bar, as I once publicly said). God is highly interested in all that interests us. We are fashioned and formed by all of life. The split between religion and life is another one of those dualisms that we have to transcend, as if here's religion and there is the rest of life. Religion then should celebrate the spiritual significance of every aspect of life. Religion and life are joined not separated. This marriage will not end in divorce.

During my extended tenure as pastor, I also celebrated my 50th anniversary as a Franciscan in 1989. In 1939, prior to my ordination as a priest, I had received the Franciscan habit that marked the beginning of my life as member of the Franciscan Order. So 1989 was my golden jubilee. We had a Mass and many people attended, including some of my family. In the homily, I tried to explain the significance of my life in the light of my religious and priestly life.

I made the point that I became a Franciscan not just for my own personal development, but to be of service to others. This is what I call prepositional living. This means that we are *among* people, to be *with* them and *for* them since we are all sent to them. I felt that God wanted me to open out to all classes of people beyond religious and social differences. I stressed the universality of my role in life. I have to be open not only to God but to all of His creation. I have a quote that I often use that captures some of what I felt on that anniversary: "We are grateful for our past; we live fully the present, and we hope for the fulfillment of the promise of a glorious future."

I am grateful that my life had turned out as it did. The outcome has been a big surprise to me. I never anticipated or had the slightest idea of the future as it has happened. Aside from my own personal satisfaction in being aided in my spiritual growth as a Franciscan, what really surprised me and gave me the most reason to be gratified was that I had never anticipated as many friends as I've had or meeting as many people from so many different walks of life including different religions. My life turned out to be much more extensive, universal, and more inclusive than I had ever expected. I was happy for that. I didn't turn out to be just a Franciscan priest serving only Catholics. I try to be open to everyone while focusing on what unites all people. This inclusive view of life challenges and guides me.

Hopefully, I had grown spiritually over these fifty years. I had studied a lot of theory in the seminary and in my graduate school years so that early on I was much more idealistic in a sense. The more recent years, by contrast, had found me much more realistic. By this I mean that I came to better appreciate the blessing of every moment, the reality of life, no matter what happens. Each concrete experience of life gives me an opportunity for growth, whether it's pleasant or unpleasant, formally religious or secular.

These years and experiences helped me to formulate my belief that the purpose of life is to be heroic in responding in faith to the reality of life. God is in reality. If I want to experience Heaven on earth, I have to embrace life as it is, human and earthly. By accepting all that is, I also accept God. How I respond to my neighbor is how I respond to God. God is not an abstraction. He's in each and every one of us and actively present in all our experiences.

Over the years, I've seen many changes in myself and in my fellow religious and clergy. But, I can still identify the same basic spirituality that I began to live in my early years. There are still the positive and negative poles of spirituality: death and resurrection, self-sacrifice and self-fulfillment, giving and receiving. This remains the same. I have to be able to respond to God in both success and defeat, joy and sorrow, approval and criticism, in virtue and in my foolishness.

I have to move from self-centerness to other-centerness, from loss to gain in life. This is the paradox of life. You find this not only in Jesus' death and resurrection – the poles of negative and positive – but also in the Old Testament. Abraham in faith went out from where he was into an unknown future on God's word. The Hebrews in Exodus moved out from slavery to freedom in a land promised by God. They had to trust in the meaning of it all as they traveled through the desert of life.

We move from our own small self; we undergo a self-emptying and we come into a more expansive world of God where we find self-fulfillment. But this transition isn't easy. We have to deny our false selves so that paradoxically we can affirm our true selves. We are more alive for undergoing a kind of dying to self. That's essential Christian spirituality. For me, it's the basic spirituality of all religions: living the tensions of two poles – negative and positive.

Jesus said "if you want to save your life, you have to lose it." This is the process of self-transformation or conversion from attachment to detachment. By giving, you receive. By dying, you live. The peace prayer of St. Francis really captures the beauty of this paradox:

> O Divine Master, grant that I may
>
> not so much seek to be consoled,
>
> as to console;
>
> To be understood, as to understand;
>
> To be loved, as to love;
>
> For it is in giving that we receive –
>
> It is in pardoning that we are pardoned;
>
> And it is in dying that we are
>
> Born to eternal life.

St. Paul added to this the notion of power in weakness. By giving up your own ambitions, desires, and ego, you free yourself and gain much more in return.

This pattern of life, of course, is not easily lived. When Jesus talked about picking up your cross and following Him, even his own apostles had trouble understanding Him. We have to grow in trusting God's mysterious ways. Some of the leaders of the Jews found it difficult to accept this message, and that is, among other reasons, why the leadership refused Jesus as the Messiah. Some of the Jews expected the Messiah to be almost like a conquering hero who would bring about peace and prosperity. Instead, Jesus promised no such things. He promised that through a radical change of heart there would be peace and salvation. Too many of us want a throne but not a cross.

Of course, I'm not saying that, as a community or as a nation or for the common good, we have to be weak or turn the other cheek. Sometimes as a group, we have to be strong. It was right and just for us to stand up to Hitler. Right is right and wrong is wrong. However, on a personal level, we have to undergo this journey of self-emptying and self-denial and of dealing with the tension between our false self and our true self.

I see this in the lives of Jesus, the saints, and the many people I have counseled. Hearing many thousands of confessions and listening to stories of testing sorrow, I have come to believe that the basic challenge in life is the same for all of us. While allowing for some differences among us, there is a spirituality common to human hearts. I have not only come to understand the universality of spirituality, but I have also seen it lived by persons of all religions and walks of life.

Overall I was pleased with the changes in the Church during those fifty years. I hope that this healthy evolution will continue into the future. My own life as a Franciscan has mirrored these changes. In 1989 I was not the same Virgil Cordano that I was in 1939. At the beginning of my novitiate, I didn't have the more integrated views of life with God and others that I developed later. In 1939 the stress on spirituality in the Church was too much on the negative and not enough on the positive, and I didn't have the ecumenical perspective and appreciation of other faiths that I would have later. My life wasn't as unified. I didn't have an overall paradigm to cover all situations. But this came through new experiences, study, and continuing reflection and reinterpretation of earlier experiences.

Gradually I became much happier and content with my life. During the earlier years there had been a sadness and even a depression in my life. I was dealing with the unknown and the old discipline. There wasn't much personal satisfaction. It was just dutifulness. Moreover, I had no assurances that it was all going to turn out well. You just trusted in blind faith. But then over the years, I became more confident, relaxed, and assured. I developed a sense of freedom that I could tolerate all sorts of situations. It doesn't have to be this way or that way. I became more carefree in a healthy way. I accepted things that were not in keeping with an earlier idealized version of life. Everything now had a meaning.

On that anniversary, I thought very much about my mother. She was the greatest influence in my life. I've always been grateful to her. I also thought of my dad, even though I hadn't really known him well. I was also thankful for my dear brothers as well as for the many friends I had made in those fifty years.

I have no regrets over my choice of a Franciscan life and the absence of marriage and family. What in the beginning was viewed as very sacrificial turned out to be a blessing. I'm supportive of marriage and family, but my vowed celibate life has given me a certain freedom to be part of an ever-expanding world. I have the wonderful experience of being a member of an ever-growing family. I am at home in many families. Now I can even joke about not being married. When I'm asked, "Why didn't your marry?" I answer, "Why marry one and disappoint fifty?" I do not believe that my calling to religious priesthood is superior to the vocation of the laity. In many ways their lives are more sacrificial and demanding than mine.

Above all, I was most grateful for being a member of many families: original home, the Church, the Franciscan brotherhood, the clergy, friends in Santa Barbara and elsewhere. My personal faith, a gift from God, sustained and comforted me during difficult times, as did the love and care of companions along the way. The ideals of St. Francis ever challenged me, although I felt that I had a long way to go in living those ideals. I learned through trial and error to trust in the many surprising events in my life, especially those that at first were painful but eventually came to be blessings.

The one thing that surprised me most after fifty years, and that I found difficult to adjust to, was my popularity as a kind of celebrity and the praise heaped upon me. This includes the recent effort to name an endowed Chair in Catholic Studies at UCSB after me. It's not easy for me, and I think for most people, to take praise and adulation. I've never felt comfortable with it. It seems to be in contrast with the so-called "hidden life" that I was supposed to follow as a Franciscan. Before, as it were, I was known only to God. On the other hand, I've accepted my popularity. I see myself as one who serves God's purposes. My theology and spirituality guide me in this understanding of myself. Jesus said, "You are the light of the world. Let your light shine before others." I also recognized that great people, such as St. Francis, got a lot of things done, despite or perhaps because of, the attention given to them.

We can be truly humble and justifiably proud if we acknowledge that by the grace of God we can do great things. God gets things done through us. Greatness is more God's gift than our achievements. Happiness and peace are before all else "inside jobs." We are who we are in God's sight. Everyone can be great and successful before God. So, I like to say we should be humbly proud and proudly humble. I long to know that everyone's dignity and worth are acknowledged. We should celebrate the person and life of all persons and not just of a few. God delights and rejoices in us (Isaiah 62, 4-5).

At my golden jubilee, some people talked about me as a role model. I'm also emotionally uncomfortable with this. I don't see myself as a role model. Role models can be crutches for some. The important thing is not to try to be like others but to be true to one's true self. Yes, we can be inspired by the goodness and even heroism of others. We have certain ideals in common but differ in the realization of these ideals. We have to find inspiration from within ourselves and let that shine before others. We can be inspired by others to achieve our own greatness. The idea of role models, at least for me, conjures up sameness or cloning each other, not physically, but symbolically. I'm more interested in the specialness of each individual and what each one of us shares with others. Others inspire us to be who we truly are.

I added to the celebration of my Jubilee by traveling to Italy to enjoy the company of my many relatives living in and near Genoa. The high point was the celebration of Mass in the very church where my mother and father were baptized, followed by a banquet of the best in Genoese cuisine. The very joyous dinner lasted almost five hours. The Italians are at their best around a table of much food and drink. I also enjoyed the hospitality of some of the individual families. I am the only priest in this large clan and they proudly expressed their appreciation of having one of their own lead them in worship at God's table and Italian jubilation around the family table.

†

One of the outreach programs that I supported as Guardian and then pastor was the Marriage Encounter movement. Vatican II called for the renewal of all walks of life including marriage, family, and the vital role of the laity. After the theological seminary moved up to Berkeley in 1968, we had to decide what to do with all these classrooms and apartments on the grounds of the Mission. We decided to use the space, in part, for marriage encounters and retreats of all kinds.

For a number of years, including while I was Guardian and pastor, we hosted many couples each weekend, maybe more than thirty or forty. It was to facilitate a new depth of communication, understanding, and honest oneness between husband and wife. They had time together as a group, time alone as husband or wife, and time together as the couple they were. They would first all meet together with two married couples and a priest as facilitator and speakers. Then they were given certain questions to be answered in a letter to one's spouse. After their individual letters were written, the couple would come together and discuss their responses. "Surprise! Surprise! So that's what goes on deep within you!" Then all would come together with the facilitators. What was hidden became revealed.

I thought that the marriage encounters were very effective and helped couples deal with their challenges in marriage and growth or lack thereof over the years. But it went beyond just the emotional and psychological. The encounters also encouraged spiritual growth and the experiencing of the spirituality of their union. Another instance of the blending of the grace of God and all that is human.

For a number of years, the encounters were very popular. They were taking place all across the country. Each year a national convention was held. I went to one of them and was quite impressed. More recently in the last twenty years or so, the popularity of marriage encounters has dropped off. I can't fully explain the reason. It's possible that this breakthrough in their lives now called for a spirituality inclusive of all of life and not just marriage.

At the same time as marriage encounters, retreats of all kinds blossomed in the Church. I initiated, for example, a program of renewal for priests who would come to the Mission for about nine weeks. I directed this renewal for nearly twenty years with the help of many others. Today, retreat work is very popular and there are all sorts. All walks of life, all human groups can benefit from time for prayer and reflection. To be truly and wisely active we have to be reflective and contemplative.

This new interest in retreats and spirituality in the 1980s and into the 1990s led me in 1997 to create a new institute for the laity. I, with the help and support of a committee of lay persons, established what is called the Institute for Adult Spirituality. The goals of the Institute are to provide busy Christians with inspiration and intellectual stimulation to foster a deeper lived faith, to promote informed dialogue within the Christian community, to link the traditions of the Catholic Church with contemporary life. There are four lectures given in September-October and also in January-February, usually on a Monday evening for two hours with time for discussion and socializing. I have been pleasantly surprised by the large number of people (usually over a hundred per session) who attend these meetings. Their minds hunger and thirst for both the truth of God's message and also deeper experiencing of God's love.

I came to believe that a major, if not the main need of the Church today, was and is the theological and spiritual education and formation of the Catholic laity, especially with the decline in members of the clergy. This is even more important in the wake of the recent sex scandals among priests that has harmed the credibility of the Church. As a result, I think that God is telling us that we need to better equip our lay people with the theological and spiritual tools that they need as they assume or should assume a greater role and voice in the life of the Church.

The themes of these classes have been prayer, ministry, personal relationships, interfaith dialogue, social justice, etc. Some of them, especially those dealing with personal spirituality, have been highly steeped in psychology. We've also focused on major spiritual figures and mystics such as Teilhard de Chardin and Thomas Merton. The themes and presentations have all been decided and arranged by lay people themselves. It hasn't always been easy to agree on topics, but the process of discussion and reaching a consensus has been necessary and important.

Spirituality is the actualization of living on a day to day basis of the Christian message. It is the lived religious faith – the spiritual meaning of all human experience. More is needed than just understanding what God reveals, what the Church says, what the Bible says. We have to understand and accept ourselves as the recipients of God's word. God meets us where we are. So where are we? Without self-understanding and self-acceptance, God is not heard truly and fully. So it's not only a question of being present to God, we have to present to ourselves the depths of our persons, where God is active. Most of the literature on spirituality today correctly stresses facing up to what stirs deep within our hearts. Grace builds on human nature. What is objective is subjectively welcomed within the heart of the recipient. There is a wonderful Latin saying that translated says: "Whatever is received is received according to the mode of the recipient." There is no such thing for us as pure and total objectivity, because the infinite grandeur of God is channeled through the limited mind of an individual or community. We must give consideration to our cultural and historical times.

In the Church of recent times, aided and prompted by Vatican II, there has been what Karl Rahner calls "a turn toward the subjective," or, we can speak of a movement from classicism to historical consciousness. According to John Courtney Murray, classicism designates a view of truth that holds that objective truth, precisely because it is objective, exists "already out there now," apart from its possession by anyone, apart from history and formulated in propositions that are verbally immutable. In contrast, historical consciousness (while still holding to the nature of objective truth) is especially concerned with the possession of truth, with human affirmation of truth, an understanding that is both circumstantial and subjective. There is changing, historical understanding of the truth to be considered in the development of doctrine in the Church. As Raymond Brown writes "every formulation that we accept as part of the contents of our faith is the product of theological reflection."

Of course, the Vatican evaluates new expressions of revelation according to what it believes to be the truth. Those who desire new expressions of the truth and more pluralism call attention to the fact that Church views and doctrines themselves have evolved over the years. Different periods have called for new understandings and new ways of formulating truth. Jesus, Himself, in His time was what we could call a revisionist. He advocated certain changes in the thought and practice of the Jewish religion. He was opposed on theological grounds because He preached a radically new message. Jesus was a threat to the establishment of His time. Other later noted Catholic theologians in their time faced much criticism and even censorship, such as St. Thomas Aquinas and, in the twentieth century, Teilhard de Chardin and Charles Curran. Change always poses a threat. It can be interpreted as opposition to so-called "everlasting eternal truths."

Change is inevitable and that is how the Church itself has evolved. You just can't keep repeating the same things in the same way. If that's the case, then we still would be practicing Jews. There would be no need for Jesus. The Bible itself has to always be reinterpreted. The interpretation of God's will changes in different historical periods although still guided by Him. In the Bible, there is the then culturally limited view of God. The Old Testament or the Hebrew Bible, for example, and to a lesser degree the New Testament also emphasizes the dominance of God and His punishment of us. There's not sufficient attention given to the exercise of free will among humans. For example, God doesn't punish us. We punish ourselves. Spirituality and theology, itself, have to always evolve in keeping with historical and cultural circumstances. But the question remains: what is true development of revelation and Church practices?

One example of some of the more recent themes we've stressed in our Institute concerns this whole question of change itself. What is true change? What is false change? There is a risk in moving beyond what has been and is now on to new thoughts and ways. However, as Cardinal John Henry Newman of England wrote "to live is to change and to be perfect is to have changed often." But this is painful. One has to give up a certain amount of security in accepting change. This is part of a conversion process. To grow spiritually and enter into a newer more fulfilling relationship with God, you have to move from where you've been and enter into a new stage. That's not easy and yet it is vital if there is to be theological and spiritual growth.

Our sessions in spirituality and theology have grown in numbers over the years and in this growth, two interesting aspects are evident. It is clear that we're not reaching enough younger Catholics in their 20s and 30s. In recent times many are leaving the Church or are not very active members. They are also more skeptical of Church authority and less willing to accept all of the Church's directions, for example, in issues such as birth control and abortion. In my youth, authority was accepted and more readily listened to, but that's no longer true. This has only been exacerbated by the loss of confidence in the way authority has been exercised by the hierarchy in the recent sexual scandals.

While many of the younger generation are leaving the Church, some recent studies indicate that maybe a good number eventually return to the Church as they get older and have their own families. How is the Church to reach out to younger Catholics? What alienates them from the Church and what will bring them back? I have not come to know the answers to these questions.

The other interesting observation about our Institute is that while they are largely attended by middle-aged and older Catholics, this does not necessarily mean that they largely represent a more conservative and traditional element. In fact, this age group leans more toward desiring change. Some of the old timers are quite liberal. They criticize the authoritarianism in the Church and have been quite outspoken, not only regarding sexual issues, but maybe more so regarding the process of decision-making in the Church. In Santa Barbara, some Catholics have formed their own chapter of Voice of the Faithful, similar to the organization in Boston that spearheaded calling to task the hierarchy for covering up the extent of the child abuses committed by priests in that area. The local Voice of the Faithful wishes to provide a prayerful voice, attentive to the Spirit through which the faithful can actively participate in what the Church is about. Their goals are: to support those who have been abused, to support priests of integrity, and to shape structural change within the Church. They desire more dialogue between clergy and laity. What has been fascinating and worthwhile is to observe this tension as we desire to create a Church that is more relevant today.

Another instance of initiative on the part of the laity has been the existence for twenty-five years of the Word and Life Study Fellowship, originally known as Word and Life Catholic Bible Study. I have been supportive of it as have other clergy. After twenty-one years of studying the scriptures, this lay group began to study the whole of developing Catholic Christian tradition. They view themselves as "a sacred dwelling place for all those who hunger and thirst for the experience of a personal God, active and present in the ordinary of everyday life." Among their topics have been an understanding of Jesus' humanity and divinity, the way in which evolution and science have informed our understanding of creation, incarnation, and redemption. Additional themes have included the way psychology and literature inform our understanding of Jesus and faith, the sexual abuse crisis in the Church, and the role of women and the feminine in the world and in the Church. Presently seventy or more register for every study.

Not only have the religious and the laity answered the call of Vatican II to renewal, the clergy have initiated renewal programs. Prompted by Father Alan McCoy, OFM (former Provincial of the Franciscans on the West Coast), I established and directed a program for the updating of priests, Franciscans to begin with and others later, here at Mission Santa Barbara. There was no earlier such program to guide us. The main professors were Fr. Alan, Anne Dunn, a member of the Immaculate Heart Community, and Professor Walter Capps of UCSB's Department of Religious Studies, and myself. I brought the priests up-to-date in recent Biblical Studies; Anne Dunn in Systematic Theology; Fr. McCoy in Moral Theology and Canon Law and Spirituality; and Walter Capps in what was stirring in theological circles outside of Catholicism.

In addition, we had visiting professors from UCSB and other academic institutions. Through a certain amount of experimentation, we offered a fairly helpful program. It was not easy for some priests, and then later brothers, to accept a theology different from what they were taught in their seminary years. A small number accused us of being heretical and even went so far as to write to the Chancery office of Los Angeles. I had to explain to the Archbishop that we were not teaching any heresy.

The program was of nine weeks duration and offered twice a year. It continued for twenty plus years from the early 1970s to the early 1990s. However, with dwindling numbers we terminated the program. Hopefully, we aided priests and brothers personally and in their ministries.

During a month in the summer, we offered a renewal program for religious sisters – again an integration of theology and spirituality.

These many new programs at Mission Santa Barbara, following the movement of the theological seminary to Berkeley, were welcomed by me. I found all of them very meaningful and also helpful in my own spiritual journey.

†

As pastor, I also enjoyed other particular activities that I initiated or participated in. For example, a delight for me was to celebrate Mass most Sundays for children. I tried as best I could to adjust the liturgy to what was appealing to them. The dialogue homily was always the highlight. I'd ask questions and listen to their insightful answers. Some were very humorous. On one occasion we talked about Heaven. "What will you most enjoy in Heaven?" I asked. Besides the answers I might expect, a very serious-looking young girl responded: "I won't have to go to church on Sunday." All laughed but not she. In response, I assured her "you won't have to sit in a church when you go to Heaven. You'll be running about in the whole world." The children enjoyed our time together as did the accompanying parents. The Friars' Chapel was used for these children's Masses and it was packed every Sunday.

Another interesting event involved Harley-Davidson motorcycle riders. In 1992 a person asked if I would annually bless his and other's Harleys. It was a practice in his former town in the Midwest. I agreed and we now have a tradition to this day. I offer a prayer for all and then bless each rider. On one occasion a young woman Harley rider asked to have her picture taken with me and her Harley. When I asked why? She responded "my mother doesn't approve of me riding a Harley and the picture of you blessing me might win her over." I bless about 300 riders annually.

†

There's no question but that the most painful experience during my years at the Mission was the sex scandal that enveloped St. Anthony's seminary in the early 1990s. This came as a huge blow to me, the Franciscan community, and to our lay Catholics. It was shocking and, at the time, affected our standing and credibility among our people. Little did I know then that this would only be one of even more extensive cases of sexual abuse throughout the Church in the United States.

Eleven Franciscans (ten priests and one brother) who taught at the seminary, were accused by ex-seminarians of having sexually abused them from as early as 1969 to the close of the seminary in 1987. During this time, there were about 44 Franciscans associated with the seminary. Actually, some of the charges also came from some who had been non-seminarian members of the Boys' Choir under the direction of a Franciscan in residence at the seminary.

The seminary closed in 1987 not due to the sex scandals, which had not yet broken out, but because we couldn't economically sustain the minor seminary anymore. The first accusation of sexual abuse occurred in 1989 followed by another in 1992. After the second one, other accusations followed. By then, the ex-seminarians and choir boys were now adults. The media here in Santa Barbara and elsewhere as well, of course, zeroed in on the scandal and widely publicized it.

Of the eleven accused Franciscans, two were actually tried in a criminal court because the charges of abuse were leveled still within the statue of limitations that, at the time, unlike today, had a shorter period. These two, whom I knew quite well, were tried and convicted. Both served some time in jail. One of them later tragically committed suicide.

How could this have happened? How could priests and a brother who had taken vows of celibacy and, more importantly, who were responsible for the education and care of young teenage boys turn around and sexually abuse them in the most sordid of ways, as the investigations revealed. How was this possible?

I don't know all of the answers. I was not personally aware of any of these incidents, even though I lived in the Mission complex all of this time. St. Anthony's Seminary where the abuses took place is physically set off from the rest of the Mission area, and I did not teach there. The Theological Seminary, where I was teaching, was housed at the Mission and not at St. Anthony's. I was not aware of any abuses since I lived and taught at the Mission. Nor, as far as I know, did other Franciscans not involved in the abuses know that this misbehavior was going on.

But our not knowing about these abuses doesn't answer the question of how all of this could have occurred.

The only thing I can say about this is that for all the Franciscans throughout our West Coast province, the revelations were shocking. They were unthinkable. We're all sinners and capable of sinning, but that this would happen right here at St. Anthony's where many of us had gone to school, and that it involved so many Franciscans, and that the rest of us didn't know about what was happening, is still a big mystery. Trying to understand this and the more current sex scandals within the Church, I try to place all this in a broader context.

What may help in better understanding the pedophile issue is to recall that in earlier days possibly the majority of seminarians entered the seminary after elementary school, about thirteen or fourteen years of age. They knew little about their own sexuality. I cannot recall any in-depth instruction on sexuality, except in the area of morality, what sexual sins to avoid. A small number of the students would be latent pedophiles and homosexuals, while the majority would be heterosexual. The issue of sexual orientation and feelings was not openly discussed. The individual student was alone in dealing with his sexual feelings. His life was very much sheltered from contacts with those outside the seminary.

Once ordained, he mixed freely with women and men of all ages. He became aware of his sexual orientation and his feelings and perhaps in most cases he sought no guidance. He discovered that he could not control his sexual urgings. He would fail now and then and struggle alone. He found that he was attracted to young children especially young boys; or he discovered his latent tendency toward homosexuality. If he taught in a seminary, or even if he was assigned to a parish, he was in contact with young boys. This became an occasion of sin.

This is especially the case in a minor seminary such as St. Anthony's. Everyone is living together. The boys as seminarians are practically members of the Franciscan family. The boys live in dormitories and the priests in their own rooms, and they're mingling with each other all of the time. I can see where gradually they would begin to feel this attraction, become friends, and then things begin to happen – unfortunate things.

I think too that beginning in the 1960s with the greater freedom in the Church as a result of Vatican II, we begin to have less separation between teachers and students. I certainly witnessed that in supervising the advanced theological students at that time. There was a tendency among some of the directors to encourage the Franciscans to get closer to the seminarians, to develop more of a family spirit, to be more father and big brother figures. Ordinarily, this family spirit is not necessarily a bad idea. However, problems began because these conditions only made it easier for some Franciscans to give expressions to their weaknesses.

As I look back at these incidents, I am proud of the way our Franciscan leadership responded shortly after the accusations were made. The friars initiated an investigation. Unlike some of the bishops more recently who tried to hide these cases under the rug, we set up a Board of Inquiry. This was set up by our Provincial Father Joseph Chinnici, O.F.M. The board consisted of five lay people and one Franciscan. One of the members was the father of one of the victims at St. Anthony's. Two were professional psychologists trained in sexual abuse, while the others had experiences working on this issue from a legal, family counseling, or religious background.

The board attempted to contact all those who had been seminarians at St. Anthony's from 1964 to 1987 to see if they had been abused or knew of others who had been abused. It, of course, examined the accusations that had already been made. It also held confidential hearings. However, before the Board of Inquiry began to function, we Franciscans listened to the sorrowful complaints of the parents of the abused young men and also others who were very angry at the friars, understandably so. This was a very painful experience. Our Provincial, and we friars, heard all of their complaints and their strong feelings. Fr. Joseph was very patient and promised that the Board of Inquiry would look carefully into all of the charges and that we would try to make some sort of recompense including offering therapy to the victims. We offered counsel to both the ex-seminarians and their parents. Also, we answered questions at a public meeting in the Community Center of Goleta, adjacent to Santa Barbara, with all the media present.

But all of this was very upsetting and filled with emotions. I'll never forget the parents anger. Some of this was justified, but the whole Franciscan Order is not to be blamed. When you belong to an organization, you can't be responsible for all that others do. You can't blame the whole Order or the entire Catholic Church. It's just like you can't blame the whole country because we have murders in our society. We didn't tolerate sexual abuse; we didn't know about it. When we found out, we right away tried to do the best we could, especially by setting up the Board of Inquiry. But nothing we could do satisfied some of the parents. They accused the Provincial of not doing enough. But what more can you do? We can't undo sin. We can't undo the past. So it was very, very painful.

The issues of who knew of these abuses and when did they know about them were key questions raised by parents and others. The fact of the matter is that the Franciscan leadership did not know it was going on. The rest of us in the Mission complex also were totally in the dark. I would see some of these priests who would come over to the Mission, and we were friends. I detected nothing that would lead me to believe that such abuses were occurring. The abused students at the time, of course, must have been intimidated and even threatened about not revealing what was going on. They were also ashamed to tell anyone. They didn't say anything until they were much older. Nothing was done then because it wasn't known to us. As soon as it was known, we tried to do the right thing.

The scandal was hard on all of us. Many of my lay friends offered sympathy for me as if someone in my family had died. These were both Catholics and non-Catholic friends. They knew how painful this was for us. Of course, we as Franciscans were not the ones who needed sympathy. We weren't the victims. It was the ex-seminarians and choir boys and their parents that needed our sympathy and support. But we Franciscans suffered embarrassment and sorrow for the victims and the perpetrators.

Needless to say, our parishioners at the Mission church were shocked. Everyone was stunned and surprised. The scandal cast a tremendous pale over the Franciscans. Morale hit rock bottom. We as friars held a number of sessions on how to deal with the crisis. Our superiors, including the Provincial, were very honest with us and kept us informed of what they were doing about this issue. We were supportive of one another, not in order to hide anything, but in order to reinforce our commitment to the Order and to the principles that we upheld that did not include condoning sexual abuse. We engaged in a form of communal crying.

Public reaction in Santa Barbara and elsewhere was very critical, as should be expected, of the Church. This criticism and condemnation came especially from those – both Catholic and non-Catholic – who went on beyond the issue of sexual abuse and pedophilia to criticize and condemn the Church's stand on sexuality across the board. What they didn't understand, and the same is true of the more recent scandals, is that these priests who became pedophiles or who abused teenage boys probably would have done the same outside of the priesthood. This is not an excuse, but it is to put things in a larger perspective. What is the best explanation of the addiction of pedophilia? It is present in all walks of life. Many studies reveal that most cases of sexual abuse of minors occur in family life. As a result of our awareness of these many instances of sexual abuse, sexual matters are today more openly discussed than they were in times past.

The cases of the two priests who faced criminal charges and were tried here in Santa Barbara, of course, received much media and public attention. I knew both of them very well. Their names are public due to their trials. It's painful enough for me to recount their trials without having to mention them by names. It's not a cover-up since anyone can find out who they are.

The trials were an ordeal for everyone – the accused priests and even more for the victims who testified and for their parents who had to sit and listen to all of these horrible accusations. In the case of one of the

Franciscans, he, himself, I was told had been abused as a young boy. So he was handicapped to begin with. When you look at the past histories of many sex abusers, you often come to some understanding psychologically of why they did what they did.

I attended the trial of one of the priests. It was sad to see him brought in dressed in his prisoner suit and with his hands and feet shackled. The worst thing about his case was that as part of his psychological examination while in jail awaiting trial, he was asked to write a diary. He was asked to describe all of his sexual fantasies regarding young boys. Unfortunately, that diary was used against him. I was surprised that it wasn't kept confidential. But it wasn't. The judge said he had never read a diary where the author was so deeply afflicted by his sexual orientation and desires.

I attended the trial because I knew the priest and as a way of supporting him not for what he did, but as a fellow human being and as a fellow Franciscan. The Order also supported him in this way. He was wrong and had committed a crime, but he was still a member of our community and we felt that we just couldn't throw him out in the cold. After all, he had nothing. He had no money to hire an attorney. So we hired one for him.

But I also attended the trial as a way of supporting the abused ex-seminarians, choir boys, and their parents. One of these families had two boys who had been abused by this priest. I visited with them. It was painful for them and for me. The victims and their parents, understandably, were very bitter. In fact, this was equally true of the other victims and their parents. Some of them left the Church and the Catholic faith.

Perhaps the best thing that came out of this tragedy was the establishment of the Board of Inquiry that made a very through investigation of the charges. The report was issued in 1993 and I attended the news conference where its findings were reported. It confirmed that abuses had taken place at St. Anthony's, but did not specifically charge particular priests. In fact, some of these Franciscans declared their innocence.

The report also did not note the names of the accused. To do so would damage their future as priests. I don't believe that any of the priests were interviewed by the Board. For the same reason, the names of the victims also were not mentioned.

The Board recommended a variety of mitigations. It called for the Order to provide at its expense psychological therapy for the victims. It also recommended new and tighter entrance procedures for those who wanted to enter the Order. These would include looking into their sexual orientations and into their personal backgrounds. As for the priests, themselves, the Board recommended that they undergo therapy and that while doing so they not be re-located where they might be tempted to abuse again. The belief of some was that they could be aided and even cured of their sexual deviance by therapy. There was no recommendation that they be laicized or stripped of their priesthood. These were hard decisions. We were dealing with human beings and we stressed forgiveness and reconciliation.

One of the recommendations that the Board made was that a permanent board of inquiry on future allegations against Franciscans be established. This was accepted by our Provincial and has been operating for over ten years. It is called the Independent Response Team and is comprised predominantly of lay people.

We didn't hide from the issues nor tried to stonewall them as some bishops have recently tried to do. All of this was a trying time for us, but we, as best we could at the time, attempted to address the problem and to institute reforms. We can't be accused of doing nothing.

The issue of the Board and of the Order not making public the names of the Franciscans other than the two who faced criminal charges was, of course, very controversial. Many of the parents reacted very harshly to this. They felt that their names should have been made public. Many of them still do. This was a difficult issue.

The majority of these priests were treated and for the most part they are serving in our monasteries or convalescent homes where they don't have access to children or teenagers. As far as I know, there have been no further accusations against most of them.

However, one exception has recently surfaced. After one of the Franciscans was charged with abuse at St. Anthony's in the early 1990s, a settlement was made with the victim, but, at the same time, the priest was exonerated on the grounds that the charges were never substantiated. As a result, he was cleared to resume his ministry, this time in a parish. However, more recently, there have been other accusations against him.

The financial settlements that were originally made in the case of this one priest were not the only one. Several other settlements also were made to compensate some of the other victims at St. Anthony's.

Besides the establishment of a permanent Independent Response Team, the Order also adopted some of the other proposed changes such as instituting sexual education for Franciscans. I think that since then the education of Franciscans on matters of sexuality has improved. After the report, we had to listen to many lectures on sexuality. We also improved our screening of candidates for the seminary. What also has helped is that we no longer recruit young boys for the minor seminary. In fact, we no longer have minor seminaries such as St. Anthony's. We also don't have any more college education. We just have a novitiate and a Franciscan School of Theology, a member of the Graduate Theological Union. Many who apply now are beyond their college years and, in some cases, even older. Presently, in our seminaries, one's sexual orientation is openly dealt with.

However, the fundamental problem still remains. It's difficult to make an assessment of someone's sexual orientation or what might happen in the future. Consequently, it's not foolproof. But we're doing the best we can. One way is by providing better sex education before ordination and better informed discussion on who is to be ordained and who should not. Today we give consideration to not only sexual morality, but also to the psychological and spiritual aspects of sexuality. Is this person mature enough to choose freely and live successfully a Franciscan and priestly life?

Some lay people at the time further criticized Cardinal Roger Mahony for not intervening in the scandal. But, the fact of the matter is that it was not in his jurisdiction. It was that of the Franciscan Order. It was our problem not the Cardinal's. He only dealt with cases of diocesan priests. Although St. Anthony's was in the Archdiocese of Los Angeles, it was juridically under the Franciscan Order. The Cardinal was sympathetic to our crisis and our Provincial kept him informed of the issues and state of the investigation, but he really couldn't do anything about it. We are all members of the same Church and we consider ourselves to be one family, but there are still separate jurisdictions within the Church.

The scandal, of course, also raised the issue of celibacy in the priesthood. Pedophilia and homosexuality are separate issues. Many today – and I agree – believe that celibacy should be optional. That's an issue still being discussed given the larger and more recent sexual scandals in the Church that broke out in 2002. Some contend that it's celibacy that is at the root cause of these abuses. They believe that if priests would be allowed to marry they wouldn't have to take out their sexual urges on young boys and, in some cases, on young women. I think the causes of these sexual abuses are more complicated and, in many cases, have to do with the particular sexual orientation of some of the abusers. However, having said that, I am one who does believe that celibacy should be optional.

We have to remember that celibacy is not something that Jesus insisted upon for his disciples. He invited those who felt called to serve Him irrespective of their marital status. In fact, many of the early priests were married with families. It was not until the 12th century that celibacy became a condition for the priesthood. Celibacy became obligatory because the Church wanted its priests to be heroic by giving up more than the average Catholic layperson. Not marrying was evidence of a great self-sacrifice. But I think this was wrong. Why is giving up sex more heroic than being married? One could argue just the reverse. Moreover, why focus on sexuality alone as heroic? In my opinion, the Church has been too fixated on the negative connotation of sexuality rather than the positive spiritual aspects of it.

Others also argue, and I don't disagree, that another key motivation for the Church's insistence on celibacy was one of power. Married priests would have to share their resources and time with their family as well as their inheritance. By not allowing priests to marry, the Church, in a sense, monopolized all of these without having to share them with the families of priests. So there's a material issue involved as well in celibacy.

In my opinion, we should consider optional celibacy. This would work by allowing diocesan priests the option of taking the vow of celibacy or not. A diocesan priest would be able to make the choice to be a non-married or a married priest. This is a logical progression from the fact that today we have married deacons who perform many functions formerly restricted to priests. These married deacons might be allowed to become priests. Moreover, optional celibacy would further help to deal with the shortage of vocations. There are a number of men who would make excellent priests if they could marry. Right now, it's celibacy that keeps some young men from entering the priesthood.

However, optional celibacy would not work with those of us who are members of a religious order such as the Franciscans. You can't be a full-fledged member of the Franciscan community and be married. In such religious orders celibacy is not optional. A member of such orders takes the three vows of poverty, chastity, and obedience, as do women religious.

With respect to future vocations, there is also the controversial issue of the ordination of women. The Vatican has taken a very strong stand against the ordination of women based on biblical authority and tradition. However, the Catholic Theological Society of America, in its 1997 meeting, stated that there are serious doubts that the Church lacks the authority to ordain women to the priesthood. I agree with this assessment. Further study, discussion, and prayer are necessary if the Church is to be guided by the Spirit on this issue.

The scandal at St. Anthony's put a great deal of pressure on all of us as Franciscans. At first I was too shy or even afraid to address the scandal myself. I didn't speak about it in my homilies until much later. In retrospect,

I should have because it was on everyone's mind. I think that we were just too embarrassed to do so. But we should have put our feelings last and instead thought of the victims who had suffered these abuses. We now have another opportunity with the wider abuse scandals rocking the Church. Recently, I and many others have spoken out publicly condemning such acts and calling for reforms within the Church to prevent future abuses.

There's no question but that the St. Anthony's scandal was one of the low-points in my career as a Franciscan. That now has been superceded by the faulty way some bishops have dealt with the larger scandals today. However, I am strengthened by my faith. Although I welcome my membership in the institutionalized Church, it is my faith in God active in the Church that above all else sustains me. I've always known that there's a human element and sinfulness in the Church. We're all sinners. This doesn't excuse abuses and crimes committed even by priests. It just puts things into perspective. But the scandal here in Santa Barbara in a way also made me focus even more on my main reason for belonging to the Church. It's the tradition of spirituality and the heroism of the saints canonized and noncanonized. It's the mystics and saints down through the years. I can live up to noble ideals. To live in imitation of Christ and to serve others is why I became a priest. I still believe in that and this belief keeps me going, even through the darkness that engulfed us in the early 1990s and today.

With regards to the more current sexual scandals in the Church, I have given recent talks at both the Institute for Adult Spirituality and the Word and Life Study Fellowship in Santa Barbara. In these talks, I offered brief histories of both sexuality and authority in our Catholic tradition. I boldly made the statement that the seeds of the present flowering of the crisis were planted in scriptural and ecclesiastical ground many years ago. We can better understand these present scandals in the Church when we look into the history, not only of sexuality, but also of the way a celibate male clergy exercised authority in sexual and other issues. I outlined the view of sexuality found in the Hebrew Bible, the Christian Bible, and ongoing Christian tradition down to present times. Then I attempted to give a brief history of the exercise of authority by the Vatican and consequently local dioceses and churches. I ended with a listing of many criticisms and calls for change heard in the Church today. These criticisms include the following:

- A clerical culture of privilege and power.
- Arrogance of unchecked authority that acts independently of laity.
- A celibate, male clergy that marginalizes the laity, and in a special way lay and religious women.
- A clericalism based on the assumption that by virtue of ordination the clergy are spiritually and morally superior to the laity.
- Lack of trust in and consultation with the laity on the part of the Vatican, bishops, and priests, resulting in a lack of trust in leadership on the part of the laity.
- Tension between Church Canon Law and civil authority and law.
- A need for collegiality, shared decision making in the diocese and parish, shared authority, consultation, accountability, transparency, visibility, openness, sensitivity.

If the scandal at St. Anthony's represented my most painful experiences as a priest up to that point, the more recent sexual scandals throughout the Church in the United States, in turn, is the lowest point in my clerical life. I know that readers will want me to say more, but the fact of the matter is that I can't due to current litigation and future potential litigation against my Order. I am pained by these scandals, and I pray for the victims and their families. I know and pray that the Church will overcome, but I also know that in the long run we can only overcome by significant and lasting reforms in the Church. I may not live to see these changes but they will and must come if the Church is to be at its best in witnessing to what God is about in society.

†

In 1994 I retired as pastor of Mission Santa Barbara. I remain as Pastor Emeritus and still am quite active in a number of areas, including working with the larger Santa Barbara community. After many, many years in administration – director of students, Superior of the Old Mission, president of a theological seminary, pastor of a parish – I, as Pastor Emeritus, have come to the happiest years of my life: to be "at large," open to all whom I encounter and whom I in any way can help. I've learned much and I am still growing in appreciation of all I receive and whatever I can give. I am most grateful for the way my life has evolved. I receive more than what I give. What I learned when I was young is clearly true: God is good and all of life is good. All this and Heaven too!

Epilogue

If we give to one another we discover our true selves.
— Fr. Virgil Cordano

As I look back over my many years of a highly diversified life, I detect a common pattern that integrates and gives a forward thrust to all the events and experiences of my life. This unifying pattern that gives meaning to my life might be called "expanding horizons," a panoply of all the colors of the rainbow of life. Thanks to the privilege of encountering persons of all walks of life, my new experiences and insights have been many. I have also been blessed – as I believe all persons are – with a mind in search of the fullness of truth and a heart longing for mutually enriching relationships. I, and not merely Martin Luther King, Jr., have a dream of what might be and should be.

For the fulfillment of this ever-present desire, I came to see that I had to advance from being exclusive to becoming inclusive of all, from particularism to universalism, from a confining state of separateness to a oneness with all persons and everything, from my own limited interests to awareness of the concerns of others, from the promotion of just my unique self to the development of my relational and communal self, from self-centeredness to other-centeredness. This opening of my true self to the true self of others, much to my surprise and although not intended, served my own self-growth.

As is true for most of us, my life began in a world much smaller than it is today. I was born into a close-knit Italian Catholic family. Life was very good. I felt very secure because of the acceptance and support I received at home, in school, at Church, and in the neighborhood. As the

Italians say *tutto e buono*, everything is good, life is to be enjoyed. Also in those early days, I was awakened to the best of values.

But then when I was about 11 or12 years of age I sensed, for reasons at the time I did not know, that I was called to become a priest. I would move beyond my own family to serve a larger family in what most mattered in life. So I went off to the seminary to study for the priesthood, to learn how to serve others as God loves and ministers to all.

During my seminary life of twelve years, I welcomed much quiet time to reflect on my true inner self, the depths of what stirs at the core of my being, my strengths and weaknesses, my talents and gifts, the meaning, purpose and goal of life as found in my faith-tradition. Living in community with others quite different from myself, I developed my relational self. Also, I had long hours to satisfy my intellectual curiosity and to engage in critical thinking. My education and faith practices guided me in understanding and living the height and depth of all my experiences and not only those of formal religion. This initial education and formation hopefully is still ongoing.

Once a Franciscan priest, I wore different hats and played a variety of roles. As seen above in the account of my life, I became a better person for the diversity of persons I met and the organizations I belonged to. I was privileged to accompany many persons in their journeys through life. Many of them shared with me their deepest thoughts and desires, their joys and sorrows, their regrets, their dreams and hopes, their new beginnings.

Much to my surprise as I listened to their stories and reflected on their lives, I gained deeper insight into my own self. Maybe I came to learn more about myself than about them. I began to perceive that, with all our differences, there is much more that we have in common – a common humanity in search of the more and more. Gradually I have been moving beyond labeling because of differences to recognize and celebrate the work and dignity of the person. I try to be open to all and to give of myself to whomever asks something of me. And I am a better person for responding to diversity of faiths and viewpoints other than my own.

There is still a way to go. I am inspired by the motto that Blessed Junipero Serra received from his parents: "always go forward and never turn back."

During the many years of my life, I have somewhat discovered and tried to live my unique and integrated (inclusive of all reality) spirituality, the lived experience of my faith. I call this a spirituality of all reality. In one and the same life, I try to integrate what God is about and what I am about, Heaven and earth, the divine and the human, grace and nature, faith and human deeds, prayer and work, gratitude for what I receive as gift and generosity in giving of myself, life alone and time with others, mind and heart, individuality and community, idealism and realism, what is and what ought to be, unity and diversity, true humility and justifiable pride, self-fulfillment and self-emptying, commitment and detachment, loss and gain. Then there is also the challenge of living the three loves of God, others and self.

I am grateful for the guidance and communal support given me by my rich Catholic tradition, its teachings, ritual and the heroism of its saints, canonized and non-canonized. Although God is a profound mystery and theological language is not fully adequate and historically and culturally limited, I am inspired by the knowledge of a God who is Love and forgiveness, a God who offers me a share in His/Her very Love-life, challenges and supports me as I try to grow in love of God and others.

Although God is hidden and transcendent, He/She is also immanent and actually present in all human reality. The Beyond is Within. I am a Christian humanist. What is human means more to me than it does to a secular humanist: it is the channel of the divine. God's Self-gift is mediated through all of my human experiences. I don't just believe in God. I believe and trust in the human manifestation or revelation of God. God is at the core of reality. God meets me where I am, at every moment and in every place. My heart does not long for just a God "up there," but a God who is lovingly present in creation "down here."

Holiness is a heroic response in faith to graced reality. In prayer and reflective or contemplative moments, it is not sufficient to be aware of and to listen to God. I must be aware of and listen to my self, my experience, or better, my response to my human experiences. God is active in what goes on deep within me. God speaks to my real and true self: "only when a person is truly present to self can that person accept the word meant for him/her by God and the deed that God wishes to accomplish in him/her" (Balthasar).

Self matters, or better, the depths of self, the heart matters. Maybe many persons never come to know God because they do not come to know themselves. If there is no intimacy with self, there is little, if any, intimacy with others and with God. Masters of the spiritual life are truly wise. St. Augustine: "let me know myself; let me know You." St. Teresa of Avila: "the treasure lies within our very selves...Let your prayer always begin with and end with self-knowledge." The author of "The Cloud of Unknowing": "humility is a person's true understanding and awareness of him/her self as she/he truly is...We must confess to ourselves our true feelings. It is wrong to say 'the feeling is not mine'...Speak out of what you know of yourself...every presence of self before the face of God is prayer...God wants us to pray and will tell us to begin where we are." Thomas Merton: "if I find God, I will find myself and if I find my true self, I will find God." Whitehead's definition of religion: "what one does with solitude."

In recent times there has been a turn toward the self, to the subjective. Fewer and fewer persons are open to listening to what formal, institutional religion teaches. We hear them say: "I am spiritual but not religious." I invite such persons to share with me what stirs deeply within themselves. My hope is that they may discover the desire and the longing of the human heart for self-transcendence, the more than human, which if experienced, may fulfill the deepest yearnings of their true selves to be one with God and also with others in a loving and accepting community. Heaven will be the fulfillment of our deepest desires and the perfection of our personal relationships.

Such is my hope and why I desire to be open to all with whom I journey. While on the journey to fullness of life with God I accept the difficult challenge of loving all who differ from me: to affirm and promote the true good of the other as other. Such is my understanding of God who deals differently with different persons who are very other than God. True love unites those who differ from one another. We can celebrate what unites us while we respect and affirm what separates us. And, much to our surprise, if we give to one another we discover our true selves.

As I come to the end of my reflections on my life of expanding horizons, my thoughts and affections again focus on my early family life of mother, father, and four brothers. All of them have gone on before me into the presence of a loving and welcoming God. The last two of my brothers have died recently. In July, 1994 the youngest son of my parents, Raymond, who told me that I was his closest friend, joined those who preceded him to the fullness of life. In February, 2003 James (Jim), the oldest of five sons, the strength and main support of the family, said goodbye to me to be with our parents and three brothers. I alone linger on earth. I believe that the close ties that unite us will continue forever. I look forward to being family with them in the very family of God.

I am grateful also for being a brother of my Franciscan family and a member of my Church-community. My gratitude extends to my many friends of all walks of life with whom I cherish a deep bond of love. I have never been alone. While I welcome the biblical, theological, and spiritual vision of my religious tradition, in great part, if not in greater part, God reveals His/Her love, acceptance, and forgiveness in the love, goodness, and beauty of the persons whom I have been privileged to know and love. Others are a blessing to me as I try to be a blessing to them. We are united in our love for each other and in our search for the fullness of truth. We support one another as the different persons that we are. With them as companions, my hope assures me of the perfection of all that is begun here on earth. As the mystic Julian of Norwich expectantly says, I believe that "all will be well, all will be well."

APPENDIX

SELECTED WRITINGS BY FATHER VIRGIL CORDANO

MAY WE BECOME CANDLES

May our task in life be to enlighten
    an otherwise darkened and threatened world.
May we be the light that enlightens and also warms
    an otherwise cold and unloved earth.
May we in family, religious groups, and business, dispel hatred with love,
    heal injury with pardon, conquer doubt through faith,
      fight off despair with hope, bring joy to saddened lives,
    and eliminate poverty by sharing our abundance.
May there be reconciliation wherever there is alienation.
May there be inner freedom where there is enslaving addiction.
May there be support where there is neglect.
May we offer acceptance where there is rejection.
May we leave the darkness of just existing to come to responsible living.
May we move from aimlessness to purpose,
    from living for oneself to life for others,
    from terror of threatening war to the calm of inviting dialogue.
May a fanatical will not obscure the light of reason.
May uncontrolled moral strength not overcompensate for the mind's
    ambiguities.
May sweet pieties not be an exchange for demanding research.
May self-righteousness not be concealed
    under a pile of quotations from sacred books
    not subjected to cultural and historical criticism.

Yes, it is better to light one candle than to curse the darkness.
May we become candles that burn from within enlightened and
compassionate hearts,
and shed the warmth of love to all who are children of the same
gracious God.
Amen.

PREPOSITIONAL LIVING

May we be blessed with the conviction that each one of us is an individual person *in* community and *for* community.

To use grammatical terms in a symbolic sense, life is meant to be prepositional: we are to live the prepositions *among*, *with*, and *for*. May we acknowledge and welcome the evident truth that we are of necessity *among* other persons with whom we interact. And more than just being among others, may we intentionally choose to be *with* one another in inviting and caring presence. And more than being among and with others, may we be *for* one another in meeting needs and promoting the true good of each other.

If we fail to live prepositional lives, we are just an unwelcoming group of isolated and often opposing *pronouns*, *nouns* and *adjectives*: I am I, you are you; this is mine and that is yours; we are "us" and "them." Or, we are natives and foreigners, invited and uninvited, favored and not favored, liked and disliked, loved and hated, chosen and rejected, winners and losers, successful and failures, strong and weak, first and last, right and wrong, true and false.

Again, grammatically speaking, some persons are more like *verbs*, often caught up in non-reflective, spontaneous, misdirected, harmful activity without any awareness of being among, with, and for others.

We are to be prepositional toward all persons and all classes of people. There are men and women, people who are brown, black, yellow and white, rich and poor, privileged and underprivileged, the powerful and the weak, the known and the unknown, a majority and a minority, and a very large number of races and ethnic peoples, Americans and foreigners, republicans, democrats, independents and other political parties, liberals, conservatives, and moderates.

Then there are Protestants, Catholics, Orthodox, Jews, Muslims, Buddhists, Hindus and many other separate and often contentious religious bodies.

May we choose to live prepositionally and be grammatically correct: I for you, and you for me, and we for all. May God, who is totally and lovingly *among*, *with*, and *for* all persons, so inspire us. To add another preposition, it is God who sends us *to* other persons to be *among*, *with* and *for* them. Summarily modifying William Shakespeare: To be or not to be prepositional – that is the question.

MAY WE CELEBRATE WHAT UNITES US

While we do what we can to promote our growth as the individuals that we are, in and through the communities of which we are members, I offer for your prayerful consideration certain basic tenets that we might hold in common, if we are to have true and responsible individualism together with the experience of community.

May we believe in, respect and promote the dignity, the worth and even the sacredness of every human person, including of course our own persons.

May we in all honesty search our minds and hearts to discover, acknowledge and to free ourselves from biases, discriminations, oppressions, violence and unenlightened and unanalyzed opinions and judgments.

May we admit in true humility that our strong assurances and convictions have their limitations. We are ever in search of the fullness of truth, the truth that is beyond simplistic answers to complicated issues.

May we not restrict ourselves to the limited and isolated visions of our own circles, especially the enclosed views of our religious organizations and ethnic and cultural affiliations.

May we welcome dialogue among ourselves in which we listen sincerely and speak honestly in an atmosphere of genuine freedom.

May we honor convictions that people live by, even though our persuasions may differ.

May we in concert with one another attempt to articulate and to live by certain basic ethical values and norms, rooted in our common human nature and confirmed and clarified in our faith-convictions.

May we share our dreams, our ideals, our deepest desires, our hopes and go on to support each other in working toward their fulfillment.

May we be united in compassion for all those in need, the poor, the sick, the lonely, the abandoned, the oppressed, the abused.

May we face up to our common frailty and mortality. Life is precarious and radically contingent. We are not in absolute control of our lives. The future is not secure. We need each other. We are dependent upon one another and God.

May we reflect on and share with one another what we believe to be the meaning of all our human experiences.

May we face up to questions and human yearnings that are felt in the depths of our hearts, including issues of intimacy and the purpose and goal of human life.

May we together go in search of understanding or an intimation of God, who is a God for all persons and not merely a God who is thought to restrict love to just one religious gathering of people. May we be open to what an educated religious faith can contribute to the moral fiber of society.

May we crown all our efforts to live in communion with one another with an all inclusive, sacrificing love for every person. We are true to our individual selves when we reach out to each other.

While we try to identify and agree upon what is our common good, of the good of all, may we be grateful for our blessings and hopeful in our struggles. We are to keep in step with and attuned to the beat and rhythm of life together. While we honor what separates us, may we rejoice over what unites us. Let us celebrate all of life as a family of citizens and of friends who move out of self-centered little worlds into a much bigger world where people love and care for each other.

EULOGY FOR ROBERT KENNEDY

I have cried over the death of Robert Kennedy. I have felt deep revulsion over the blackness of the crime. I have been anxious about the moral health of my country. And now, as I believe I am expected to, I wish to view this national tragedy in the context of religious faith. I hope that what I say is confirmatory of and complementary to what is being said by others about this Senator's political and social achievements, for I speak of a faith that is not divorced from political ambition and social involvement, but a faith that calls for such ambition and involvement. I find a close analogy, or better, an intimate link between this man's public life and the challenge issued by his God and my God and, I hope, the God of all who would listen to their true selves and meet the demands of life with others. This message of faith gives me hope, which I sorely need at this time, and I wish to share it with you.

The God of Robert Kennedy, if rightly understood, is the God of all who take the risk of faith. He comes upon the historical scene with a challenge to Abraham and to all believers: "Go forth; raise up your eyes and from where you are now look to the north and the south and the east and the west; Arise, walk the length and the breadth of the land, for I will give it to you; Then, look at the heavens and count the stars." He is a God who opens out to man a vision that is without limit. He is a God who gives us a dynamic and progressive view of our personal and social history. He is a God who challenges and empowers us to be truly men, to gain mastery of ourselves and of the world. Through free and creative action, He says, take steps to better yourselves and your world. Where you go will depend largely on where you *decide* to go. The new world has to be *willed* by you.

Ever since this call was heard such has been the pattern of faith and of human life itself. Again, when man was enslaved, he was told to go out in exodus, in faith and trust and in risk to his life. Later prophets spoke out against complacency and smugness. They were zealous for change. They criticized what was too long established. Keep life open and moving, they thundered. Go forth again and again. Hasten the day of the Lord, the coming of the great age. There is ever need of new creation and a new exodus.

Then in the history of believers a Jesus of Nazareth said that it was necessary that he go forth, all the way to the Father, to one greater than he. And his life was taken from him.

This zeal for change and new discoveries inspired President John F. Kennedy and Rev. Martin Luther King. It caught up in its rushing thrust forward the person of Robert Kennedy. Such, I believe, was the ambition of this true visionary, this frontiersman, this rightly ambitious one. He was willing to leave all behind and to press on. Why? He had the vision of the promised land, the same vision that thrilled the courageous heart of the prophet Martin Luther King. For Robert Kennedy's witnessing to such ambition we are humbly grateful. We shall cherish the message written in his own blood. And this is the message: in the final analysis the question asked of us is: in what direction do we go? We are not to look at each other in sentimental repose and possess one another, but we are together to look ahead. "As if there could be love without hope for the beloved." Though we are one in origin, in our living we go our separate ways, and because of the barriers of blood, color, religion, social status, nationality, we begin to segregate and often hate. Robert Kennedy's death warns us that we must rise above crippling, paralyzing heritage of past divisions and enmities. The sins of our fathers are not so much visited upon us children, as they are insanely willed by us children. We forget that we are united in something bigger than any two of us and any number of nations. We are one in origin and we should be one in vision, ambition and goal.

The realization of a common goal, for the attainment of which we work and, if necessary, risk life, alone makes possible the creation of a true community among us, a solidarity with all others who are also on the way to the goal of all men. In the acknowledgement of a common vision and goal there is hope.

It is this sense of direction that challenges us to make the most of the present time. We are not to lose ourselves in the present with the static frigidity. Rather, we are to be creatively active in the present age. We are to love with a love that builds and builds and never ceases to build, with a love that fulfills and does not destroy.

Also, this vision of a common goal of love and peace among all men demands and justifies criticism of our present failure to move ahead with purpose, to live up to prophetical roles assigned us by a God who also sits in judgment of present institutions and men who remain entrenched in age-old hatred and enmity and disregard of the true needs of others.

God speaks this message through his prophets, men like Robert Kennedy and Martin Luther King. But it is to our shame that as prophets are sent to us, we kill them. What will happen to our vision and ambition if we keep on killing the Kennedys and the Kings and all other prophets? We send them back to their God before their time, to the God who sent them to us to speak in His behalf. The day may come when no one will speak and on that day *we* shall die. Then these words of Christ, spoken as he was being destroyed will be bitterly understood: "Weep not for me, but weep for yourselves and for your children."

However, and this is our hope, even though we kill the prophets, we do not kill their spirit. Through the death of a historical man comes life. Jesus won the Spirit for his followers through his dedication in death. Also, we believe that God will send more prophets. Those who have vision will see. Those who love will hope. Others will remain in darkness, foolishly prolong ancient rivalries and enmities and again try to still the voices of those who love and criticize because they love.

Today we repent of our ill treatment of this prophet. We pray that God will rid our hearts of evil thoughts and of hatred, for from the heart, as Christ has said, comes murder. And, then, may we be attentive to what St. Francis of Assisi often said to his followers: "Let us now begin, for up to now we have done nothing." Robert Kennedy would want us to move ahead. Let us go forth together.

University of California, Santa Barbara, June 7, 1968
Memorial Service for Robert Kennedy

A MESSAGE FOR PEOPLE OF ALL FAITHS

Since Christmas means all sorts of things to all kinds of people, there are many expressions of the message of Christmas. I respect and welcome all of them and I find meaning in every one of them. Among these many understandings of Christmas there is the basic Christian message – God enters into our human life.

Even this Christian message is open to many interpretations and expressions. Without denying this faith-meaning of Christmas – it will be my concern in church services – I am in search of a message for persons of all faiths. I am in search also of a message for individuals caught up in the spirit of giving at Christmas.

Maybe this universal message of Christmas will be heard if we reflect on what happens at Christmas.

People come together, greet each other, sing carols, travel long distances to come home or to be with friends. They are in touch with one another in letters, greeting cards and telephone calls. Then there is the exchange of gifts, enjoyed especially by children.

All that we do at Christmas time speaks of an implied belief in the goodness of human life. There is something profoundly good about being a human person in a loving exchange with other persons. People are at their best in reaching out to others and being concerned for those in need.

For a season of the year the world is close to being all that it could be.

The universal message, then, is not just about God far off in Heaven and angels descending from above. Christmas is a celebration of Earth itself.

Christmas is not only good news about God, but also joy-filled news about ourselves. It tells us what is good about us and how blessed we are in being human persons in this actual world of ours.

We can be thoughtful of one another. We can be welcoming to the presence of each other. We can give generously to each other. We can receive with gratitude gifts from one another.

We need and welcome Christmas to counter the threat of frustration and despondency that hangs over us and spews anger, abuse and violence.

We cannot agree with what someone wrote recently, "The dominant fact about our world today is that life is no longer loved."

This cannot be true. We will love life and celebrate its goodness at Christmas time.

And yet there are too many people who think poorly of themselves. And there are too many condemnations of people. We hear too many bad things said about us and we respond in speaking in a similar way about others.

This deluge of pessimism and criticism lures us into doubting that there is value in ourselves. It lures us into doubting the meaning in all that happens in our lives.

May we, then, be grateful that every year at Christmas we are invited to listen to and to be inspired by a simple yet profound three-part message:

First, life is good.

As a brilliant sun breaks through dark skies to brighten the land and to warm the bodies and hearts of women and men, Christmas returns in the threatening cold and darkness of our personal winters to renew us, to remind us that life is worth living.

We believe all are capable of loving heroically. We are grateful that we are recipients of unconditional love. There are endless possibilities for achievement in life. We can experience thrilling moments of happiness and continue in the pursuit of a greater happiness.

Second, there is value in our human tasks.

The goodness of life is to be experienced in the fulfillment of given and chosen human tasks. Each of us is a story made up of specific events at particular times and places. The story of each one of us asks for commitment to persons and a generous response to the reality of our lives.

For our inspiration and to guide us in our search for meaning, the Christmas message is told in a story. It is the story of a man, Joseph, a woman, Mary, and a child, Jesus.

Briefly, a young woman and a young man lived in the same village, met, fell in love, got married and then the wife had a baby boy. In the story there is everything that is very human – conception, birth, growth, tension, trial, waiting, searching, surprise, wonder and discovery.

It wasn't an easy life. They were away from home, had a hard time finding lodging, and they had to make difficult decisions. They did not find it easy to trust in God and in each other. Yet, they were faithful to their calling in life.

Third, there is beauty in personal goodness.

Many of the details of that story of this family are not appealing – poor quarters, coldness, lack of recognition and even opposition from others.

But there is great beauty. It is captured in the beauty of the persons of husband and wife to whom God entrusts the care of a child. It is the goodness of this family that attracts the simple shepherds as well as truly wise persons.

May we be in admiration of persons who open themselves to welcome others into their lives, persons who are true, faithful, dedicated to the fulfillment of their given and chosen roles in life. The heavens sing in praise of such beauty.

Such then is the three-fold message of Christmas for all persons –

believe in the goodness of life, the lasting value of all that is human, and the beauty of goodness.

If something like this three-fold guide is the universal message of a Christmas and explains its overwhelming popularity, may we:

• Renew our faith in the dignity and worth of our persons and every person.
• Be interested in and be concerned with all truly human issues and activities.
• See through and beyond all the tinsel of life, listen to our inner selves and discuss with others the deeper questions of life.
• Search for meaning, purpose and direction of all that happens in our lives.
• Be open to the possibility that we are invited to transcend all that is human, especially human limitations.
• Stop regretting who we are not, and celebrate who we are, feel happy about the good we do and not falsely guilty about what we cannot do.
• Experience something good and beautiful being born in us when we welcome other persons and their concerns into our lives.
• Discover new reasons to say "yes" to God – as we understand God – and to others in need of our loving and caring presence.
• Welcome the privilege of giving and the joy of receiving much more in return. Generosity never impoverishes a person and the best thing we can do for our true selves is to give to others.
• Recognize our giftedness and feel called to have our own talents and gifts released within the families and communities to which we belong.

And may we who claim to believe in the true God and are members of religious organizations rethink just who our God is. May we grow in respect of people of all faiths and persons who have no explicit ties to religion but often are more considerate, gracious and God-like than we are.

There is a way in which we can be true to our own religious beliefs and at the same time welcome the religious, ethnic and racial differences among us. In this way we may remove some of the scandal given by those who, with falsely presumed approval of God, hate and vilify others.

Each one of us might ask him or herself, who is God? Isn't my God the God of all persons?

"Whoever loves God must also love brother and sister." (1 John 4:21) Is God for all or just for some? Is God working through all or just through some?

A Happy Hanukkah to my Jewish friends and for all of us a renewed faith in the goodness and profound meaning of our human lives.

BECOMING A GLOBAL COMMUNITY OF RELIGIONS

In all aspects of human life we experience tension between diversity that separates us and our need and desire to discover and live what unites us. This diversity exists among our religious traditions. What do we have in common? We are aided in this search for religious harmony by a growing new consciousness, an awareness of the interdependence of all creation and a developing knowledge and appreciation of the treasures in all religious traditions. We live in an age of *interspirituality*. Indicative of this spiritual convergence has been the World's Parliament of Religions in 1893, 1993, 1999 and 2004. In these gatherings common statements were made toward a *global spirituality and ethic*.

To better understand interspirituality, the sharing of the experiences of differing traditions, we should reflect on the interrelated meanings of *religion, spirituality, and mysticism*:

1. *Being religious* connotes belonging to and practicing a religious tradition, its ritual, theological teaching.

2. *Being spiritual* is to be committed to growth as an essential ongoing life goal. The person is primarily inner-directed by the experiences of the heart (depth of one's being), nurtured and supported by a tradition, if one has such; not overly dependent on an institution; takes responsibility for one's spiritual life. Often the religious and the spiritual coincide, when authentic faith and religious practices embody an individual's spirituality. Yet, not every religious person is spiritual (although he/she should be)

and not every spiritual person is religious. The tradition should nourish the inner life beyond perfunctory observances. There is a difference between being rooted in a tradition and being stuck in it.

3. Experiencing mysticism: at the very heart of spirituality is a grace-filled experience of a deep personal union with God and in God with all of creation. God invites all persons of all times to experience union here on earth and the full experience of a loving union in Heaven. Spirituality opens us toward a direct, immediate experience of Ultimate Reality (union and communion with God). Everyone has a mystic heart (the deepest part of who or what we are) that awaits our awakening to the mystery within, without, and beyond us. Nothing is closer to me than my awareness of my self, my consciousness. God is there at the core of my being. "Be still – and know that I am God (Ps. 46:10)." The purpose of prayer, especially contemplative prayer: an awareness of and an experiencing of union with God, with whom we are always united, whether we are aware of it or not.

What is called for today: Interspirituality and Intermysticism

For the unity of our human family we must be in dialogue and in communion with everything of value in our spiritual and mystical traditions. At the same time this reaching across traditions need not submerge our differences. The task of interspirituality is not "instead of" but "in addition to." We should not be against diversity of expressions, when they are based on authentic inner experience. Our true experiences often are given differing theological and cultural interpretations. What matters the most is inner (contemplative) and outer (actions) transformation. All of us must struggle with the problem of the ego-driven life and the false self. Life is a journey from hypocrisy to sincerity, from self-centeredness to other-centeredness and love, from self-deception to self-honesty, from ignorance to clarity, from illusion to truth.

FIESTA'S MISA DEL PRESIDENTE, 1996

Old Spanish Days Fiesta means different things to different persons. For some people Fiesta is a time to recall our historical past and its traditions. Or, Fiesta is an occasion to express in song and dance our pride and appreciation in being citizens of this city and county. Or, we just wish to have a good time at the many social events of Old Spanish Days.

In the setting of this historical Mission I wish to reflect on what I might call the social-spiritual meaning of Fiesta. How does this view of Fiesta add a depth and a height to our celebration? In answer, have you ever taken time to reflect on the reasons for the basic tension that under-lies many, if not all, of our conflicts – personal, social, ethnic, political, economic and religious? The answer to this inquiry is simply that we are different individuals and we belong to a diversity of groups. Given our personal differences and allegiances, we have difficulty in coming to deci-sions, in agreeing on solutions to our problems, in achieving community. In our personal journeys we are at different places. Yet we want to walk together toward the same goal. We desire to identify the common good, the good for all that considers and represents our differences.

We must admit that this task is not an easy one. It never has been. In early Santa Barbara there was the painful clash between European culture and the way of life of our Native Americans. Also, the early Spanish mis-sionaries and the Spanish civil authorities argued over many issues. St. Augustine in his day identified 288 different philosophies of life. He offered his own. But today not everyone accepts Augustine's view of life!

We also experience in our own ways the tension between existing diversity and hoped for unity, the issue of the one and the many, the inter-relatedness of "I" and "You" and "We," separateness and closeness, a true love of self and love of and concern for others. We dance different steps, sing different tunes, and have differing tastes. And yet, we want to be members of the same dance team and of the same vocal group, and sit around the same table.

What does all this talk about the tension between individualism and community have to do with Fiesta? In a limited but meaningful way we witness to what the world needs now: we live community. Fiesta brings together persons who otherwise would remain apart in their own walks of life, professions, interests, ethnic groups and religious affiliations. We meet at the same places, we greet each other, we sing and enjoy the same songs, we try to dance in step with one another, we eat the same food and drink together, although we select different drinks. This morning we pray together, each in his/her own way around a ritual that goes back to much earlier times.

We have to admit that to live community beyond Fiesta week is not easy. For some time there has been a loss of confidence in our ability to agree over vital issues. We doubt that we can unite in sharing a common vision and working toward the same goal. There are so many lines of difference. Take notice of the proliferation of confusing proposals and biting criticism of nearly everyone and everything channeled to us through our media. Read the letters to the editor for a wild medley of ideas coming from the left and from the right and from I know not where. There are excesses in the camps of both those who stress individualism and the rights of individuals and those who speak of the rights of all persons and our obligations to fulfill the desires of others and not just our own. While some take as their theme song "I gotta be me" and "I have to do my thing" there are others who are members of newly created social and ethnic groups who tend to stifle individual initiative and would permit little freedom to those who disagree with them. There is a growing number of narrow-minded, closed, exclusive communities that are concerned with only one issue. Disappointment with our two major political parties has moved many citizens to dream of a utopia to be realized in the formation of a third major party. Then, of course, we always suffer the dire consequences of the distortions of limited and biased human wills.

The differences among us will remain. We retain our national and cultural and ethnic identities. They are even strengthened in and through our communal worship and our communications with one another. But these differences need not keep us apart nor create opposition among us. We are challenged to expand our hearts, to broaden our vision and to grow in unrestricted love and service. No one of us, no group of ours knows it all and can do it all. We need the complementation and support afforded by others. Then we can better give to others what is uniquely ours and to receive from others what is their special contribution to our lives. We can experience unity, brother/sisterhood without complete uniformity, a leveling of all to the same monotonous level. Differences invite cooperation rather than destructive divisiveness. Universal brother/sisterhood can be realized in the actual and real respect of and love for neighbor. As Jesus says, every person is neighbor.

Fiesta brings all of us together. We who have celebrated many Fiestas have welcomed many new brothers and sisters, persons not met in our churches and in our different professions and walks of life. Our coming together as members of one large universal human family in food and drink, song and dance has brought us to this Mission where we are united in prayer to the same God of us all. We celebrate the mystery of a God of unconditional love and we are in respectful and reverential awe of the wonderful mystery of our persons and the persons of all. How blessed are we. How grateful we should be!

GOD'S BLESSING IN BASEBALL LANGUAGE

The same God of us all, we are grateful that you assign each one of us an important *position* on your *team* and on other many teams – teams of family, Church, country, city, school, sports, neighborhood, business and social life. We are always in the *starting line-up*. We just don't *sit on the bench*. You ask for *team effort*. We are to cooperate with others in the *game* of life. May we come to believe that on a team each *player* and each *player's position* matter to you and to all on the team. It is only team effort that makes all the players winners. May we gratefully acknowledge that we need the help of others if we are to succeed. In baseball the *pitcher* needs the *catcher* to *catch* the *best pitch*. The *infielders* need the *first baseman* to catch the *throws*, especially when they are *in the dirt*. Every player needs the *good play* of the others.

May we believe that each one of us can *make a hit* on your team and maintain *a good average* throughout the *season* of life. May personal hits *double* and even *triple* our joy and the joy of all on the team.

May we learn to wait patiently for *the best pitch*, the opportunity to do what we do best. May we willingly *sacrifice* that others might advance from *base to base*, from advancement to advancement. May we hurry to back up persons when they *err* or *throw* wildly. Once in awhile we may hit *foul balls* but may we never *foul out*. Keep us from prolonged sadness over an occasional *error* or *bad call*. You always give us another *time up*, another *swing*, another *throw* to make. You give us more than *three strikes* or attempts to *knock in the winning run*.

May we be grateful for *winning* and gracious in *losing* an occasional game, knowing that we have given it our best, our best *pitch*, our best *swing*. We are always given another *inning* or *game to play*. Our game is not limited to *nine innings* but to *extra innings* that can end not in a *tie* but in a *win*. There are many *relief pitchers* and *pinch hitters*. There is always *another game to play* and *another season*. Life is a series of new beginnings. May we never give up hope of winning it all. There are other *positions* to play.

May all the players, those on *winning teams* and those on *losing teams*, know that they can always *win* and *win big* before you. We have only to listen to you, our *manager* and *pick up the signals* you or your *coaches* give us. And may we believe that before we play our *last inning*, or have our last time *at bat* or make our last *pitch*, we can, after each game of every day, *run home* to family and to friends, where win or lose, we know we will be *cheered* by our loved and loving ones. And when the game of life on earth is over may we *run all the way home* to you and receive a *standing ovation*. AMEN.

GOD'S WORDS TO GOLFERS

It seems to us that as we play golf you are trying to tell us in a symbolic way something of great importance. We can hear you speaking as the best of *pros*:

Now, listen carefully to what I am telling you out of love and care for you. Each of you can play the game of life well. You have only to walk the straight and narrow path as far as you can. May all your ways be *fair-ways*.

You'll hear me shout *"fore"* when your actions are misdirected. May you never be *out of bounds* or remain too long in the *rough*. May you not get stuck in the *trap* of just *puttering* around without any sense of achievement. May you believe that with my help you can overcome whatever your *handicaps* are and give life your best *swing*. May you come to experience my compassionate understanding of you and my forgiveness of your occasional *bogies*.

May you keep on *qualifying* in life and never be *cut* from me, family or friends. May you play in *fields* open to me and to others, fields wider than your own small and narrow worlds, fields as high as the sky above and as expansive as the horizon before you. May each round of life be better than an earlier *round* and may your final round be your best. May you, after many years of work and play come to a *course* of everlasting play where all are winners and there are no losers.
AMEN.

A BLESSING

We find ourselves between praying seas and kneeling mountains, in a setting sacred to our native citizens and dear to peoples from across the seas. With respectful remembrance of ancient traditions, we call down your blessing, the same God of us all, upon this monument of dolphins at our waterfront that challenges us to be friends to one another, since we are brothers and sisters of the same human family.

We gratefully welcome your kindness, which, like these dolphins, encircles and protects peoples of different lands surrounded by the same seas.

From the very birthday of creation when your joyous Spirit danced over the waters, you have never ceased to call your children to play together as members of the same family.

May we be each to each a beacon of light so that our days may not be passed in shadows. May our lips speak peace to all. In sharing may we find our happiness expanded and our sorrows divided. May we, like the waters of this fountain, reach up to you the God of us all. And may we like the sea before us, stretch out in all directions to embrace in friendship the people of different lands touched by the same waters of life.

One thousand trade paperback copies of *Padre* were printed by Capra Press in 2005. Of the one hundred hardcover copies printed, twenty-six copies in slipcases have been lettered and signed by the author, Fr. Cordano, and Congresswoman Capps.

ABOUT CAPRA PRESS

Capra Press was founded in 1969 by the late Noel Young. Among its authors have been Henry Miller, Ross Macdonald, Margaret Millar, Edward Abbey, Anais Nin, Raymond Carver, Ray Bradbury, and Lawrence Durrell. It is in this tradition that we present the new Capra: literary and mystery fiction, lifestyle and city books. Contact us. We welcome your comments.

155 Canon View Road, Santa Barbara, CA 93108

www.caprapress.com

Mario T. García is Professor of History and Chicano Studies at the University of California, Santa Barbara. He is also an affiliated faculty member of the Department of Religious Studies. He is the author of numerous books, including *Desert Immigrants: The Mexicans of El Paso, 1880-1920; Mexican Americans: Leadership, Ideology & Identity, 1930-1960;* and *Memories of Chicano History: The Life and Narrative of Bert Corona.* He is a recipient of a Guggenheim Fellowship.